Borland Pascal:
Step-by-Step

CORIOLIS GROUP BOOK

Borland Pascal: Step-by-Step

Keith Weiskamp

John Wiley & Sons, Inc.
New York • Chichester • Brisbane • Toronto • Singapore

Library of Congress Cataloging-in-Publication Data

Weiskamp, Keith.
    Borland Pascal : step-by-step / Keith Weiskamp.
      p. cm.
    Includes index.
    ISBN 0-471-30429-8 (alk. paper)
    1. Pascal (Computer program language)   2. Borland Pascal.
    I. Title.
    QA76.73.P2W418   1994
    005.26'2--dc20
                                              93-37078
                                                    CIP

Printed in the United States of America

10 9 8 7 6 5 4 3 2 1

Contents

Introduction

With the release of Borland Pascal 7.0, the Pascal language has evolved into the programming language of choice for the 1990s and beyond. Unfortunately, in the past, learning a programming language such as Pascal required a great time commitment and usually a lot of work. The problem was that available programming environments weren't all that easy to use. Borland has now removed the barriers by creating Borland Pascal 7.0—the complete Pascal programming environment that provides an interactive debugger, a mouse-controlled window and menu system, a sophisticated help system, and graphics and object-oriented programming capabilities. To help you learn how to use Turbo Pascal and write useful Pascal programs, *Borland Pascal: Step-by-Step* provides a practical "hands-on" approach to programming.

Some major highlights of this book are:

- Emphasizes the learn-by-doing approach to writing and debugging Pascal programs

- Incorporates exercises throughout the book to help you learn at your own pace

- Includes a set of programming exercises at the end of each chapter along with an answer key to help you check your work

- Provides a solid introduction to object-oriented programming

- Covers the new features of Borland Pascal 7.0 including the Borland Graphics Interface (BGI) and object-oriented programming tools

Who Should Read This Book

If you've always wanted to learn Pascal, but have been put off because you thought programming was difficult and mysterious, then you've come to the right place. Throughout the book, short, easy-to-follow programs are used that demystify Turbo Pascal programming. You'll learn how to write, edit, compile, run, and debug the kind of programs that you can use. If you're the kind of person who likes to learn at your own pace, you'll especially benefit from the exercises that are provided in each chapter.

What You'll Need

To use this book you'll need Borland Pascal 7.0, as well as an IBM PC XT, AT, PS/2, or compatible computer system. Because some of the programs take advantage of Turbo Pascal's graphics features, you'll need a computer capable of displaying graphics such as a CGA, EGA, or VGA system in order to run the graphics programs.

A Quick Look Inside

This book progresses from the basics to more advanced topics—in a way that lets you put previously learned skills to use quickly. In each chapter, you'll find a set of exercises to help you review the material that has been presented. Also throughout the book are special notes and tips that point out important programming issues.

Chapter 1: *Turbo Pascal's Environment Up Close* shows you how to use the latest TP environment—including the menu system, the help system, the editor, the compiler, and the debugger. You will learn everything you need to know to start writing programs.

Chapter 2: *Writing Your First Programs* explains the basic components you'll need to write TP programs including program structure, the basics of simple and compound statements, screen I/O operations, and controlling the execution flow of programs.

Chapter 3: *Variables and Data Types* explores the basic techniques for using TP variables and the different data types that are available for declaring variables, such as **Integer**, **Real**, **Char**, **String**, and **Boolean**.

Chapter 4: *Expressions and Operators* shows how to build expressions so that you can effectively use constants and variables to process your data.

Chapter 5: *Program Control: Decision-Making and Loop Statements* covers all of the TP decision-making and looping statements. The cast of players includes **IF-THEN**, **CASE**, **GOTO**, **FOR**, **WHILE-DO**, and **REPEAT-UNTIL**.

Chapter 6: *Console Input/Output* presents the basic TP screen and keyboard I/O features. Here you'll learn how to use powerful routines, such as **Readln** and **Writeln**, to control program I/O.

Chapter 7: *Static Data Structures* shows you how to use the static data structures, such as sets, enumerated types, strings, arrays, and records, to help you write more useful programs.

Chapter 8: *User-Defined Functions and Procedures* explores the techniques for writing and using Pascal procedures and functions. In addition, the two methods for passing arguments—pass by value and pass by reference—will be covered.

Chapter 9: *Working with Units* shows how custom units are created to perform specialized tasks. Some of the topics covered include the interface and implementation sections of a unit, how a unit is compiled, and how to use the units provided with TP.

Chapter 10: *An Introduction to File Input/Output* examines TP's file system. In this chapter you'll learn how to open, close, read, and write text and binary files.

Chapter 11: *Dynamic Data Structures* explains how memory allocation techniques are used to create dynamic data structures. A complete discussion of how to use pointer variables is provided.

Chapter 12: *Object-Oriented Programming* presents the basic concepts of OOP and shows you how to use the object-oriented features provided with TP 6.0. In this chapter you'll learn how to master the OOP building blocks, including objects, instance variables, methods, messages, and inheritance.

Chapter 13: *Explorations with Graphics* shows you how to put TP's powerful graphics features called the Borland Graphics Interface to work.

Chapter 14: *Using the Debugger* explains Borland's powerful built-in debugger and shows you how to put the debugger to work.

Contacting the Author

I always enjoy hearing from programmers who have read one of my books. Your comments and suggestions are always greatly appreciated because they help me write the kinds of books that help you the most.

If you have a question or two, find a bug, or would like to share some of your ideas for future editions of this book, please contact me. If you use MCI, you can send a note to KWEISKAMP. By mail, write to me in care of *PC TECHNIQUES Magazine*, 7721 E. Gray Road, Suite 204, Scottsdale, AZ 85260.

Turbo Pascal's Environment Up Close

In 1984, when I first encountered Turbo Pascal (TP) I thought my days of struggling with Pascal programs were over. The interactive, lightning-fast, and easy-to-use compiler had the right stuff to help bring programming into the twentieth century. But now that version 7.0 has evolved into such a powerful, fine-tuned programming tool, it's going to transform your experience of learning both Pascal and personal computer programming. Never again will you have to struggle along with inadequate tools as programmers did years ago.

This chapter will introduce you to TP's powerful integrated development environment. As you'll quickly discover, TP is much more than a Pascal compiler. It's a user-friendly, window-based system that provides a built-in text editor, hands-on debugger, compiler, and a help system that can save you from spending your valuable programming time looking things up in a reference manual.

In this chapter, you'll encounter the menu system, the help system, the editor, the compiler, and the debugger. You won't have to write any real programs in this chapter, but you will learn everything you need to know to start writing programs in Chapter 2. If you're already experienced with the TP environment, you should feel free to skip this chapter.

After completing this chapter, you'll know how to:

- Start TP's integrated development environment
- Use the TP menu and window system
- Use both the mouse and the keyboard to get around
- Customize your working environment
- Use the TP help system
- Use the TP compiler

What Is an Integrated Development Environment?

Imagine that someone took away all of the desks, chairs, and even computers in your workplace. You probably wouldn't get much work done. In order to be productive, you need to have all of the necessary working tools at your disposal. Of course, it's no different with programming. In fact, that's why personal computers were invented in the first place—to help us create our own productive, customizable working environments. The advantage of using a product such as TP to develop and test programs is that it provides all of the tools needed to make programming as easy as possible. As Figure 1.1 indicates, TP allows you to write programs with the built-in editor, compile them with the compiler, run them without having to leave the environment, and then you can even closely inspect a program with the interactive debugger as it runs. Together these components are called the integrated development environment (IDE). As this chapter unfolds, you'll learn the basics for using the different components of the IDE.

Figure 1.1   Using the IDE to create programs.

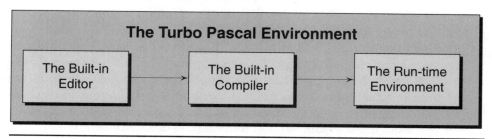

A Special Note About Versions

Just like the personal computer, Turbo Pascal has evolved in the years since its introduction. There are currently several different versions of TP: Turbo Pascal, Turbo Pascal for Windows, and Borland Pascal. These different programs offer different tools and environments to suit the needs of a wide range of programmers, from beginners to professional. Turbo Pascal (Turbo) runs only under DOS, or in a DOS compatibility box inside Microsoft Windows. Turbo Pascal for Windows (TPW) runs in Windows. Borland Pascal (BP) offers both DOS and Windows programming environments. Despite these differences, there's much to these different products that is the same, including the language. Throughout the book, we will refer to all versions of the Turbo Pascal program as TP. The focus of this book is to show you how to program using the Turbo Pascal language. To do this, you will learn using examples which are applicable to all flavors of TP. You may also see special notes that describe differences between the environments to help to get the program examples working.

The IDE's Components

Let's start with the window-based editor—the component you use to get most of your programming work done. The editor allows you to enter, save, and modify programs. However, this TP editor isn't exactly your run-of-the-mill word processor. It provides two important features that reduce the difficulty of writing programs. First, it allows you to compile the file that you're editing without having to return to the operating system (probably the biggest time saver yet known). Second, it is a mouse-driven, multiple-window editor that allows you to easily create and modify your program files. You can even work with more than one file without having to save one file in order to open another. In addition, the editor has a special feature called *pair matching* that helps you tell at a glance if something, such as a misplaced quote or parenthesis, is going to be misinterpreted by the compiler. You'll learn the basics for using the editor a little later in this chapter.

The *compiler* is the tool that actually converts your Pascal programs into machine instructions so that they can be understood by your computer. When Pascal compilers were first developed, they required a source program to be located in one disk file so that the entire program could be compiled at one time. This philosophy had two major disadvantages. First, large and complicated programs required large files, which meant that editing was a real nightmare. Second, the compiler had to recompile the entire file (which could take up a lot of time and disk space) even though the only correction made to the program may have been the insertion of a missing semicolon on one line!

To avoid these irritants and to improve the efficiency of programming, TP allows programs to be represented as independent files that can be compiled separately. This provides two distinct advantages: (1) The file size can be kept small in order to provide faster editing and compilation, and (2) functions that have been written and compiled can be used in more than one program without needing to be recompiled each time.

The *debugger* is an extremely powerful tool that allows you to inspect a program as it executes. If you have errors in a program that are difficult to find, you can define markers called *breakpoints* to instruct a program to stop at specified points so that you can examine the program variables. The debugger also provides a useful tracing feature to help you monitor the execution flow of your programs.

The last tool in the TP IDE is the online context-sensitive help system. If you've used software packages before on a personal computer, you're probably familiar with the way context-sensitive help systems work. What's unique about TP's online help is that it provides different levels of useful help information: help on a specific topic, help using a table of contents, help using an index, help by searching for a topic or keyword, and even help on the help system. The help system also provides a powerful hypertext feature so that you can easily access help information that is related to a given topic. For example, if you are viewing help on the Edit menu, you can select the phrase "Restore Line" to display information on the Restore Line.

Installing and Starting TP

Before getting too far into the technical details of TP's IDE, let's look at how TP is started. If you haven't installed TP yet, you should do so by using the automated installation program called INSTALL that comes with your distribution disks. This program loads all of the necessary files onto your system. During the installation process, new directories are created on your hard disk to store the program and sample TP source files. Here are the basic steps you should follow to install TP:

1. Insert the installation disk (disk 1) into one of your floppy drives such as drive A.

2. Type

   `A:INSTALL`

   and press Enter.

3. Follow the instructions given by the installation program. As long as you have enough free memory on your hard disk, you shouldn't encounter any problems installing TP.

Up and Running

After you have installed TP, get into the subdirectory where the installation program stored your program files (the default directory is C:\TP; for Borland Pascal, the default is C:\BP) and enter the following command at the DOS prompt:

`TURBO`

or

`BP`

To start from the Windows environment, simply double-click on the proper icon (labeled TPW or BPW, depending on your version). You'll then see the window shown in Figure 1.2. Notice that the window opens with a default file, nonname00.pas, in the editor. If you already have a file that you want to use, enter this command:

`TURBO <filename>`

or

`BP<filename>`

For example, the command

`TURBO GIZMO1`

starts TP with the source file GIZMO1.PAS.

If you are using TP from DOS, you can change your AUTOEXEC.BAT file so that it contains the name of the full directory path where TP is installed. You can then run TP from any directory.

As Figure 1.2 shows, the IDE consists of three main visual components. At the top of the window is the main menu bar which is used to access the menu

Figure 1.2 The BPW environment.

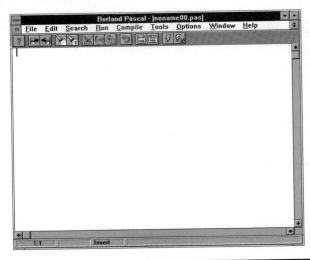

commands and dialog boxes. The area in the middle of the window is called the *desktop*. This is where dynamic windows are displayed so that you can edit, modify, compile, and debug your Pascal programs. In this area you can use the mouse and/or the keyboard to navigate and perform editing commands. The status line at the bottom of the window provides information to help you use the IDE, such as a list of available function keys or program status information.

 This book contains many questions and answers to help you test your knowledge about the commands and techniques you have just learned. Occasionally, they will provide a "sneak preview" of features that will be presented in the section that immediately follows.

1. How do you start the IDE?
2. What happens when you select the menu bar by clicking on it with the mouse or pressing F10?
3. What happens when you press F1?
4. What happens when you press Esc?
5. What happens when you quit the IDE by pressing Alt+X?

 1. Move to the directory where TP is installed, type

TURBO

and press **Enter**.

2. The menu bar becomes active. You should see a highlighted menu bar on one of the menu items.
3. A help window is displayed for the online help system. The F1 key is the shortcut key for accessing the help system.
4. The help window is removed.
5. Control returns to the DOS prompt. The Alt+X sequence provides a shortcut for quitting TP. Whenever you see an *Alt key combination* (the Alt key followed by a letter key), it is an indication that you can press both keys at the same time or press the Alt key first and then the other key listed.

Startup Options

In addition to specifying a source file, you can also include a configuration option to instruct TP to make use of different hardware and software settings such as selecting expanded memory, loading EGA colors, and loading a configuration file. These options are listed in Table 1.1. The correct sequence for including a configuration option with one or more filenames is illustrated by the following general syntax:

```
TURBO [options] files
```

or

```
BP [options] files
```

For example, if you type

```
TURBO /G GRAPH1
```

you are telling TP to call up GRAPH1 and to select the full-graphics memory save feature.

Likewise, when you type

```
TURBO /D /N GRAPH1 GRAPH2
```

you are telling TP to call up GRAPH1 and GRAPH2, toggle the snow checking on or off for CGA monitors, and work in dual monitor mode.

Determine the display hardware that is installed with your computer and execute TP with the proper configuration option. If you're not sure which option to use, test the different options until you're happy with the way your screen looks.

Table 1.1   Command-Line Options for Starting the IDE

Option	Description
/C	Specifies that a configuration file will be loaded to initialize the IDE. A configuration filename must be included with this option. This feature is handy because it allows you to easily customize the IDE.
/D	Instructs the IDE to work in dual monitor mode if hardware is detected to operate two monitors. This option is especially useful if you have both a monochrome and color graphics display card.
/E	Changes the size of the editor heap from the default of 28K. A value must be included with this option ranging from 28 to 128. (Turbo only)
/F	Instructs the IDE to use a swap file for compiling very large programs. Valid sizes for the swap file range from 1024K to 16384K. (BP only)
/G	Selects the full-graphics memory save feature to improve the performance of the debugger when debugging graphics programs.
/L	Selects a Liquid Crystal Display monitor as the active display.
/N	Disables or enables snow checking for CGA monitors. Snow checking is enabled by default.
/O	Changes the IDE's overlay heap size from 64K to 256K. The default setting is 90K. (Turbo only)
/P	Controls palette swapping on EGA hardware when a program modifies the EGA palette registers.
/R	Tells TP to "remember" the last directory you were in and make that the current directory.
/S	Specifies the drive and path for a fast swap area (RAM disk).
/T	Disables loading of the file TURBO.TPL.
/W	Changes the window heap size from 24K to 64K. The default setting is 32K. (Turbo only)
/X	Disables the use of expanded memory (EMS). This setting is enabled by default. (Turbo only)

Note

To help you remember which startup option is best for your computer, you might want to create a .BAT file and include the TURBO command with the configuration option. For example, if you're using a CGA system and you always want to disable snow checking, place this command in a .BAT file:

```
TURBO /N
```

Also, examine the README.DOC file that comes with TP to see if there are any last-minute updates. Use the following command to view the file:

```
README
```

Working with the Menu System

Now that you've been introduced to the basic features of programming environments, we'll move on and look at the TP menu system. The window that appears when TP is called up, which was previously shown in Figure 1.2, contains a menu bar that identifies the different operations (menus) that can be accessed from this window. From left to right, these menus are File, Edit, Search, Run, Compile, Tools, Options, Window, and Help. With the exception of Options and Help, these menu options are arranged more or less in the order in which you would use them to develop a program. Here is a short description of each menu's function:

File
: Provides the set of commands and options for managing your files. Operations available include creating, opening, saving, and printing your Pascal files. You can even change directories and access DOS from this menu.

Edit
: Provides all of the necessary editing operations such as cut, paste, and copy for creating and modifying files.

Search
: Allows you to search for text and perform search and replace operations.

Run
: Provides the necessary commands to run programs and start the debugging process.

Compile
: Provides commands and options for compiling, making, and building a program displayed in the active window.

Debug
: Provides the commands and options for controlling the integrated debugger. This menu command is available in the DOS version only, which is why it is not displayed in Figure 1.2. In Windows versions of TP, the debugger is included as a standalone program (*Turbo Debugger*).

Tools
: Provides access to source-tracking commands and user-installed utilities.

Options
: Provides a set of options for configuring the built-in compiler, linker, debugger, and the environment.

Window
: Provides the basic commands for accessing and controlling the various windows that the IDE provides.

Help
: Allows you to access the online help system.

Selecting Menus and Commands

The easiest way to open a menu or select a command in a menu in either the TP or BP environment is to use a mouse. To open a menu, simply click the left mouse button on the desired entry in the menu bar. Once the menu is open, you can select a command by clicking on it. You can also quickly select a command by dragging the highlight bar down to the desired command and releasing the mouse button. If a command is followed by an ellipsis (...), a dialog box will be displayed when the command is selected. TP uses dialog boxes to query you to enter information and select options. If a command is followed by a right-pointing arrow, another menu will appear when the command is selected. This feature is called *cascading menus*.

After a menu has been opened with the mouse, you can easily open another menu by holding down the mouse button and dragging the mouse pointer along the menu bar to the right or left.

If you don't have a mouse, you can select the main menu bar by pressing F10. Individual menus are then opened by highlighting the menu name with the Right or Left Arrow keys and then pressing Enter. As a shortcut, you can also open a menu by pressing Alt and then the unique highlighted letter for the desired menu. For example, the Run menu is displayed by pressing Alt+R. After a main menu is opened, you can then select a command by highlighting the command with the Up or Down Arrow keys and then pressing Enter.

Even if your computer has a mouse, you might encounter problems if your mouse driver software (called MOUSE.SYS for the Microsoft mouse) is not properly installed. Without the mouse driver, there is no way for the hardware to get mouse commands to the TP environment, so the system will only respond to the keyboard selection commands. When this happens, you can quit TP by pressing Alt+X.

Note To get help information on the help system itself, open the Help menu and select the Help On Help option. You can also view this help information by pressing F1 twice.

Using the mouse or the cursor keys, take a few minutes to examine the menus that are assigned to each of the menu bar items. You can get help on any of the menu commands by first highlighting the menu option with the mouse or cursor keys and then pressing F1.

1. What happens if you try to select a menu command that is shaded?

1. You cannot select the command. A menu command is shaded to indicate that it is currently not available.

Notes on Keyboard Shortcuts

After experimenting with the menu system, you'll discover that menus and commands are easy to select using either the mouse or the keyboard or a combination of the two. To help you to be even more productive, the IDE provides a number of keyboard shortcuts so that you can select a command or open a dialog box without having to first open a menu. For example, you can select the Open... command in the File menu by pressing F3 while you work with a window. The full set of shortcut keys are listed in the Appendix.

Using Dialog Boxes

As I mentioned earlier, some of the menu items are followed by an ellipsis (three dots after the item's name)—for example, the Find... item listed under the Search menu.

What is this trying to tell you? The item is attached to a special dialog box that is displayed when the item is selected. As an example, if you select Find..., you'll see the Find Text dialog box, which is shown in Figure 1.3. Notice that the name of the dialog box is displayed in the top center of the dialog box—the title bar. Because dialog boxes are essentially windows that allow you to select options and enter information, they also contain a close box in the upper-left corner. If you click on the close box, the dialog box will be removed and TP will ignore the options you have selected.

Take another look at the Find Text dialog box and you'll see that a number of components called *controls* are provided. Starting from the top, the first control, which is labeled Text to find, is called an *input box*. This type of control allows you to type in and edit text using the mouse and the cursor movement keys. The next group of controls (labeled as Options) are called *check boxes*. These controls are similar to the check boxes you encounter when filling out forms such as your IRS tax forms. In a group of check boxes, you can select as many boxes as you like. The third group of controls (labeled as Direction) are called *radio buttons*. Although they look like check boxes, radio

Figure 1.3   The Find Text dialog uses a number of different types of controls.

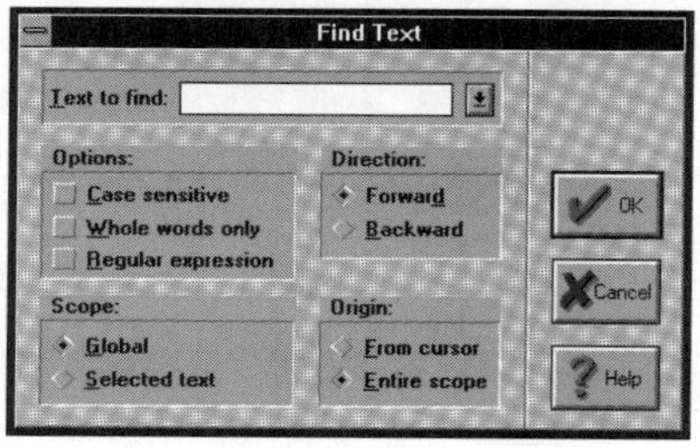

buttons are slightly different because only one radio button in a group can be selected at one time. The fourth type of control (labeled as OK) is called an *action button*. As you might guess, when this type of button is selected an action occurs.

To see the last type of control, we'll need to pop-up another dialog box. Figure 1.4 shows the File Open dialog box, which is displayed when you select the Open... command from the File menu. The control we're interested in (labeled as Files) is called a *list box* or a *scrollable field*. Its name should clue you in to its function. With a list box, you can scroll through a set of items to find the one that you want to select. These controls are often provided in dialog boxes to help you select a file or directory name.

Getting Around

To move from one control to another in a dialog box, you can either use the mouse or press Tab. (Pressing Shift+Tab allows you to select controls in a reverse order.) You can also select a control from the keyboard by pressing the highlighted letter of the control.

In each dialog box, one of the action buttons is designated as the default button—usually the OK button. To find this button, look for the right-pointing arrow (if you are using a monochrome monitor) when the dialog box first appears. The default button will be highlighted if you are using a color monitor. In Windows, the default button will have a dark outline surrounding it. You select the default action button by pressing Enter.

When you have finished selecting options in the dialog box, move the cursor to the OK or Cancel button to select the new settings or to discard them if you made an error.

Figure 1.4   The File Open dialog contains a list box control.

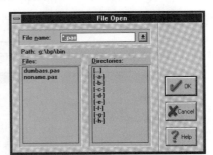

Tips on Using Controls

The following discussion is a useful summary of techniques for working with the five control groups found in TP's dialog boxes.

Action Buttons   To select an action button with the mouse, simply click on the desired button. From the keyboard, keep pressing Tab (or Shift+Tab) until the desired button is highlighted, then press Enter. As a shortcut, press the highlighted letter of the button to select it.

Check Boxes   Remember that you can select as many check boxes in a group as you want. An X within a check box indicates that it has been selected. To select or deselect a check box, click on it with the mouse. From the keyboard, press the highlighted letter of the desired check box.

Radio Buttons   To select or deselect a radio button, click on it with the mouse. A dot will appear when a button is selected. From the keyboard, press the highlighted letter of the desired radio button to select it.

Input Boxes   You can use any of the standard editing keys (Del, Backspace, Arrow keys, etc.) to edit text in an input box. To select the entire line with the mouse, double-click the left button. You can also click and drag the mouse to select text.

List Boxes   The easiest way to scroll the items in a list box is to use the mouse. To select an item in a list, double-click the left button. You can also use the cursor movement keys (Left Arrow, Right Arrow, etc.) and the Home, End, PgUp, and PgDn keys to navigate in a list box.

Remember that TP provides help information for each dialog box. The help information is displayed by selecting the Help button in the dialog box.

Customizing Your Working Environment

Now that you've learned about the basic interface components of the IDE, you'll want to find out how you can set up your own working environment. For this task, you'll primarily be working with the Options menu, which is shown in Figure 1.5. This menu is used to customize all of the major components including the compiler, linker, debugger, editor, display, mouse, memory, and your directories. All of these features will be covered next except the editor which will be covered later in this chapter.

Figure 1.5   Use the Options menu to make modifications to your environment.

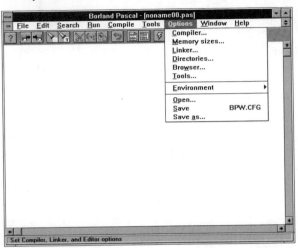

The environment settings that you select from the Options menu can be saved in a file and then later retrieved. To save your settings, select the Save command from the Options menu. The settings will be saved in a file named TURBO.TP if you're using TURBO.EXE or in a file named BP.TP if you're using BP.EXE. When you start TP at a later time, the program will automatically load this file.

The Display

Before you get too far into the DOS IDE, you'll want to ensure that your display is set up to your liking. This is especially important if you are using a color display. The DOS IDE provides a useful dialog box called Colors to help you set your screen colors. To access this feature, select the Environment command in the Options menu. This cascading Environment menu provides access to special environment settings such as the mouse and the display.

To bring up the Colors dialog box select the Colors... command. Notice that this dialog box provides two list boxes. The first list box, Group, contains the names of the IDE's interface components, and the second list box, Item, contains the set of attributes that can be set for each item in the Group list box. These two list boxes allow you to define attributes for the different types of display objects, such as windows, buttons, scroll bar icons, and even selected menu items. For example, if you select the Editor item in the Group list and then select the Scroll bar icons item in the Items list, you can select any of the colors available as the background and foreground colors for this object.

A good way to set up your display is to first select each item in the Group list and examine how its different components are displayed in color. When an item is selected, its foreground and background color is shown in the lower-right corner of the dialog box labeled as "Text."

After you view the colors for an object, try changing the background and foreground colors by selecting desired colors from the Foreground and Background palette. After you have selected the desired colors for the different objects, you can accept the new attributes by clicking on the OK button at the bottom of the dialog box. The display will immediately change to reflect the new colors that you have selected.

The Mouse

To customize the mouse, select the Mouse... command from the cascading Environment menu. As Figure 1.6 shows, three different options are available for configuring the mouse: disabling the right mouse button, setting the mouse to the topic search feature, or setting the right button to access the browse feature.

Special Preferences

Another important feature you'll find available from the cascading Environment menu is the Preferences... command. When you select this command, TP displays the Preferences dialog box. Here several groups of options are provided: Screen Sizes, Source Tracking, Auto Save, Desktop File, Desktop File Options, SpeedBar, and Command Set. The groups that appear will depend on the version of TP you are using. For instance, the Screen Sizes radio buttons allow you to select the number of lines displayed on your screen when running the DOS IDE. The default is 25 lines. In Windows, the number of lines displayed is dependent on the operating system fonts and the size of the window, so this option is not in the Preferences dialog.

The Source Tracking option allows you to specify how you want the IDE to open windows for locating errors. When the New window radio button is selected, the IDE will open a new window whenever it needs to open a file in

Figure 1.6   Use this dialog to set up the mouse.

order to mark the location of an error. If Current window is selected, however, the new file will be displayed in the current window. In the Windows IDE, a new window will always be opened to display errors.

The Auto Save option allows you to instruct TP to automatically save changes that you make while working with the IDE. If you select the Editor files check box, TP will save the source file in the Edit window when you run your program or debug it. (This is a very useful safety feature because it will keep you from losing a program that locks up your computer if you forget to save it before attempting to run it.) The Desktop check box allows you to save your desktop information in the file TURBO.DSK (or BP.DSK or BPW.DSK depending on the program version you're using). This file contains information related to your desktop environment, such as the position of all windows on the desktop, edit window information, history lists, and so on. To instruct TP to save your environment settings before you quit the IDE, select the Configuration check box.

The Desktop File group allows you to specify where you want the IDE to save the desktop file (TURBO.DSK, etc.). The Desktop File Options group lets you select whether to save symbolic information from your last compile in the desktop file. Although this takes up more space in the file, this option can sometimes greatly speed up debugging sessions.

The SpeedBar options allow you to configure the shape and position of the Windows IDE SpeedBar. The SpeedBar is a collection of buttons that allow you to choose frequently exercised menu commands by clicking with the mouse. The Vertical bar option places the SpeedBar along the left edge of the IDE, while selecting Horizontal bar puts the SpeedBar across the top of the IDE. Selecting the Popup radio button makes the SpeedBar a floating palette that you can move around the IDE. Selecting Off hides the SpeedBar until you turn it back on again by choosing one of the other options.

Command Set is another Windows-only IDE option group. The CUA option tells the editor to use the Common User Access guidelines for shortcut keys. The Alternate command set uses the normal Borland defaults. For instance, to exit the IDE you use the Ctrl+F4 key combination with CUA and Alt+X with the Alternate command set selection. Use whichever is more comfortable for you.

Selecting Directories

Another command listed in the Options menu is Directories.... When you select this command, TP brings up the dialog box shown in Figure 1.7, which lets you select the directories TP uses to locate important files. The first file type (.EXE) should be familiar to you; however, the .TPU, include, unit, and object files are special types of files that TP uses. Files with extension .TPU are compiled unit files created by TP. Include files are used to help you write more modular programs. You can define program data and structures in an include file and

---

Figure 1.7   The Directories dialog box helps you to access the directories that TP uses to store special file types.

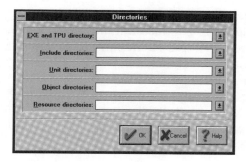

then use the file with different source files. Units are used to package program data structures and code into separate files that can be shared by other programs. The object file types are the precompiled .OBJ files that store binary information. Versions of TP that are capable of compiling programs for Windows have a fifth Directories option: Resources. Resources are descriptions of parts of a Windows program's user interface. These items include menus, cursors, bitmaps, dialog boxes, and accelerator keys.

Note ▼

When you specify a directory, make sure you include the disk drive and full path name. For example, if you plan to store your program files in the directory TP\TPEXE on drive D, enter the following text for the Source option:

```
D:\TP\TPEXE
```

The Tools Menu

The Tools menu is new to TP in version 7. It gives you access to utility programs from inside the IDE. This is generally not such a problem for Windows programs, but when using TP's DOS IDE, the ability to execute a program without leaving the environment can be a great benefit. Although you can install your own utilities into the DOS IDE using the Options/Tools dialog box, one tool comes already installed: Grep. Grep is a powerful text search utility that can help you quickly track down the location of a text string inside other files. Suppose you wanted to find all the other places in which the **Writeln** procedure was called from other TP programs. You would click on the Tools menu and select Grep. You are then prompted for a command line to pass to Grep. You would enter:

```
Writeln *.PAS
```

Grep would then search through all the files with the .PAS extension in the current directory and return lines that contained the string "Writeln." Such a feature can be very useful when tracking down references to a variable or procedure inside of multiple files.

Grep is designed to interface with the Message window inside of TP, which allows you to see the output of Grep inside the environment as well as use this information to open additional files. See the UTILS.DOC file inside TP's \DOC subdirectory for more details on Grep.

Utilities that might appear on the Tools menu in the Windows IDE include Turbo Profiler, WinSight, Turbo Debugger, and the Turbo Resource Workshop depending on which version of TP you have. These programs can also be invoked outside of the IDE.

The Compiler

Figure 1.8 shows the Compiler Options dialog box, which is displayed when you select the Compiler... command from the Options menu. Although this information might look unfamiliar to you at this point, the options are actually very straightforward (i.e., you don't need a Ph.D. in computer science to understand how they work). All of these options simply tell the TP compiler how to process your source files. At this point, the default settings should be adequate for your needs. As we develop programs throughout this book, you'll learn how some of these options are used in practice.

Figure 1.8   The options in this dialog box will tell TP how to process your source files.

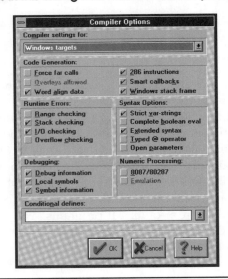

The Linker and Debugger

Working down the list of options, you'll next come to the Linker... and Debugger... options. As Figure 1.9 illustrates, these features allow you to control how TP performs when you build (link) and debug your programs. The Linker dialog box provides options for optimizing the linking process of your programs. If you have enough memory, you can select the Disk radio button in the Link Buffer File section, and TP will use a memory buffer to link your programs instead of a disk buffer.

TP's DOS IDE allows you to select from two main debugging options: Integrated or Standalone debugger. If you are planning to only debug your programs within the IDE, you should select the Integrated check box. If you plan to use the standalone Turbo Debugger, ensure that you select the Standalone option. In Windows, the Debug option is not available. The debugger is always run as a standalone program.

The Debugger dialog box also allows you to select how the integrated debugger will swap your screen with debugging information.

Using the Help System

Now that you've had a chance to customize the screen to your personal tastes, the next logical area to explore is the extensive online help system. Help can be accessed in various ways. The simplest is to either click on the Help menu name on the menu bar or to press Alt+H to select the Help menu. In the DOS IDE, if the Index item is selected, a general index of keywords is displayed in a dialog box, as shown in Figure 1.10. By double-clicking on the appropriate keyword (or pressing Enter when one is highlighted), the help system will take you to the information box that corresponds with the word you selected.

The Contents command in the Help menu provides another useful feature for obtaining help information. This option allows you to access help information

---

Figure 1.9   Linker options allow you to specify the details of building your programs.

Figure 1.10   The Help Index dialog box is used to locate help topics.

---

from any of five categories in the DOS IDE: How to Use Help, Menus and Hot Keys, Editor Commands, Functions and Procedures, and Miscellaneous topics such as directives, error messages, reserved words, Turbo Vision, and so on.

How to Use Help provides a set of useful text and figures to show you how to use the help system. If you're looking for information on how to use TP's menus and hot keys, test any of the topics listed under the Menus and Hot Keys category. The Editor Commands category provides a set of help screens for the window editor that TP provides. This is a good place to check when you are looking for a technique for removing a line of text from a file or undoing a previous editing command. The Functions and Procedures help section provides a list of program parts that are included with TP to help you in writing programs. Functions and procedures are covered in depth in later chapters. The last category provides a set of basic options to help you program in TP. For example, if you want to look up information on how to use the command-line compiler, locate and select the command-line topic.

The Windows version of the TP IDE uses the Windows Help system to provide online help. Figure 1.11 shows the five categories listed when you click the Categories option under the Help menu. They include: Essentials, Language Reference, Tasks, Menu Commands, Keyboard. Clicking on one of these items with the mouse will provide you with specific help information for that item.

As you are viewing help information, keep in mind that you can press Alt+F1 or click on the Alt+F1 text in the status bar to backup a level and view a previous help window.

Also available on the Help menu are the selections Compiler directives, Reserved words, Standard units, TP Language, Error messages, and About. Most of these items are shortcuts into specific groups in the help system. The Error messages selection, for example, allows you pick a particular error message and provides an explanation of how the error occurred and likely steps to correct it. TP Language provides a brief description of the essential elements of TP's syntax. The About choice displays the program's copyright and version number.

Figure 1.11   The contents help window under Windows is used to view help contents.

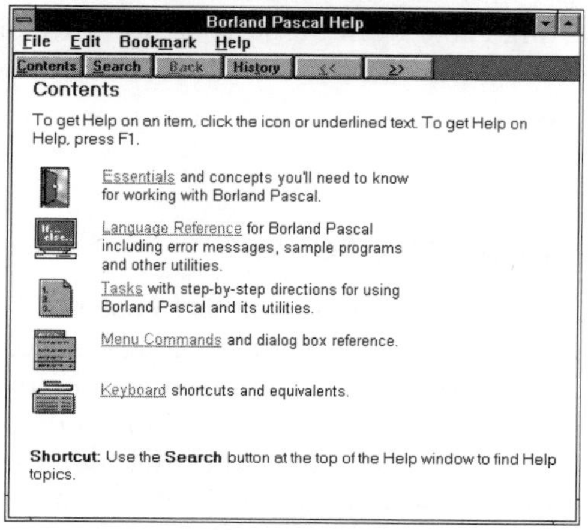

Using TP Help Examples

The help system allows you to copy information and save it to another file for later use. The best part of this feature is that you can actually select any one of the code samples from the help screens and place it in the TP editor so that you can compile and run it. If you see some code you like, feel free to test and use it. To copy help text, follow these simple steps:

For the DOS IDE:

1. Highlight the text by clicking and dragging the mouse, or move the cursor to the beginning of the text you want, hold down Shift, and move the cursor to select the text.

2. Copy the text to the editor buffer by selecting the Copy command from the Edit menu or press Ctrl+Ins.

3. Move the cursor into an edit window and paste the copied text to the TP editor by selecting Paste from the Edit menu or by pressing Shift+Ins.

For the Windows IDE:

1. Open the Sample Code example by clicking on the name of the sample code file listed under "Sample Code" (for instance Abs.PAS for the Abs—absolute value—function).

2. Select Edit, then Copy from the Help system menu.

3. Highlight the text by clicking and dragging the mouse, or move the cursor to the beginning of the text you want, hold down Shift, and move the cursor to select the text.

4. Copy the selected text to the Clipboard by clicking the copy button.

5. Move the cursor into an edit window, and paste the copied text to the TP editor by selecting Paste from the Edit menu or by pressing Shift+Ins.

After code has been copied to the TP editor, it can then be modified or compiled and executed "as is."

Using the Keyword Help Feature

A more interesting way of invoking help is to use the TP keyword help feature. This allows you to quickly get help on a Pascal keyword, function name, procedure name, operator, or constant. As an example, assume that you have a file in the TP editor. You can move the cursor so that it is on, or next to, the item you want to get help on and then click the right mouse button. Next, select the Topic Search command from the Help menu (or pressing Ctrl+F1) to provide information about the word in the edit screen next to the cursor.

Note

If you have your mouse configured properly (see *The Mouse* earlier in this chapter for details), you can press Ctrl while clicking the right mouse button to invoke the Topic Search command.

Figure 1.12 shows the help window that is displayed when the cursor is positioned next to the keyword **BEGIN**. After the help window is displayed, use the mouse cursor to select the window so that you can view the help information. When you're done reading the help text, double-click on the close box in the upper-left corner of the help window.

Figure 1.12   TP allows you to get help with keywords.

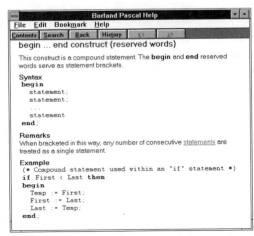

Note

> When using help, keep in mind that the TP help system is a hypertext-based system. This means that you can double-click the mouse or press the Enter key to receive more information about a highlighted key word, which is called a *link*. If you don't have a mouse, you can select keywords by pressing Tab.

When using the DOS IDE, you can switch between the help window and the editor window by using Shift+F6 and F6. When the help window first appears, the cursor is positioned in the help window. To return to the editor window, press Shift+F6. Then pressing F6 will then take you back to the help window. You can resize the help window by pressing Ctrl+F5.

In the Windows IDE, the Alt+Tab key shortcut will take you back and forth between the help window and the editor window.

If you're still uncomfortable using the TP environment, you might want to select the Contents command from the Help menu and explore on your own. To access specific help, double-click on a highlighted item:

1. Access the help system and determine which window lists the special TP editing and shortcut keys?

2. Load in one of the TP sample programs, move the cursor to different Pascal keywords, and press Ctrl+F1 or click the right mouse button to access the context-sensitive help. What happens if the cursor is next to a word that is a Pascal keyword?

1. Press **Alt+H**, then select Contents. From this window select the Editor Commands topic to display information on TP editing and shortcut keys..

2. Help information is displayed for the keyword that has been selected.

Using the Editor

You've now been introduced to many of the basic features of the IDE; however, you haven't seen the TP editor—the component you use to create your programs. Since you'll be spending a lot of time using the editor, you'll want to learn as much as you can "up-front" about how to get the most out of the TP editor. Let's quickly explore some useful techniques for performing the key editing operations, such as opening and saving files, entering and deleting text, and so on.

Loading Files

The first thing you'll need to know in order to create TP programs is how to open and save source files. When you call TP from the DOS prompt with the command

```
TURBO
```

or

```
BP
```

an editor window opens with the default file NONAME00.PAS. To open a different file, just call up TP and include a filename. For example, the following command opens the file named GRAPH1.PAS:

```
TURBO GRAPH1
```

If the file specified does not exist, TP will display a new window with this filename.

Once you're in the TP environment, a different file can be opened at any time by selecting the Open... command from the File menu. Figure 1.13 shows the dialog box that TP displays when this command is selected. If you have .PAS files in the current directory, they'll be listed in the Files list box. To open a file, first highlight it by moving the mouse to select it or by using the Arrow keys, and then select the OK button. (As a shortcut, use the mouse and double-click on the filename.)

What do you do if the file you want to open is in a different directory? That's easy. Just scroll through the Directories list box and select the directory you want. You'll then see the list of files for the selected directory displayed in the Files list.

The File Open dialog box provides a useful feature called a *history list* that allows you to select files that have previously been opened. To access this feature, click on the down arrow that is displayed to the right of the Name input box.

Saving Files

After you're through editing a file, you can save it in one of two ways:

Figure 1.13   Use this dialog box to open files.

- Select the Save command from the File menu to save the file with its current name. (This command can also be selected by pressing F2.)
- Select the Save As... command to save the file with a new name. This command will display a dialog box so that you can give the file a new name.

The more you program with TP, the more you'll find that the Save As... command comes in handy for creating new versions of a program that you are building.

Note

If you have multiple files open, you can save them all by selecting the Save All command from the File menu.

Working with Editor Windows

When a file is opened, TP creates a window to display the file. Each window contains a number of components that you can access to control how a file is displayed. Notice that the keyboard equivalents for the mouse actions are included so that you won't get in trouble if you don't have a mouse installed.

What's useful about windows is that not only can you change their size and move them around, you can also open multiple windows. This means that you can edit multiple source files at the same time. Each time the Open... command is selected from the File menu, a new window is automatically created. You can then change the size of the windows so that multiple files can be viewed. To access a window, click the mouse within the window you want. Inside the DOS IDE, use F6 and Shift+F6 to switch to the next or previous window, respectively. Inside the Windows IDE, use Ctrl+F6 and Shift+Ctrl+F6 to cycle through the open windows.

In the DOS IDE, each window has a unique number assigned to it. You can easily activate a window by pressing Alt and the number of the window. Look in a window's upper-right corner for its ID number. The list of all open windows can be activated by pressing Alt+0.

Selecting, Copying, and Deleting Text

The TP editor is similar to many of the other editors that are available for writing PC programs. In fact, if you're familiar with WordStar commands such as Ctrl+Q or Ctrl+Y, you can use these keyboard sequences to navigate the cursor and insert and delete text. Of course, if you have a mouse, you'll really be able to take advantage of the powerful editing features. Let's take a look at what we can do.

To select a text block, simply click the mouse at the beginning of the block, hold the mouse button down, and drag the mouse until you reach the end of your text block. This same operation can be performed from the keyboard by moving to the beginning of the block, pressing Shift, and using the Arrow keys.

There are also shortcuts you can use, such as pressing Shift+PgUp to select a screen full of text. The complete set of these keyboard shortcuts is listed with the editing hot keys window. (In DOS, select the Contents command from the Help menu, then select Menus and Hot Keys; finally select the Hot Keys topic. In Windows, select the Contents command from the Help menu, then click on the Search button. Enter "hot keys" as a search topic, click on the Show Topics button, and then click on the Go To button.)

After a text block has been selected, it can easily be copied, deleted, or moved by using the Clipboard. The Clipboard is a temporary buffer that stores data for you while you're running TP. Here are the methods for storing data in the Clipboard:

Copying text: Select a block of text and then select the Copy command from the Edit menu or press Ctrl+Ins.

Deleting text: Select a block of text and then select the Cut command from the Edit menu or press Shift+Del.

Moving text: Mark a block of text, cut the text, move the cursor to the starting location where you want to move the text, and select the Paste command from the Edit menu or press Shift+Ins.

The TP editor provides only one Clipboard buffer for deleting, copying, and pasting text. However, it's easy to simulate a multiple clipboard buffer by using multiple windows. That is, you can create windows by opening temporary files, and then use the windows as buffers.

Customizing the Editor

Like the other features of the TP environment, the editor can be easily customized to help you create and edit your programs. To customize the editor, select the Editor command from the cascading Environment menu. (Remember that this menu is found under the Options menu.)

As Figure 1.14 shows, there are 13 different configuration options available. It is recommended that you make sure the first check box, Create backup files, is selected. This ensures that TP will automatically make a backup copy of each file that you edit. Working down the list, the Insert mode check box allows you to toggle the text insert mode for the editor. If this check box is deselected, the text that you type in will overwrite existing text.

To make the editor automatically indent your programs as you type them in, you'll want to select the Auto indent mode check box. The editor also provides the Use tab character check box so that you can store the tab characters that you enter as a true tab character (ASCII 9) or a sequence of spaces. The Optimal fill option uses the least number of characters (tabs and spaces) to perform auto indentation.

Figure 1.14   Using the Editor configuration options.

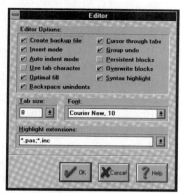

Backspace unindents is used to align lines of program code when the auto indent function indents a line more than you would like. If you press Backspace with this option set, TP aligns the line of code with the previous level of indentation. Cursor-through tabs controls how the text cursor moves when it encounters a tab character.

Group undo controls how much is "undone" when you select Undo from the Edit menu. Version 7 of TP has a near infinite amount of undo/redo control. Persistent blocks check box control whether a block of text remains highlighted when the cursor leaves the block. The Overwrite blocks check box controls whether highlighted blocks are replaced by the next text entry (either from the keyboard or the Clipboard).

The next check box, Syntax highlight, indicates whether the various elements of your TP programs will be highlighted in various colors. This can improve readability of your program code and make it easier to understand. You can change the colors of various syntactical components with the Environment menu option.

The remaining check box options are found only in the DOS IDE. The Block insert cursor check box controls the shape of the text cursor inside the editor. The final check box, Find text at cursor, indicates whether the Search/Find and Search/Replace dialogs default to the previous value or uses the text at the cursor in the current editing window.

For more information about the editor options, click on the control in question and press the F1 key.

Using the Compiler

After you have written a TP program using the editor, you'll need to compile the program before you can run it. A program can be compiled from inside the

TP environment or from the DOS command line. Let's first explore how a program is compiled from the TP environment. Then we'll look at the command line version of the compiler.

Assuming that you have a program in the editor, all you have to do is select the Compile command from the Compile menu or press Ctrl+F9. If your program compiles without any errors, you can then run it by selecting the Run command from the Run menu or press Ctrl+F2. Because it's likely that some of your programs are going to have errors, you might be wondering what happens when the compiler finds an error. To illustrate, let's go over an example.

Figure 1.15 shows a sample session with the compiler. In this figure, the compiler has detected an error in the source file. Notice that a highlighted error message is displayed to indicate the nature of the error. If you need help information about the error, you can press F1 or select the Help text line in the status bar. Before continuing, you must fix the error that has been detected.

The method described for compiling and running programs with the TP environment is the one you use to process programs that require only one source file.

To use the command-line version of the TP compiler, enter the following command at the DOS prompt:

```
TPC <filename>
```

or

```
BPC <filename>
```

Figure 1.15   The compiler has detected an error in this program.

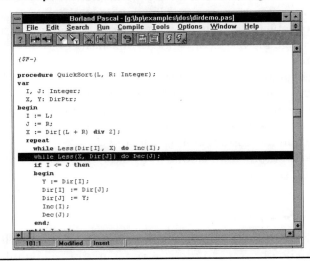

Here the filename component must be the name of your Pascal source file. For example, the command

```
TPC SORT.PAS
```

compiles the SORT.PAS file and creates an executable version of this file (.EXE) if no errors are found.

A Quick Look at the Debugger

Once you get past the compiler, the battle is half won. But what happens if your program doesn't do what you think it should do? Of course, you can print out your program and stare at each line of code until you either fall asleep or you discover your problem. There is, however, a much better way to find your errors—put the built-in debugger to work.

The menu used to invoke the debugger provides three separate types of operations that can be performed: Evaluate/modify, Watches, and Breakpoints. The Evaluate/modify... command is used to help you evaluate and modify the contents of selected variables that your program uses. The Watches option allows you to specify an expression that you want to "watch" as your program is running. When you select this option, a special menu is presented to allow you to add, delete, edit, and remove all watches. The last two options in the Debug menu, Toggle breakpoint and Breakpoints..., allow you to define and change breakpoints so that you can stop your program at a specific line and take a close look at what is going on. These features can help you identify when your program takes a "wrong turn." When a breakpoint has been reached, another TP debugging feature allows you to single-step through your code. This stepping method is very powerful because it can help you isolate those hard-to-find errors. By setting a breakpoint at the beginning of the section of the code that you suspect is guilty of the serious crime (not doing what you told it to do), you'll be able to step through each line until you find the problem.

We'll take a much more in-depth look at TP's powerful debugging tools in a later chapter.

Summary

We've now completed our quick exploration of the TP environment. We started by looking at the basic components of the interactive development environment (IDE) including the editor, compiler, help system, and debugger. Then, we explored how the menu system is used to access the TP features. You also learned how to customize the display, keyboard, mouse, and the editor.

In Chapter 2, you'll be able to put the information presented here to work as you start writing TP programs.

Exercises

1. Which special key is used to select the main menu bar?
2. How can you call up TP so that it will run in a dual monitor mode?
3. How can you compile a TP program from the DOS command line?
4. Try to compile the following program:

```
PROGRAM Test1;

BEGIN
 Writeln("This is a test");
END;
```

What two errors does the compiler give you? How can you fix them so that the program will compile?

5. When running the program from step 4, how can you switch back and forth from the editor screen to the output screen?

Answers

1. The F10 key.
2. Use the command

```
TURBO/D
```

at the DOS prompt so that TP will come up in the dual monitor mode.

3. To compile a TP program from the DOS prompt, use the command TPC. For example, the following command compiles the file TEST.PAS:

```
TPC TEST.PAS
```

4. The two errors the compiler will find in the sample program are:

• The output string specified with the **Writeln** statement is formatted incorrectly.

• The program does not terminate with a **.** after the **END** keyword.

A correct version of the program is:

```
PROGRAM Test1;

BEGIN
 Writeln('This is a test');
END.
```

5. Press the Alt+F5 to switch between the run-time environment screen and the editing screen.

Writing Your
First Programs

In this chapter, I'll show you how to get started writing your own programs. But don't worry if you're new to TP programming. Writing and running a program in this highly structured language is much easier than you might first think—especially with the powerful integrated environment on your side. Once you learn how to use the basic components of the Pascal language, you'll find that the real work in writing programs involves knowing how to plan and knowing how to apply basic problem-solving skills.

This chapter explains the basic components you'll need to write TP programs. It begins by examining the basic structure of a Pascal program and the main building blocks that are required to compose programs. Next, we'll write a complete, working program that includes a user-defined procedure and a function. As you work through this chapter, you'll learn the basics of writing simple and compound statements, performing screen input/output (I/O) operations, and controlling the execution flow of programs. In the last part of the chapter, some important techniques for programming with style are discussed.

After you complete this chapter you'll know how to:

- Apply structured programming concepts
- Write, compile, and run a basic TP program
- Perform simple I/O operations
- Use loop control and decision-making statements

Words, Rules, and Structure

Pick up any textbook on Pascal programming and the first paragraph will probably tell you that Pascal is a structured language. Unfortunately, this description really doesn't tell you a lot about Pascal programming—especially if you've never written a program before. *Structured language* simply means that there are certain structural rules you must follow in order to write programs that will compile and run. In practical terms, the different components that make up a program, such as constants, variables, assignment statements, decision-making statements, procedures, and so on, must be written in a certain order. The Pascal language is so big on structure because it was designed to help programmers approach programming in a methodical, structured manner instead of with the haphazard approach that other languages allow.

You can think of the structured programming approach in terms of good planning. For example, assume that you were going to take a trip from your home town to the Himalayas. With the structured approach, you would sit down and work out the details of your trip before you jump in your car and drive to the airport. Now compare this to the unstructured method, where you wander around the world, making your plans as you go, until you get to your destination—if you're lucky.

Before examining the structural aspects of Pascal programs in more detail, you'll need to see what elements are actually used to create programs. The important thing to keep in mind is that Pascal is a language, and therefore consists of a set of words and "grammar" rules that make everything work. Of course, the words that you use to write TP programs aren't exactly the same as the words you use in day-to-day conversation. The TP vocabulary actually consists of a set of *reserved words*, *standard identifiers*, and *user-defined identifiers*. For example:

```
IF Total <> Max THEN Writeln('The total is ', Total);
```

First, don't be scared away if this example code looks unfamiliar to you— it's supposed to. This simple statement contains words from the three categories just introduced. The words **IF** and **THEN** are reserved words because they have special meaning to the TP compiler. That is, they serve as sign posts to help guide the compiler as it works its way through a program. The word **Writeln**, however, is a standard identifier—it refers to a built-in Pascal function. Finally, the words **Total** and **Max** are user-defined identifiers. In this case, the TP compiler will treat these words as names of variables or constants because of the way they are used.

Note

In the program examples presented in this book, the TP reserved words will be written with all uppercase, boldface letters (e.g. **BEGIN**, **END**, **IF**, **THEN**, **WHILE**). The standard and user-defined identifiers will be written with an initial uppercase letter and then all remaining letters will be lowercase (e.g. **Read**, **ClrScr**, **Total**, **Writeln**).

To further understand how reserved words and identifiers are used by the TP compiler, let's look at how the compiler might process a simple **BEGIN-END** statement. The code for our example is:

```
BEGIN
  IF X > 20 THEN Writeln('The number X is out of range');
END;
```

Figure 2.1 illustrates the step-by-step process the compiler uses to compile this code. The **BEGIN** keyword tells the compiler that a statement block is about to start. The **IF** keyword then directs the compiler to prepare to process an **IF-THEN** decision statement. As the compiler processes this statement, it first expects to find a conditional expression (**X > 20**) and then an action clause (**Writeln(...);**). As you can see, the components of each statement must follow a specific order.

Figure 2.1   The compiler processes a statement in a structured manner.

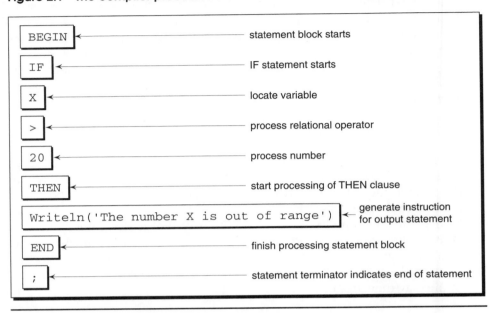

A Program Template

You might now be wondering, "What does a complete Pascal program actually look like?" Figure 2.2 provides a detailed template of the components that make up a Pascal program. You can use this template to help ensure that your programs are structured correctly. Notice that the first line in Figure 2.2 consists of the keyword **PROGRAM** followed by the "user-supplied name" that you assign to the program. The **PROGRAM** keyword tells the compiler that the file it is processing is a valid Pascal program. If you forget this keyword, the compiler won't know what to do with your file.

If you skip to the bottom of Figure 2.2, you'll see the other major section that every Pascal program source file must provide called the *main program block*. This component is bracketed by the two keywords **BEGIN** and **END**. Notice that the main program is terminated by the keyword **END** followed by a period. The main program block is the section where all of the instructions for the main body of your program reside. When your program runs, the instructions in the main program block are executed in the order that they are listed.

Another requirement of the Pascal program structure is that compiled units, program labels, constants, data type definitions, and variable declarations used by the main program must be defined at the beginning of the file—before any code is written. These elements are placed in the different sections called **USES**, **LABEL**, **CONST**, **TYPE**, and **VAR** in Figure 2.2. These labeled components

Figure 2.2 **This figure illustrates the structure of a TP program.**

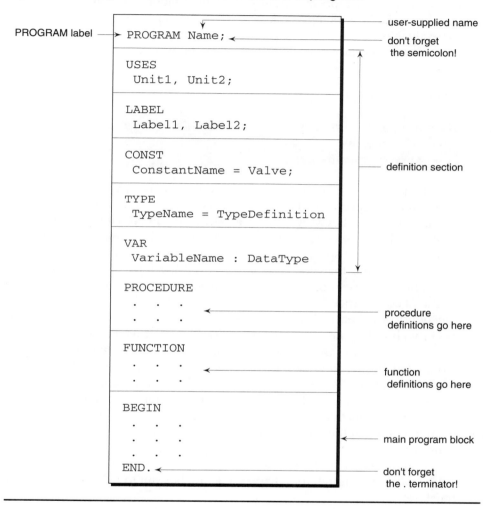

taken together are called the *definition section* of a program, and are needed to help the compiler determine how it should process the instructions in the body of a program. Let's look at an example.

Imagine that you have a program that contains this statement to add the number 3 to a variable named **Sum** in the program body:

```
Sum := Sum + 3;
```

Until **Sum** is defined as some sort of variable or constant, the compiler won't know what to do with the word **Sum** because it isn't a keyword. Of course, it is easy to see that **Sum** is a simple variable. Unfortunately, there are several different ways to represent numbers. Thus, unless the compiler knows what type of variable is being used, it won't know how to process the statement correctly. Now a variable declaration statement is placed in the **VAR** section of the program, as shown in the following program:

```
VAR
  Sum  : Integer;
```

Note

Because the TP compiler can't read your mind, you must always remember to define an element such as a label, constant, or variable before you try to use it in the program body.

The last group of building blocks used to create programs includes procedures and functions. As Figure 2.2 shows, these components must also be defined with the keywords **PROCEDURE** and **FUNCTION** before the main program block. Procedures and functions generally contain sections of code that are either very specialized or that are used repeatedly by the program. For example, assume that you're going to write a simple database management program to keep information on electronic-like index cards. This program might need a procedure to display each card "image" on the screen, or a function to read each data record from disk storage. Both types of definitions begin with either the keyword **PROCEDURE** or **FUNCTION** , followed by its user-supplied name and an argument list, if any. These *subprograms* are always terminated by the keyword **END**, followed by a semicolon. Procedures and functions will be discussed in greater detail later in this chapter.

Any constants, variables, and so on that are intended to be used only by the procedure or function must be defined within the procedure or function. But keep in mind that the order for defining these components is the same as in the main program.

A summary of each program component listed in Figure 2.2 follows. As you're working through this chapter, you might want to refer to this section as a quick reference.

PROGRAM marks the beginning of a TP program source file. For example:

```
PROGRAM CountNum;
```

In this case, the text "CountNum" represents the program name.

USES tells the compiler which separately compiled files, called *units*, are used by the main program. This statement illustrates how two built-in units (Dos and Graph) are included in a program:

```
USES Dos, Graph;
```

LABEL defines the labels that are used with **GOTO** statements. The format for this section is:

```
LABEL 20, 1000, 120;
```

CONST marks the beginning of the constants declaration section. The required format is:

```
CONST
  Low  = 0;
  High = 1000;
```

TYPE defines a type declaration section. In this section, you place all of the user-defined types such as ranges, sets, records, and objects. An example of a type section is:

```
TYPE
  Vowels = ['A', 'E', 'I', 'O', 'U'];
  Range = 1..10;
  Template = ARRAY[1..10] OF Integer;
```

VAR marks the beginning of the variable declaration section. An example is:

```
VAR
  Sum, Count : Integer;
  Numbers : Template;
```

PROCEDURE/FUNCTION is used to define a procedure or a function.

BEGIN marks the beginning of a procedure, function, or main program block.

END marks the end of a procedure, function, or main program block.

1. Write a variable declaration section to declare the variables **X** and **Y** as **Integers**, and **Total** as a **Real**.
2. What will the compiler do if you reverse the order of the **CONST** and **VAR** sections in a program?
3. Why does Pascal require you to declare variables before they are used?
4. Why are procedures and functions useful for structured programming?
5. True or false: The **PROGRAM** keyword is optional.

1. ```
   VAR

     X,Y  : Integer;
     Total: Real;
   ```
   ```

2. The compiler will still be able to compile your file.
3. A variable must be declared before it is used in a program so that the compiler will know the data type of the variable.
4. Procedures and functions are useful devices for structured programming because they help you group code that performs a specific operation.
5. False

Getting Your Feet Wet

Now that we've explored the basic structure and components of a TP program, let's put together an example that uses many of the components we've been discussing. Although this program isn't very fancy, it does show how the key components of a TP program interact with each other. Type in the program in the Turbo editor, compile it, and then run it, and you'll discover that it displays 10 lines and includes the line number on each line. (If you're not sure how to compile the program, you'll be shown how a little later in this chapter.) Here is the complete program:

```
PROGRAM Greeting;
{ Program displays numbers on 10 lines }
USES Crt;    { The Crt unit is provided with TP }
CONST
  Max_lines = 10;
VAR
  Loop_count, Line_num : Integer;

FUNCTION LineCounter(J : Integer) : Integer;
BEGIN
  LineCounter := J + 1;
END;

PROCEDURE ScreenOut(U : Integer);
BEGIN
  Writeln(U);
END;

{ Main program body }
BEGIN
  ClrScr; { Clears the entire screen }
  FOR Loop_count := 0 TO Max_lines-1 DO
  BEGIN
    Line_num := LineCounter(Line_num);
    ScreenOut(Line_num);
  END;
END.
```

Windows Tip: If you've got Turbo Pascal or Borland Pascal for Windows, you may wish to try this program inside of Windows. To get this program to compile and run in Windows, simply replace the line

```
USES Crt;
```

near the top of the program with

```
USES WinCrt;
```

WinCrt is a TP unit that provides a text-like screen for outputting in Windows.

Notice that the program consists of a main program body that houses the instructions **ClrScr**, **FOR Loop_count := 0 ...**, and so on, a procedure (**ScreenOut**), and a function (**LineCounter**). If you look closely at the program, you'll notice one important difference between a function and a procedure: The function returns a value of a specific type. This is why the function definition contains the keyword **FUNCTION**, its name, a parameter list enclosed in parentheses, a colon, and the type of the result of the function. A procedure, however, doesn't return a value; it simply performs an expected operation and returns control to the statement that called it. You'll learn a lot more about procedures and functions in Chapter 8.

One component of this program that may need some explanation is shown by the following code:

```
{ Program displays numbers on 10 lines }
{ Clears the entire screen }
```

What are the these lines used for? They're actually comments, which allow us to document the program. The TP compiler always ignores text that is placed within braces { }. You can also write comments by putting text between the symbols (* and *). For example, this line is a valid comment:

```
(* Clears the entire screen *)
```

Our sample program also includes a number of other statements—including assignment statements, loop statements, output statements, and others—that we haven't explained yet. We'll go over these statements during the remainder of this chapter to give you a handle on the basics of TP programming.

1. Show the output that the GREETING program will produce if you change the **Max_lines** constant to:

```
CONST
  Max_lines = 20;
```

What happens if you set this constant to 30?

2. What compiler message do you get if you remove the '.' from the final **END** statement in the GREETING program?

1. Twenty line numbers will be displayed if **Max_lines** is set to 20; thirty line numbers will be displayed if **Max_lines** is set to 30.
2. Error 10: Unexpected end of file

Starting with the Assignment Statement

The simplest type of statement to write in Pascal is the *assignment statement.* As an example, the statement

```
K := Counter + 1;
```

tells the TP compiler to generate an instruction to take the value of **Counter** from memory, add 1 to it, and to store that value in the memory location assigned to the variable **K**. This operation is illustrated in Figure 2.3. The symbol **:=** indicates that the result of the evaluation of the expression to the right of that symbol should be assigned to the variable to the left of the symbol. The semicolon at the end of the line is a statement terminator, which tells the Pascal compiler that it can stop processing at that point in the statement and interpret what it has seen so far into machine-executable code.

If you've never written an assignment statement before, you'll need to get used to the fact that you can use the same variable name on both the right and left side of the assignment operator. For example:

```
Counter := Counter + 1;
```

Figure 2.3 **Here is an example of how the compiler processes an assignment statement.**

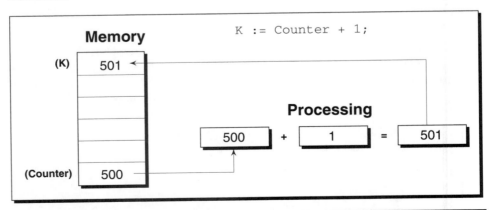

As Figure 2.4 shows, this statement instructs the compiler to generate an instruction to take the value from **Counter**, add 1 to this value, and place the result back into **Counter**. This type of statement is called an *increment statement* because it increments the value of a variable.

Other Simple Statements

In addition to assignment statements, our sample program contains other simple statements to define and initialize such components as constants and variables. These statements are found in the declaration section of the program. For example, the statement

```
CONST
  Max_lines = 10;
```

defines a constant called **Max_lines** and sets this constant to the value 10.

Note   A constant can be defined only once in a program. If a constant has been defined in the **CONST** section, you cannot later assign it a new value.

A **TYPE** declaration section wasn't included in our sample program; however, the following example illustrates the format required for creating a **TYPE** definition:

```
TYPE
  Workdays = (Monday,Tuesday,Wednesday,Thursday,Friday);
```

Figure 2.4   An example of incrementing the value of a variable.

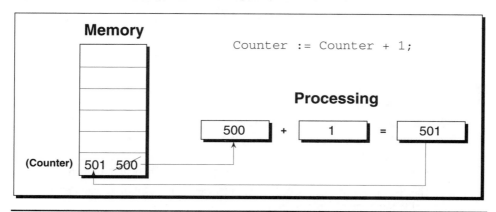

This simple statement tells the compiler that we are defining an *enumerated* data type called **Workdays,** which will consist of the values **Monday** through **Friday**.

The last type of simple statement found in the declaration section of our sample program is used to declare the variables that the program needs:

```
VAR
    Loop_count, Line_num : Integer;
```

Notice that each variable name must be separated by a comma. A colon is placed after the last variable, followed by the name of the data type for the variables. In this case, the compiler is instructed to store the variables as **Integer** data types. Whenever a value is assigned to one of these variables, the TP compiler checks to ensure that the value assigned is an integer. If we tried to execute an assignment such as

```
Loop_count := 1.5;
```

we would get a compiler error because the value being assigned is a different data type.

1. What are the differences between these two statements?

   ```
   X := 10;
   X = 10;
   ```

2. How many assignment statements were used in the GREETING program presented earlier?

3. What is the difference between a constant and a variable?

4. Why can't a constant and a variable be given the same name?

5. What will the compiler do if you add the following statement to the body of the GREETING program:

   ```
   Max_lines := 15;
   ```

1. The first statement is an assignment statement; the second statement is a comparison statement.
2. Two assignment statements are used.
3. A constant does not change during the execution of a program, whereas a variable may be assigned many different values.
4. The compiler would not be able to tell the difference between the two.
5. This statement will produce an error because a value cannot be assigned to a constant inside the body of a program.

The Compound Statement

Another powerful statement available in Pascal is the *compound statement.* Such statements can always be identified by the presence of the keywords **BEGIN** and **END**. All of the statements contained by a particular **BEGIN-END** pair are considered one compound statement. Thus, even the code sections of procedures, functions, and programs can be thought of as one large compound statement.

Normally, compound statements are used to associate statements into groups that will be executed only if a specific condition has been satisfied. For example:

```
IF K > 0 THEN
   BEGIN
     X := X + 1;
     J := 10 DIV K;
   END
ELSE J := 20;
```

The two statements between the **BEGIN-END** pair will be executed only if the requirements of the **IF** statement are satisfied; otherwise, the statement following the **ELSE** statement will be executed. Keep in mind that a different compound statement could also have taken the place of the **J := 20** statement if several things needed to be done when the **IF** statement failed. For example, we could add this new **ELSE** clause:

```
ELSE
   BEGIN
     J := 20;
     X := 0
   END;
```

Figure 2.5 shows how the complete **IF** statement block actually consists of two groups of statements, which themselves consist of separate statements.

Note   In TP, a compound statement can be used anywhere that a normal assignment statement is allowed.

A Quick Look at I/O

If you've ever had a computer program "wander off" to some unknown place while you're running it, you know the uneasy feeling of waiting for the program to do something, anything, to reassure you that it's still "alive." The problem is that we all expect a program to generate some form of output—no matter how simple the program is. For this reason, you're going to want to learn some of the basics of writing statements that make your programs communicate with the outside world.

Figure 2.5 A compound statement diagram.

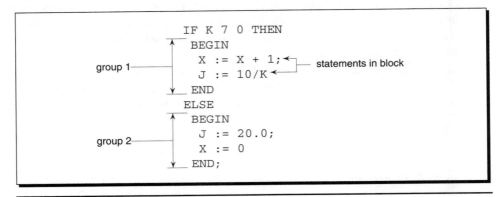

The simplest forms of I/O on personal computers are keyboard input and screen output. The procedure used most often to perform screen output is **Writeln**. The general format for this procedure is:

```
Writeln(<identifier>:<width>:<decimals>);
```

You replace *identifier* with the name of the variable or string that you want to display. Because **Writeln** is a general purpose output routine, you can output a variable of any standard Pascal data type, such as **Integer**, **Real**, **Char**, and so on. The component *width* specifies an optional number that indicates how many columns you wish to allocate to the data that is being displayed on the screen, and *decimals* is an optional field that indicates how many digits should be shown after the decimal point for floating-point numbers (reals). If you are printing an integer, only the width should be specified (there's no fractional part to integers). Some sample approaches for using **Writeln** to print data of different types are:

```
VAR
   X   : Integer;
   Ch  : Char;
   Sum : Real;

BEGIN
   X   := 10;
   Ch  := 'C';
   Sum := 100.73;
   Writeln(X);           { Prints an integer value }
   Writeln(Ch);          { Prints a character }
   Writeln(Sum : 6 : 3); { Prints a real value }
```

The **Writeln** statement can also be used to print character strings by applying the format

```
Writeln('Print out this string');
```

What's really useful about **Writeln** is that you can combine constant strings with variables to display output. For example:

```
Writeln('The answer is ', X);
```

If **X** had the value 100, this statement would produce the output

```
The answer is 100
```

Another handy thing about **Writeln** is that the output from each call to the procedure begins in the first column of a new line. This means you don't have to worry about moving the cursor to a safe position before sending out your data. In Chapter 6, we'll explain the I/O commands in more detail.

Note

The **Writeln** procedure always advances the screen cursor to the next line after it displays its data. If you don't want to advance the cursor, you can use the **Write** statement instead.

Inputting Data

We've taken care of simple output, but what about input? That is, how do we read data into a program? Fortunately, TP provides a set of procedures called **Readln** and **Read** that are similar to **Writeln** and **Write**, except that they read data instead of outputting data. Here is the basic format for a **Readln** statement:

```
Readln(<variable>);
```

In this case, all you have to do is provide the name of the variable where you want the input data to be stored. When the procedure executes, it waits for you to enter your data and then saves the data in the specified variable. A sample program for inputting data is:

```
PROGRAM ReadIt;
{ Reads a character and converts it to uppercase }

VAR
  Ch : Char;
```

```
BEGIN
  Writeln('Enter a character');
  Readln(Ch);
  Writeln('The uppercase version of this character is ', UpCase(Ch));
END.
```

The first **Writeln** instruction displays a message and then the **Readln** instruction waits for you to type in a character. Keep in mind that you must enter a character and then press Enter to instruct **Readln** that the data has been entered. The character that you enter is stored in the variable **Ch**. In the last **Writeln** instruction, the built-in function **UpCase** is used to convert the letter stored in the variable **Ch** to its uppercase equivalent.

Another useful input command is **ReadKey**. It always returns one character that corresponds to the key currently being pressed. It also does not echo the pressed key to the screen. Imagine that you had to write a program that required a user password before it would run. You certainly wouldn't want the password to show up on the screen, so you could use the **ReadKey** command to read in each keystroke. The result of the **ReadKey** command could then be used to build up a string that could eventually be compared to the valid password.

Note

Because **ReadKey** is defined in the Unit **Crt**, you must include the following statement in the **USES** declaration section of your program in order to use **ReadKey**:

```
USES Crt;
```

If you are programming in Windows, you must include

```
USES WinCrt;
```

instead.

1. Show the output that the following program will produce:

```
PROGRAM OutTest;
VAR
  Num : Integer;

BEGIN
  Writeln("Enter a number from one to 10");
  Readln(Num);
  Writeln("The number is ", Num);
END.
```

2. How can you fix the program in step 1 so that it will compile properly?

1. The program will not compile because double quotation marks (" ") are used to delimit the output strings.
2. Change the double quotation marks to single quotation marks.

Controlling Program Flow

Imagine that you had to restart your editor for each line of code you wanted to modify in your program. You would lose interest in programming very quickly! Fortunately, your editor was programmed so that it could repeat tasks. After all, computer software is uniquely suited to the job of performing routine tasks repetitively. In order to repeat an operation, however, you must be able to control program flow.

The most common way to control program flow is to decide whether a condition is true or false and then perform the appropriate processing. In Pascal, this is easily done with an **IF** statement. The simplest **IF** statement looks like:

```
IF Count > 0 THEN
   Writeln('The count is greater than zero');
```

As Figure 2.6 shows, there are four distinct parts to the **IF** statement: the keyword **IF**, an expression that can be evaluated to true or false, the keyword **THEN**, and a statement that will be executed if the expression evaluates to true. As you will recall from our previous discussion of compound statements, the **Writeln** statement above could have been replaced by a group of statements bracketed by a **BEGIN-END** pair. An important point to remember here is that if we had wanted to test the variable **Count** to determine if it was equal to 0, we would have used = rather than := since we were not trying to assign the value 0 to **Count,** but were only trying to decide whether it already contained that value.

Another common method for controlling the flow of execution in a program is to use a loop. For now, we'll concentrate on the simple **FOR** loop. This type of loop is written using the following format:

Figure 2.6 The four different parts of an IF statement.

```
                    logical expression
                          |
   IF keyword          THEN keyword
      |      |<------>|    |
      v      |        |    v
      IF  Count  7  0  THEN
expression--> Writeln('The count is greater than zero');
```

```
FOR I := 1 TO 10  DO
  BEGIN
    K := I * I;
      . . .
  END;
```

The **FOR** loop is similar to the old **DO** loop that's been around since FORTRAN days. It assigns an initial value to an integer loop index variable, and then increments this variable by one for each pass through the loop until the end value is exceeded. (In our example above, the variable **I** would contain the value 10 on the last pass through the loop.)

Another common type of loop that we'll be using in many of our examples is the **WHILE** loop. How is this loop different from the **FOR** loop? Instead of repeating for a fixed number of times, it repeats until an initial condition is no longer true. As an example, the following loop repeats until the variable **X** becomes greater than 100:

```
WHILE X <=100 DO BEGIN
  Writeln('Enter a new value');
  Readln(X)
END;
```

These *constructs* and others are explained in detail in Chapter 4.

1. Change the following **IF-THEN** statement so that it will be more efficient:

   ```
   IF (X > Y + 10) AND (X <> Y) THEN ...
   ```

2. Explain how to convert the following **FOR** loop into a **WHILE** loop:

   ```
   FOR I := 1 TO 10 DO
     Writeln('The loop count is ', I)
   END;
   ```

1. IF (X > Y + 10) THEN ...
   (The second comparison expression was not needed.)
2. The converted loop is:

   ```
   WHILE I <= 10 DO BEGIN
     Writeln('The loop count is ', I);
     I := I + 1;
     END;
   ```

Creating Programs

Now that you've had a brief exposure to the basic components of Pascal programs, we should pause to discuss how to enter a program so that TP can execute it. Three menus will be of concern to you. First, select the Directories... command from the Options menu. This allows you to display the dialog box for specifying the default directory for the types of files you'll need to write TP programs. Remember that the .PAS files are Pascal source files, the .EXE files are the compiled versions of your programs, and the .TPU files are compiled unit files. Make certain that the directories point to where you want your files to go.

After you've modified and saved the Directories dialog box, go to the File menu and select New to indicate that you want to create a new program. A blank screen will appear. You can now begin to enter a program. As an exercise, you may wish to enter the extremely brief program shown next, which is called BLANK. This program simply clears the screen and then slowly moves a character around the screen to indicate that the computer is still on.

```
PROGRAM Blank;
{ Program clears the screen and moves a character }
USES Crt;
CONST
  Lines_per_screen = 24;
  Time_delay = 300;
VAR
  Count, Switch : Integer;

BEGIN
  Switch := 0;
  ClrScr;
  WHILE Switch = 0 DO BEGIN
    FOR Count := 0 TO Lines_per_screen DO BEGIN
      Writeln('');   {Generates a blank line}
      Delay(Time_delay);
    END;
    Writeln( '    *');
    IF KeyPressed THEN Switch := 10;
  END;
END.
```

Windows Tip: Don't forget to use the **WinCrt** unit instead of **Crt** if you want to run this program in Windows.

Now that you've invested at least a few minutes of your time to type in the sample program by this point, you should next save the file so that you don't lose your work. Do this by selecting the Save As... command from the File menu, typing the name of the file, and selecting OK. Notice that the title bar of the window displaying your program now shows the filename that you entered.

Compiling the Program

Now that you have a program in the editor that has also been saved to disk, you're ready to compile, then run the program. To do this, select the Compile... command from the Compile menu. A special dialog box will appear in the center of the screen to indicate how many lines have been processed by the compiler. If your program does not have any compile-time errors, TP will simply return to the main screen. At this point, select the Run command from the Run menu to start program execution. That's all there is to it!

If you did have compile-time errors, TP returned you to the point in the program where it thought an error had occurred. The actual cause of the problem may sometimes lie above this point in the program. If you encountered an error while compiling the sample BLANK program, recheck the text carefully for misspelled keywords, missing semicolons, and so on.

If you didn't have any compile-time errors, this may be a good point to introduce you to the compiler's reaction when it encounters a mistake. Let's start off with something simple, such as omitting a semicolon. If you used the BLANK program as an example, remove the semicolon after the line

```
Writeln( '    *');
```

When you tell TP to compile the modified source, the compiler should indicate the error and return to the screen at the point where you inserted the error.

Debugging the Program

Thus far we've only seen what TP will do if there are no compile-time errors. I mentioned earlier that TP has a powerful debugger that allows you to set up breakpoints or to monitor the values attained by a particular variable. Chapter 14 contains useful information on using the Debugger to find and debug logic errors in your programs.

Summary

In this chapter, I've shown you how to work with the TP environment to create, compile, execute, and debug your first Pascal program. Along the way, you saw how TP is a structured language and how programs are written by placing statements in a certain order. You also now know how to write basic statements for assigning values to variables, reading and writing data to the keyboard and screen, and controlling the execution flow of programs.

In Chapter 3, we'll continue our exploration of the Pascal building blocks as we learn how to use variables and data types.

Exercises

1. Modify the GREETING program (page 38) so that it does not need the **LineCounter** function and **ScreenOut** procedure.

2. Explain the advantages and disadvantages of using the procedure and function in the GREETING program.

3. Explain what is wrong with the following variable declarations:

```
VAR
  X, Y : Integer
  CH : Char
  Sum : Real
```

4. Write a program to input three numbers and calculate the average of the three numbers.

5. Explain why the following statement will not compile correctly:

```
Counter = Counter + 1;
```

Answers

1. Here is the modified program:

```
PROGRAM Greeting;
{ This program displays numbers on 10 lines }
USES Crt;
CONST
  Max_lines = 10;
VAR
  Loop_count, Line_num : Integer;

BEGIN
  Line_num := 0;
  ClrScr; { This clears the entire screen }
  FOR Loop_count := 1 TO Max_lines DO
    BEGIN
      Line_num := Line_num + 1;
      Writeln(Line_num);
    END;
END.
```

2. The procedure and function make the program more modular. However, because they are short and called within the body of the loop, we can get by without them.

3. Semicolons are missing from the variable declaration statements. The correct

version is:

```
VAR
   X, Y : Integer;
   CH   : Char;
   Sum  : Real;
```

4. The program would be written as follows:

```
PROGRAM ComputeAvg;
CONST
   TotalNum = 3;
VAR
   Num1, Num2, Num3 : Integer;

BEGIN
   Writeln('Input the first number');
   Readln(Num1);
   Writeln('Input the second number');
   Readln(Num2);
   Writeln('Input the third number');
   Readln(Num3);
   Writeln('The average is ', (Num1 + Num2 + Num3) Div TotalNum);
END.
```

5. The assignment statement is written incorrectly. The colon must be added:

```
Counter := Counter + 1;
```

3

Variables and
Data Types

Now that we've explored the basics of creating and compiling a TP program, we can turn to the subject of *data representation*. All the information stored in your computer is represented by a sequence of 1 and 0 values. In order for TP to differentiate between different types of data, (for example, the number 65 and the letter A), the compiler must know the attributes of the type of variable with which it is working. Needless to say, we would all be in serious trouble if the compiler were to get confused and display the numerical values of each letter in our program, rather than the characters themselves!

In this chapter, you'll learn about the basic techniques for using TP variables and the different data types that are available for declaring variables. You'll learn how to use the five basic data types: **Integer**, **Real**, **Char**, **String**, and **Boolean**. You'll also be introduced to the other data types for representing integers, which include **ShortInt**, **LongInt**, **Byte**, and **Word**.

After you complete this chapter, you'll know how to:

- Declare and initialize simple variables
- Use the five basic data types
- Select the proper representation for the numbers that your programs use
- Use constants
- Convert data from one type to another

Working with Variables

In the sample programs presented thus far, simple Pascal variables have been used to store data temporarily. Each time you see a declaration statement, such as

```
VAR
  X : Integer;
```

the TP compiler reserves a unique memory location to store the data for the variable (**X**, in this case). But how does the compiler know how much memory to set aside? In the above example, that's where the data type **Integer** comes in. This keyword tells the TP compiler that the variable you are declaring is an integer, which in turn tells TP how to use the variable within the program. As long as you assign integer values to this variable, you won't get any complaints from the compiler.

Before you start working with the different variable types, you'll first need to know a little about how the computer's memory is organized. The smallest entity within personal computer memory is the *bit*. A bit represents one physical location in memory and is capable of containing only two values: 1 or 0.

The fundamental unit of memory in most personal computers is the *byte*. You've probably heard a great deal about kilobytes or megabytes of memory or disk storage. A byte is simply 8 bits of memory available at one storage location, which is called an *address*. This relationship is shown in Figure 3.1.

Due to the bit and byte approach to data storage, data is represented in numbers of the base 2 system, called the *binary number system*. Therefore, a kilobyte of data indicates 1,024 bytes (1,024 is 2 to the 10th power). A megabyte consists of 1,048,576 bytes (which is 2 to the 20th power). Unless you really need to count bytes in detail, think of K as representing 1,000 (1 kilo) and *M* as representing 1,000,000 (1 Mega) of something. Let's now investigate the various ways you can use bytes to represent different data types.

Integer Data Type

The simplest type of numeric variable utilized by TP is the **Integer**. An integer is a positive or negative whole number (only floating-point numbers can have a fractional part). Integers are types of numbers you normally use to count things. TP supports five different flavors of integer numbers: **ShortInt**, **Byte**, **Integer**, **Word**, and **LongInt**.

If you were to sit down and write all of the unique 1 and 0 combinations that can be held in 8 bits (1 byte), the count would reach 256 (which also happens to be the value of 2 to the 8th power). Since there isn't anything magical about the different bit patterns, we could allocate the available bit patterns in several arbitrary ways. For example, we can insist that a pattern of eight zeros stands for the number 0 and that other patterns represent increasing whole numbers. This counting scheme allows us to count from 0 to a positive 255 and is represented in TP by the variable type **Byte**.

Another way to allocate the 256 possible patterns is to pick the leftmost bit as a sign bit (indicating a positive or negative value). This means that, when the leftmost bit is *on* (set to 1), the number being represented is negative. This allows us to represent positive numbers from 1 to 127 and negative numbers from −1 to −128. (The reason for the asymmetry is that 0 must also be repre-

Figure 3.1 This illustration shows the makeup of a byte.

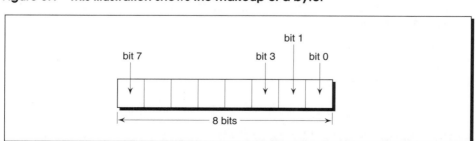

sented, and takes a bit pattern of all zeros.) This counting scheme is represented in TP by the variable type **ShortInt**.

Imagine that instead of using only 8 bits to represent a number, we can use 16 bits (2 bytes attached end-to-end). It turns out that 65,536 different permutations of 1 and 0 values can be represented with 16 bits. If we choose to count only from 0 to a maximum positive value of 65,535, the variable type is represented in TP by the type **Word**. If we use the same bit patterns to represent numbers from +32,767 to 0 to –32,768, we describe a variable type called **Integer**.

The last integer type supported by TP is called **LongInt**. This type of variable uses 4 bytes to represent a number (32 bits total) and is capable of representing signed numbers in the range 2,147,483,647 to 0 to –2,147,483,648. Needless to say, this integer is large enough to tackle any integer computations performed in this book! As a review, Table 3.1 provides the ranges of the integer family of data types.

Figure 3.2 provides a summary of the five different integer types that TP supports. Notice that the first item consists of the general format used to store a binary number (a 1 or a 0) in a byte (8 bits). The rightmost bit, bit 0, represents 1, bit 1 represents a value of 2, bit 2 represents a value of 4, and so on. If you add up all the bit settings in a byte, you get the following:

```
128 + 64 + 32 + 16 + 8 + 4 + 2 + 1 = 255
```

Note

> TP provides two built-in functions called **Hi** and **Lo** that allow you to access the high and low bytes of a standard **Integer** type. We'll discuss these functions in more detail later.

Using Integers

Normally, integers are represented with standard decimal digits. For example, assume the variable **X** is declared as an **Integer** variable. You could assign a positive or negative integer to this variable by using the following notation:

```
X   :=   25;
X   :=   -25;
```

Table 3.1   Integer Data Types

Type	Range
Byte	0 to 255
ShortInt	-128 to 127
Word	0 to 65,535
Integer	-32,768 to 32,767
LongInt	-2,147,483,648 to 2,147,483,647

Figure 3.2   This figure illustrates how integers are represented in the binary number system.

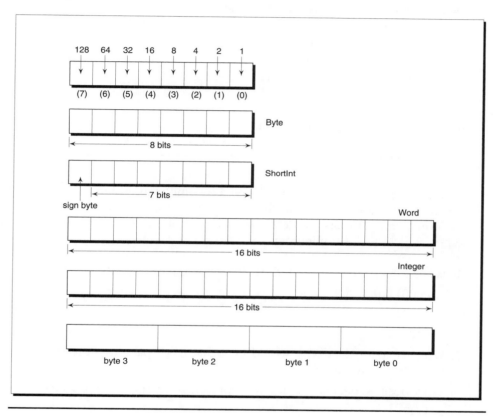

However, TP doesn't stop here. You can also represent your integers as hexadecimal numbers (base 16). To do this, you simply place the $ character in front of the number. For example:

```
X := $10;
```

In the hexadecimal number system, the characters A through F and 0 through 9 are used to represent a number—16 in all. Table 3.2 shows this numerical relationship.

Equivalents

The best thing about integers is their accuracy. As long as the result of an addition or subtraction operation never exceeds the limits of the integer type

Table 3.2 Hexadecimal Digits and Decimal Number Relationship

Hex	Decimal		Hex	Decimal
0	0		8	8
1	1		9	9
2	2		A	10
3	3		B	11
4	4		C	12
5	5		D	13
6	6		E	14
7	7		E	15

you are using, the answer will always be completely accurate. Unfortunately, integers often aren't useful in the real world because most quantities contain fractional parts of units. To describe such quantities, TP supports floating-point types, which we'll examine next.

1. What values are represented by the following binary numbers?
   a. 00001110
   b. 10001010
   c. 01010110
2. Which integer data type would take the least space to store numbers that range from –100 to 100?
3. What positive decimal values are represented by the following hex numbers?
   a. $FE
   b. $55
   c. $1A

1. The decimal numbers are:
   a. 14
   b. 138
   c. 86
2. ShortInt
3. The decimal numbers are:
   a. 254
   b. 85
   c. 26

Introducing Floating-Point Numbers

Floating-point numbers, which are commonly called *real numbers*, can contain both a whole-number part and a fractional part. A few examples are:

234.51
−432.05
10.99

As you can see, floating-point numbers are different from integers. Of course, you can still use floating-point numbers for counting purposes; however, the fractional part provided with these numbers makes them ideal for performing such tasks as balancing your checkbook, calculating how much you owe the IRS, or determining the results of your latest scientific experiment.

There are, however, certain limitations to floating-point numbers. The limitations stem from a simple characteristic of storage: The accuracy of a floating-point number is restricted by the number of bytes used to store the number. What does this really mean?

Floating-point numbers can be viewed as large integers with scaling applied. For example, assume that you are writing a program to store food recipes and you need to represent the quantity 4 1/2 cups of flour using a **ShortInt**. As explained previously, a **ShortInt** is capable of counting from −128 to 127. Because the data type can't directly store fractional parts, we'll have to resort to scaling to make the **ShortInt** work. How is this done? We could define a **ShortInt** variable called **Halfcup** that will count units of 1/2 cup. Since we need to represent four 1/2 cups for a particular recipe, we'll assign the value 9 to the variable **Halfcup**—there are nine 1/2 cups of flour in 4 1/2 cups. We have now "cheated," or scaled, to make a small integer hold a number that includes a fraction of a unit.

Unfortunately, there is a slight problem with this approach. Assume that you have another recipe that specifies 3/4 cup of milk. Obviously, the "mental" scaling that we assigned to the variable **Halfcup** is inadequate to represent this new measurement. We'll need to define a different variable called **Qtrcup** to count the number of quarters in one cup. Notice that we could use this new variable to represent the amount of milk (where **Qtrcup** would be assigned a value of 3 to represent 3/4 cup). Of course, we could also use **Qtrcup** to represent the amount of flour.

As you can see, this approach can become rather complicated. That's why we need floating-point variables, which can continually adjust the "size of unit" (in the above examples, "sizes of unit" were 1/2 cups, 1/4 cups, and so on). By making this adjustment, the variable always represents the desired quantity with the smallest possible units. This is why floating-point numbers always maintain the maximum possible precision.

In most modern programming languages, this manipulation is done by splitting the number of bytes reserved for a particular variable into two parts:

one part to count the number of units, and another part to keep track of the scaling that is being used. Unless you have a math co-processor installed in your system, TP performs all of these adjustments using internal software routines.

As with most things in life, there's a trade-off: Floating-point numbers take appreciably more time to add, subtract, and so on, than integers. Thus, they not only take up more memory (which could be a problem if your program must process extremely large amounts of data), but the computational time can increase dramatically as well. For this reason, it is important to understand the characteristics and limitations of the various types of floating-point numbers.

Note

Any of the different floating-point types that TP supports can be used even if your computer doesn't have a math co-processor. If your computer has a math co-processor, you should include the following compiler directive at the beginning of your source file:

```
{$N+}
```

This directive tells the compiler to generate math instructions for the co-processor chip, which will speed up the execution of your program.

If you don't have a math co-processor, you can instruct TP to use special math libraries to emulate the co-processor by including both of these directives:

```
{$N+}
{$E+}
```

Floating-Point Types

Now that you've been introduced to floating-point numbers, let's examine the data types that TP provides. The smallest floating-point number type is the **Single**, which takes up 4 bytes of storage and is capable of storing numbers in the range 1.5E–45 to 3.4E38. (The uppercase E followed by a number indicates the power of 10 of the number.) Thus, a variable declared to be **Single** is capable of representing a positive number that would be written as 34 followed by 37 zeros. (The 4 takes up one of the positions.) Unfortunately, this limited size means that a **Single** can represent only numbers that are accurate to seven or eight digits. Thus, if you wrote an accounting program using **Single**s, you would have to make certain not to exceed $99,999.99 (seven digits long) to guarantee that you would be accurate to the penny. Since this tends to be too limiting for most realistic business applications, you will probably want to use a larger type of floating-point number for these kinds of programming situations.

The next larger (and therefore more accurate) type of number is the **Real**. This type uses 6 bytes of storage to represent numbers in the range of 2.9E–39 to 1.7E38 with 11 to 12 digits of accuracy. As you can see, the number of bytes used to represent the scaling is approximately the same as the number used for scaling the **Single** type. The reason: Both types cover approximately the same magnitude of numbers. TP assigns the extra 2 bytes to the "number" part to increase the precision significantly. Using **Reals**, our accounting program could safely process numbers up to $999,999,999.99, which is certainly large enough for many business applications.

If you need to write accounting packages for multi-national corporations, you should consider using the **Double** type, which can represent the range 5.0E–324 to 1.1E308 with 15 digits of precision or better. The **Double** provides 8 bytes of storage per number. Unfortunately, this floating-point type isn't large enough to keep track of the U.S. national debt. We need something even larger.

The largest floating-point number that TP supports is the **Extended** variable type. This type takes up 10 bytes of storage per number and can represent numbers in the range 3.4E–4951 to 1.1E4932 with 19 to 20 digits of accuracy. Thus, use the **Extended** if you need a great deal of precision and an extremely wide range of possible values.

One last type of floating-point number, **Comp**, is the same physical size as the **Double** (8 bytes long), but has more bytes allocated to the number part to give it higher precision. For this reason, **Comps** are capable of handling numbers only in the range 9.2E–18 to 9.2E18, but have the same precision (19 to 20 digits) as the **Extended** data type.

Finally, we've included Figure 3.3 to help you see how the different floating-point numbers are stored in memory.

Figure 3.3 Floating-point numbers allow you to perform precise computations.

| byte 3 | byte 2 | byte 1 | byte 0 | Single |

| byte 5 | byte 4 | byte 3 | byte 2 | byte 1 | byte 0 | Real |

| byte 7 | byte 6 | byte 5 | byte 4 | byte 3 | byte 2 | byte 1 | byte 0 | Double |

| byte 9 | byte 8 | byte 7 | byte 6 | byte 5 | byte 4 | byte 3 | byte 2 | byte 1 | byte 0 | Extended |

| byte 7 | byte 6 | byte 5 | byte 4 | byte 3 | byte 2 | byte 1 | byte 0 | Comp |

1. What would be the most efficient floating-point type to represent numbers in the range −3,200,000 to 3,200,000?

2. What will happen when you try to compile the following program:

```
PROGRAM RealTest;
VAR
   Num1 : Real;
   Num2 : Integer;
   Num3 : Single;

BEGIN
   Num1 := 3400.00;
   Num2 := 100.00;
   Num3 := 1.5E+10;
   Writeln('The first number is ', Num1);
   Writeln('The second number is ', Num2);
   Writeln('The third number is ', Num3);
END.
```

3. How can you fix the program in step 2?

1. Real
2. The statement *Num2 := 100.00;* will generate a compiler error.
3. Change the variable Num2 to a Real.

Characters

Numbers aren't the only type of data that you can store in TP. In fact, you'll find that TP's ability to store and process character-based data such as single characters and sets of characters called *strings* is quite advanced. Let's start with single characters and then we'll go on to strings.

To store a single character, you use the data type **Char**. Because only 8 bits are required to store a character, this data type reserves only a single byte of memory.

Typically, characters are represented by placing each character within single quotation marks, for example:

```
Ch := 'A';
```

However, if you know the ASCII code value of a character, you can use this value to represent the character by including the **#** symbol. Here is an example of how the character A is assigned to a **Char** type variable using the ASCII code:

```
Ch := #65;
```

This approach comes in handy when you want to work with the graphics characters supported with the computer's character set. (These characters start with the ASCII code 176.) As an example, let's write a program that displays a box using double-line characters.

The complete program is shown here, and the output is displayed in Figure 3.4.

```
PROGRAM DrawBox;
{ Draws a simple box using ASCII characters }
CONST
  BHeight = 10;
  BWidth  = 40;
VAR
  I, J     : Integer;
  DrawChar : Char;

BEGIN
  Writeln;                { Starts with a blank line }
  DrawChar := #201;       { Upper-left corner }
  Write(DrawChar);
  DrawChar := #205;       { Straight line }
  For I := 1 TO BWidth-2 DO
    Write(DrawChar);
  DrawChar := #187;       { Upper-right corner }
  Writeln(DrawChar);
  FOR I := 1 TO BHeight-2 DO
    BEGIN
      DrawChar:= #186; { Side character }
      Write(DrawChar);
      FOR J := 1 TO BWidth-2 DO
        Write(' ');
      DrawChar := #186;
      Writeln(DrawChar);
    END;
  DrawChar := #200;       { Bottom-left corner }
  Write(DrawChar);
  DrawChar := #205;       { Straight line }
  For I := 1 TO BWidth-2 DO
    Write(DrawChar);
  DrawChar := #188;       { Bottom-right corner }
  Writeln(DrawChar);
END.
```

Windows Tip: If you included the **WinCrt** unit to run this program under Windows, you may have noticed some funny output. Instead of the box-drawing characters you see in Figure 3.4, you probably saw a bunch of funny characters with accents. This is because Windows uses a different set of charac-

Figure 3.4   This is the ouput produced by the program DRAWBOX.

ters for ASCII codes above 127 than does DOS. To get something that looks like a box in the **WinCrt** text window, replace the first **#205** with **#175**, replace the second **#205** with **#95**, and replace the other character assignments to **#124**.

Notice that the graphics characters are displayed using the standard **Write** and **Writeln** routines. The constants used in the program are declared in the **CONST** section and the variables are declared in the **VAR** section.

Note ▼

Control characters can also be represented in TP by using the caret symbol (∧) along with the symbol that designates the control character. For example:

```
Ch := ^J;   { linefeed }
Ch := ^G;   { bell }
Ch := ^H;   { backspace }
```

Strings

In addition to single characters, TP allows you to store a string of up to 255 characters. String variables are declared using the **String** keyword, for example:

```
VAR
  NewStr : String;
```

Like **Char** variables, **String** variables can easily be used to read, write, and process text data. After a **String** variable has been declared, you can assign data to the variable by using the following format:

```
NewStr := 'This is a string';
```

Notice that the string must be enclosed in single quotation marks.

One byte is needed to represent each character in a string. When a string variable is declared, such as **NewStr**, TP sets aside 255 bytes to store the string. What if you don't need that much storage space to store your string? You can limit the amount of memory allocated for a string variable by including a size parameter with your declaration. For example:

```
VAR
  Str15 : String[15];
```

In this case, the variable **Str15** is declared to have a maximum size of 15 characters. Once such a variable is declared, you can assign it any string having 15 characters or less. If you try to assign it a string that has more than 15 characters, such as:

```
Str25 := 'This is a string with more than 15 characters';
```

only the first 15 characters would be stored:

```
'This is a strin'
```

Because strings are similar to arrays, they will be discussed in much more detail when we look at Pascal data structures in Chapter 7.

1. What ASCII characters are represented by the following codes?
   a. #74
   b. #63
   c. #43

   (Hint: The ASCII chart is available from the TP help system.)

2. Run the following program to display the standard ASCII character set. How can you change this program to include display of the graphics characters?

```
PROGRAM ShowASCII;
{ Displays standard ASCII characters ! to ~ }
VAR
  I         : Integer;
  DrawChar : Char;

BEGIN
  Writeln('Standard ASCII characters');
  Writeln;
  DrawChar := #33;     { Start with the ! character }
  FOR I := 33 TO 126 DO
    BEGIN
      Write('The ASCII code is ', I);
      Writeln(' The Character is ', DrawChar);
      Inc(DrawChar)
    END;
END.
```

3. What does the **Inc** function do?

4. How many bytes does it take to represent the following string:

```
'Turbo Pascal is fast'
```

1. These are the characters represented by the ACSII codes
   a. t
   b. c
   c. C

2. To display all the ASCII characters, change the loop statement

   ```
   FOR I := 33 TO 126 DO
   ```

   to

   ```
   FOR I := 33 TO 255 DO
   ```

3. **Inc** increases a variable's value by 1.

4. 20

The Boolean Type

Imagine that you want to write a simple program that asks the user a series of yes/no questions and then saves the responses for subsequent processing. One way to save such information would be to use **ShortInt** or **Byte** variables and to assign arbitrary values to stand for true and false. However, it would be nice to be able to process the information by making direct comparisons with true or false, rather than by comparing each variable to zero for false, and so on.

TP and many other modern languages permit this kind of direct comparison through the use of a special data type called a **Boolean**. A **Boolean** is a bytewide variable that can be used in **IF** statements to determine whether certain conditions exist. Here is an example of how a **Boolean** variable is declared:

```
VAR
   Test_check : Boolean;
```

Such a variable could then be assigned the value True or False, for example:

```
Test_check := True;
Test_check := False;
```

Boolean variables can also be manipulated by special *boolean operators*, such as **OR** or and **AND**. For example, imagine you are writing a program to diagnose automobile air-conditioning systems. Your program instructs the technician to connect pressure gauges at the inlet and outlet of the compressor and asks that the two readings be entered for analysis. Based on the readings, the program is able to conclude that the compressor is fine and that the problem must be elsewhere. Thus, a **Boolean** could be set to keep this information for later use:

```
Comprsr_Ok := True;
```

Later in the program, you may want to execute a section of code only if the compressor is working correctly. To do this, you would precede the group with this **IF** statement:

```
IF Comprsr_Ok = True THEN
  BEGIN
    { Code to be executed goes here }
  END;
```

Again, note that in the **IF** statement only, an equal (=) sign was used rather than a colon-equal (:=) sign since you are comparing rather than assigning a value. In reality, you can make the statement even simpler by writing:

```
IF Comprsr_Ok THEN
```

Here, it is implied that the result of the **IF** expression is tested to determine whether it is true. This makes for more elegant and readable programs and is always encouraged. Now imagine that, instead of executing a section of program when the compressor is good, you actually want to execute a section of code if the compressor is bad. You can modify the **IF** statement to do this by using the **NOT** operator, for example:

```
IF NOT Comprsr_Ok THEN
```

The **NOT** operator negates the logical value of the variable when it evaluates the **IF** expression. Understand, though, that a **NOT** doesn't change the actual contents of the variable (if **Comprsr_Ok** was true before the **IF** statement, it will still be true afterward); it simply negates the answer for the evaluation of the **IF** expression.

Creating Identifiers

Recall from Chapter 2 that identifiers are the names you create to represent such elements as variable names, constant names, function names, and procedure names. As an example, in the statement

```
NewTotal := Abs(Sum) + NewSales(Day5);
```

the names **NewTotal**, **Sum**, and **Day5** are identifiers. But what about **Abs**? Isn't it also an identifier? No, because it is the name of a built-in function. Identifiers can be only names that you create. Any terms reserved for use by the compiler can't be used as identifiers.

Here are the basic rules you must follow in creating an identifier:

- An identifier can be any length. However, only the first 63 characters are used by the compiler.
- The characters that you can use to create an identifier include 0 through 9, A through Z (or a through z), and the underscore character (_).
- The first character must be a letter or the underscore character.
- Each identifier must have a unique name.
- An identifier can't use the same name as a Pascal reserved word.
- The compiler does not make a distinction between uppercase and lowercase letters. (**Total** is the same as **TOTAL**.)
- Spaces are not allowed in an identifier. (Usually, the underscore character, _, is used to represent a space in a Pascal identifier.)

As long as you follow these basic rules, you shouldn't have any problems. From time to time, though, you might accidentally create an identifier that has the same name as one of the standard Pascal identifiers. Of course, this mistake is easy to make. When it happens, the compiler will warn you with an error message.

It's usually a good idea to use identifiers that are as descriptive as possible. Don't be afraid to use long names if they are necessary to get the job done. For example, if you're creating a variable to calculate the total sales for socks during the month of July, the following identifier

```
Sales_Of_Socks_For_July
```

is certainly more descriptive than

```
Sosfj
```

Be as creative as you like when making up your identifier names; but remember, someone else might have to read and understand your program!

Putting Constants to Work

One of the most annoying problems in maintaining a program is the occurrence of an unexplainable constant. Usually, such constants are embedded in formulas within the code.

For example, if you are maintaining an employee benefits program, you might see a number such as 1992 in calculations to prorate annual benefits expenses per working hour. At this point, you probably wouldn't have any idea where the number came from. However, if you take 52 weeks in a year and multiply that by 40 work hours per week, you get 2080 hours per year. If you now subtract 88 hours for 11 paid holidays per year, you get 1992. But what happens if the company policy changes to allow for 12 paid holidays per year? How could you be sure that all numeric constants that were affected by the number of paid holidays have been updated? This clearly illustrates the value of providing readable, understandable constants in programs.

Now imagine that the employee benefits program had been written by someone who used constants with a little more care. In the code, you might find the following constant definition:

```
CONST
  Hours_per_year = (52 * 40) - (8 * 11);
```

Now, the numbers used are at least visible. However, even this isn't descriptive enough; the definition line should be preceded by a set of comment lines that explain what the individual constants mean.

The preceding example introduces a few interesting points. First, the value was assigned to the constant using just an = rather than the := we normally use to assign values to variables. This is done to differentiate *compile-time* operations from those done at *run-time*. In simpler terms, this means constant evaluations are performed when the program is compiled. Our sample statement will not use up any computer time when the program is actually executed.

Second, if you made a mistake in entering code for the programs in the previous chapters, you may have been given an error message associated with the missing colon. So, how does the compiler know that you are defining a constant? If you recall the program template presented in Chapter 2, you will remember that both programs and other procedures and functions have a section before the actual code identified as **CONST**. Constants definitions are valid only within these program blocks.

Up to this point, you've only seen how simple constants are defined. The problem with this approach is that the compiler will assume what type of constant it is supposed to handle. For example:

```
CONST
  Const_one = 42;
  Const_two = 42.0;
```

Most Pascal compilers would treat **Const_one** as an integer and **Const_two** as a real. This can lead to all kinds of problems and can result in a compile-time error if you try to use both of these constants in the same expression. For example, assume that you have a variable **Sum,** which is declared as

```
VAR
   Sum : Integer;
```

and you place the following assignment statement in the body of your program:

```
Sum := Const_one + Const_two;
```

The compiler would not accept this statement because the data types of **Const_one** and **Const_two** are different. (Remember that Pascal is a strongly typed language.) The main problem here: The compiler can't know ahead of time what the result of the computation will be. For this reason, it is usually best to control, whenever possible, the types of variables that the compiler uses for calculations. We already control variable types through explicit definitions. TP takes the Pascal standard one step further by allowing you to declare *typed constants.* You do this by inserting the constant type identifier between the constant name and the equal sign, as follows:

```
CONST
   Const_one : Integer = 42;
   Const_two : Real = 42.0;
```

Some examples of valid constants, both typed and untyped, are:

```
CONST
   MsgStr : String = 'Please enter your name';
   MaxNum = 150;
   Resp : Char = 'Y';
   IntVect : Integer = $A4;
   Status : Boolean = True;
   MinNum = MaxNum - 100;
```

Note

A typed constant operates more like a variable than an actual constant because it can be reassigned a new value within the body of a program. For example, if a program contains the following constant declaration

```
CONST
   AnsChar : Char = 'Y';
```

the constant can later be assigned a new value:

```
AnsChar := 'N';
```

Remember that untyped constants cannot be changed.

1. Which of the following names represent valid Pascal identifiers?
   a. 1High
   b. Level1
   c. Total_Of_Sales*
   d. True
   e. Ship&Date

2. Which constant declarations are incorrect? Fix the invalid declarations.

```
CONST
    P : Integer = 2.5;
    Msg = "Please press the Enter key";
    Avg : ShortInt = 100;
    Ch = #65;
    Sum = P + Avg;
```

3. What is the difference between typed and untyped constants?

4. What is wrong with the following variable declaration?

```
VAR
    Unit : Integer;
    Area : Real = 45.75;
```

1. b

2. The following constants are incorrect:

```
P : Integer = 2.5;
Msg = "Please press the Enter key";
```

The correct versions are:

```
P : Real = 2.5;
Msg = 'Please press the Enter key';
```

3. A typed constant is defined with its data type, while an untyped constant does not include a data type. Also, a typed constant can be reassigned a new value inside the body of a program.

4. The variable **Area** cannot be assigned a value when it is declared. Variables can only be assigned values with assignment statements.

Declaring Variables

As explained in Chapter 2, all variables must be defined near the top of the program in a section of the program that starts with the keyword **VAR**. Each variable to be used by the program is listed along with its data type. As I mentioned previously, this provides two benefits: (1) The data type informs the compiler in an unambiguous manner what kind of variable we expect it to be, and (2) it simplifies the compiler design quite a bit by eliminating the "guess factor" associated with other languages. If TP assigns the wrong type to a variable, you have only yourself to blame!

Converting Data Types

In some situations, you may need to convert data from one type to another. Because Pascal is such a strongly typed language, you can't assign a variable a value that is of a different type and expect the compiler to make the conversion for you. For example, if you declare the following variable

```
VAR
  Sum : Integer;
```

and then try to assign it a character, such as

```
Sum := 'A';
```

you will get a compiler error message.

So, how can we convert data from one type to another? For this job, TP provides a few conversion functions such as **Ord**, **Chr**, **Frac**, **Hi**, **Int**, **Lo**, **Str**, **Trunc**, and **Val**. Let's briefly explore each of the conversions that are supported.

Converting Integers to Characters

The two built-in functions used to convert between integers and characters are:

```
Ord(<ordinal-type>);
Chr(<integer>);
```

The **Ord** function takes a character or any other ordinal type (a type that can be represented with a integer value) and converts its argument to an integer. For example, the statement

```
Sum := Ord('A');
```

converts the character 'A' to the value 65, which is its ASCII representation number.

To proceed the other way, that is, to convert a number to a character, use the **Chr** function. For example:

```
Ch := Chr(97);
```

Here, we're converting the value 97 to its ASCII character equivalent, which is 'a.' Keep in mind that when you use this conversion function you must use numbers that represent valid ASCII characters. For example, the statement

```
Ch := Chr(395);
```

wouldn't make much sense because there isn't an ASCII character with the code 395. (The highest ASCII code is 255.)

Note

> Because the **Ord** function works with any ordinal type, you can also use it to convert a **Boolean** to an **Integer**. As an example, the following statement converts the argument **True** to a value of 1. (**False** would be converted to 0.)
>
> ```
> Ans := Ord(True);
> ```

Converting Strings to Numbers

Another useful conversion involves converting strings to numbers or numbers to strings. The routines you'll need are:

```
Str(<number :width :decimals, string>);
Val(<string, number, error-position>);
```

These routines are procedures, not functions, which means they don't return a value. Instead, **Str** and **Val** use what are called *VAR parameters* to return a value. To explain how these parameters work, we'll need to look at the formal definitions of these procedures:

```
PROCEDURE Str(<formatted-number>; VAR RetStr: String);
PROCEDURE Val(SrcStr : String; VAR <number>; VAR Code : Integer);
```

The keyword **VAR** indicates that a parameter will return a value. For example, with the statement

```
Str(578, NewStr);
```

the variable **NewStr** would store the string '578' after the procedure call. Perhaps the best feature of **Str** is its ability to also convert a real number into a string. For example:

```
Str(102.78:5:2, RlStr);
```

In this case, the variable **RlStr** stores the string '102.78.'

Converting a string to a number is not much different than converting a number to string. The only difference: You must include an error code variable to test the results of the conversion. Here is an example that illustrates how a string is converted:

```
Val('22', Num, ErCode);
IF ErCode <> 0 THEN Writeln('The string cannot be converted');
```

If the number can be converted, **ErCode** is set to 0.

Converting Reals to Integers

There is actually only one function that allows us to convert a real number into an integer. The function is:

```
Trunc(<real-number>);
```

In this case, the real-number argument is converted to an integer by removing its fractional part. For example,

```
X := Trunc(577.87);
```

returns the value 577. The return type is an integer.

If you're working exclusively with real numbers, two other functions are available for use in breaking a real into its components:

```
Int(<real-number>);
Frac(<real-number>);
```

The **Int** function returns the whole number part of a real number, and **Frac** returns the fractional part. A few examples are:

```
IPart := Int(1234.56);
FPart := Frac(1234.56);
```

The variable **IPart** would contain the value 1234.0, and **FPart** would contain 0.56.

Working with Integers

In addition to converting numbers from one data type to another, there are a few techniques you can use to represent integers in different ways. As discussed earlier, a standard integer is represented in memory as 2 bytes. How can we access the two different bytes of an integer? The built-in functions **Hi** and **Lo** provide a way to do this:

```
Hi(<integer-data>);
Lo(<integer-data>);
```

As you might guess, the **Hi** function returns the upper byte of an integer (bits 8 through 15), and the **Lo** function returns the lower byte (bits 0 through 7). The result returned is of type **Byte**. An example that shows how each function is called is:

```
Lo_Byte := Lo(2027);   { returns EBh or 235 }
Hi_byte := Hi(2027);   { returns 07h or 7 }
```

Note

> The **Hi** function ignores the sign bit of a negative number. For example, the function call
>
> ```
> Hi(-3047);
> ```
>
> returns the value 244 or F4h.

Summary

This chapter has shown you how to use two important building blocks of the Pascal language: data types and variables. You now know how to represent program data using data types from the five major families, including **Integer**, **Char**, **Real**, **Boolean**, and **String**. You learned that variables are declared using the **VAR** statement and that, once declared, they can be assigned only data that corresponds with the declared data type of the variable.

In Chapter 4, you'll learn how to use variables to process program data by creating expressions.

Exercises

1. Modify the DrawBox program presented in this chapter so that it draws a box using single-line characters when run in DOS.
2. Write a program that allows you to type in an ASCII code and then returns the ASCII character.
3. Write a program that converts a real input to an integer and then displays the converted number.

Answers

1. To change the program, set the **DrawChar** variable to the following codes where appropriate to draw the single-line border characters:

   #218, #196, #191, #179, #192, #217

2. This program allows you to type in an ASCII code and have the equivalent character returned:

```
PROGRAM ShowChar;
VAR
   InpCode : Byte;

BEGIN
   Writeln('Enter an ASCII code');
   Readln(InpCode);
   If (InpCode < 0) OR (InpCode > 255) THEN
     Writeln('The ASCII code is out of range');
   Writeln('The ASCII code is: ', InpCode);
   Writeln('The character is: ', Chr(InpCode));
END.
```

   (Be sure to use **WinCrt** when running this program in Windows.)

3. This program converts a real input to an integer and then displays the converted number:

```
 PROGRAM ConvtReal;
VAR
   InpVal : Real;
   Intval : Integer;

BEGIN
   Writeln('Enter a Real value');
   Readln(InpVal);
   Intval := Round(InpVal);
   Writeln('The real number is: ', InpVal);
   Writeln('The converted value is: ', Intval);
END.
```

   (Be sure to use **WinCrt** when running this program in Windows.)

Expressions and Operators

Y ou've now learned about the basics of writing TP programs and the techniques for defining and using data types and variables. What's missing? Actually, you haven't seen how to build expressions so that you can effectively use constants and variables to process your data. In this chapter, we'll explore the two basic components that TP provides for constructing expressions: operands and operators. After introducing you to the basics of creating expressions, the remainder of this chapter will present the complete set of TP operators.

After you complete this chapter, you'll know how to:

- Write simple expressions
- Use Pascal operators
- Combine operators with constant and variable operands
- Work with operator precedence and the rules for evaluating expressions

What's in an Expression?

Before beginning our detailed tour of TP operators, we need to take a brief look at TP expressions. In general terminology, an *expression* is simply a statement that combines data elements with operators and evaluates to a single value. For example:

```
X := (Total + 20) / May_Avg;
```

This expression combines the data elements **Total**, **20**, and **May_Avg** with the operators **+** and **/**. Thus far, quite simple. There are, however, some special terms you need to understand. When data elements are combined with an operator, they are called *operands*. For example, in the subexpression

```
Total + 20
```

the variable **Total** and **20** serve as the operands. In TP, operands are created using variables and constants. You can use any data type to construct your operands, including integers, reals, characters, strings, and so on. However, you must follow one important rule. *The operands used in an expression must all belong to a related data-type family.* After all, it wouldn't make much sense to perform this expression:

```
'Jon Adams' + 25
```

If you need to use operands of different data types, you must first convert the operands to a uniform type before you try to evaluate them in an expression.

Many different types of expressions can be constructed in TP. The expression just introduced, **(Total + 20) / May_Avg**, is called a simple arithmetic expression because it performs a numeric computation—in this case, an Integer. You can also construct expressions to produce other results, such as Boolean values or string data. However, before you learn how to build different types of expressions, you'll need to be introduced to the complete set of operators that TP provides.

Introducing TP Operators

The second component of expressions, as just stated, is the *operator*. Fortunately, TP provides a number of operators to allow us to process data from the different data-type groups. Operators are the symbols that instruct the compiler to generate an instruction to process an operand. They are divided into seven basic groups:

1. Arithmetic operators
2. Relational operators
3. Boolean operators
4. Bitwise operators
5. Set operators
6. String operators
7. Pointer operators

The different operators fall into two categories of usage. The first operators category, called *unary operators*, requires only a single operand. For example, in a statement such as

```
X := -10;
```

the – serves as a unary operator and operates on the single operand 10.

The second category includes the *binary operators*, which require two operands. An example of a binary operator is:

```
X := 24 * 5;
```

In this case, the operator * operates on the operands 24 and 5.

When you use operators to build expressions, keep in mind that TP applies special rules, called *precedence rules*, to determine the order in which operators should be evaluated. You'll see how these rules work after we cover the complete set of operators.

Arithmetic Operators

A good way to begin our discussion is to examine *arithmetic operators*. If you've studied basic algebra, you may already be familiar with these types of operators. As the name implies, arithmetic operators are used to perform such commonplace math operations as addition, subtraction, multiplication, and division. A few other arithmetic operators are provided by TP to perform special actions, such as calculating only the whole-number part of an integer division or the remainder. Table 4.1 lists the complete set of arithmetic operators available with TP. Notice that the table includes a type category to indicate whether the operator is unary or binary.

The two unary operators (+ and –) are used to tell the compiler the sign of a number. In addition, the unary minus sign has the duty of negating the value contained in a variable:

```
Days_left := -Days_left;
```

This statement will actually change the contents of the variable by making it a negative number if it was originally a positive number, and vice versa.

The numeric addition, subtraction, and multiplication operators can be used with integer and floating-point operands. These operators always return a result that is of the same data type as the operands used. An example of each operator is:

```
I := I + 1;    { I is an integer—returns an integer }
Total := Sales - Cost;
{ Sales and Cost are integers—returns an integer }
Area := Height * Width;
{ Height and Width are reals—returns a real }
```

Table 4.1   The Arithmetic Operator Set

Operator	Description	Type
+	Unary plus sign	Unary
–	Unary minus sign	Unary
+	Numeric addition	Binary
–	Numeric subtraction	Binary
*	Multiplication	Binary
/	Floating-point division	Binary
DIV	Whole number result of integer division	Binary
MOD	Residue of integer division	Binary

If you combine different types of operands in an expression, and one of the operands is a floating-point type, you must assign the result of the expression to a floating-point type variable. For example, consider this statement:

```
Base := July_Sales * ScFactor
```

If **July_Sales** is a real and **ScFactor** is an integer, the variable that stores the result, **Base**, must be a real.

Note

> Operands of the same data-type family, such as **Integer**, **ShortInt**, **Byte**, **Word**, and so on, can be combined in a numeric expression; however, the result of the expression should be assigned to a variable that has enough range to hold the result. For example, if **X** is a **ShortInt**, the following expression would produce incorrect results because **ShortInt** operands can hold values only up to 127:
>
> ```
> X := 120 * 2;
> ```

The division operand (/) can be used with both integer and floating-point operands; however, it always produces a floating-point value. For example:

```
Day_Wage := 10000.55 / 365;
```

As long as the variable **Day_Wage** is declared as one of the floating-point types, this expression will compile correctly.

One final point about using the basic arithmetic operators to build numeric expressions must be made. If you're building expressions that use multiple operators, it's a good idea to include parentheses so that you can separate the different parts of the expression. For example, the parentheses in this statement ensure that the subexpression **Height * Width** is evaluated first:

```
Area := (Height * Width) / 2;
```

The natural order of evaluation for operators within an expression will be explained when operator precedence is looked at.

Integer Division

You've seen how the / operator is used to perform division and produce floating-point results, but how do you perform integer division? Two operators available to you for this purpose are **DIV** and **MOD**. Imagine that you wish to divide an integer that contains the number of days in a year (365) by the integer constant 7 in order to find out how many weeks there are in a year. Because 365 is not an even multiple of 7, we have a small problem if we want to save the result in another integer.

The **DIV** operator tells the TP compiler not to worry about the remainder of such an operation. The result of the division operation is always truncated so that only the whole number part is computed—it makes little or no difference whether the answer is closer to 53 than 52—and the result is always rounded down. Therefore, the result of the expression

```
365 DIV 7
```

is 52.

Now assume that you want to know the magnitude of the remainder (the number left over after the integer division); TP will provide this through the **MOD** operator. Since 52 times 7 is 364, the instructions

```
Rem_one := 365 MOD 7;
Rem_two := 370 MOD 7;
```

would provide a result of 1 for the first line and 6 for the second line.

1. What are the results that the following expressions produce?
    a. (200 * 12) + (11 * 3)
    b. (57 / 12) + 87
    c. 2092 / (12 * 2)
2. What data types can be used to hold the results of the expressions in step 1?
3. What are the results that would be produced by the following expressions?
    a. 28 DIV 7
    b. 28 MOD 7
    c. 100 MOD 12

1. The expressions in step 1 would produce the following results:
    a. 2,433
    b. 91.75
    c. 87.1666
2. The following data types can be used to hold the results of the expressions in step 2:
    a. Integer
    b. Real
    c. Real
3. The expressions in step 3 would produce the following results:
    a. 4
    b. 0
    c. 4

Relational Operators

In addition to operators for constructing numeric expressions, you'll also need operators to compare operands. This type of operators, called *relational operators*, are important because they allow us to construct decision-making statements. Table 4.2 lists the set of relational operators available with TP. Each of these operators takes two operands and returns a Boolean value (true or false).

Here are some examples that show how relational operators are used:

```
20 > 15        { Compare two integers }
'A' < 'Z'      { Compare two characters }
'one' <> 'two' { Compare two strings }
49.76 <= 201.9 { Compare two reals }
```

Notice that any of the standard data types can be used as an operand. If you're comparing numeric operands, you can use operands of different data types. For example, the following expression is valid:

```
275.89 <> 300
```

1. Which expressions evaluate as true?
   a. ' one' = 'one'
   b. 'A' > 'a'
   c. 47 <> 47
2. Which of the following are arithmetic operators?
   a. ++
   b. %
   c. /
   d. *

Table 4.2 The Basic Relational Operators

Operator	Indicates that:
=	The two operands are equal
<>	The two operands are not equal
>	The left operand is greater than the right operand
<	The left operand is less than the right operand
=>	The left operand is greater than or equal to the right operand
<=	The left operand is less than or equal to the right operand

3. Which of the following are relational operators?

a. >

b. –

c. :=

d. =

1. All of the expressions are false.
2. The correct answers are c and d.
3. The correct answers are a and d.

Boolean Operators

Although, technically, Boolean operators are also relational operators, they belong to a branch of mathematics that may be unfamiliar to you. For the most part, these operators, which are also called *logical operators*, are used to implement logic decisions. As Table 4.3 shows, the four Boolean operators are **AND**, **NOT**, **OR**, and **XOR**.

Figure 4.1 illustrates how the various Boolean operators work. Notice that **NOT** is the only unary operator. (Again, this means that it only operates on one value at a time.) The other three operators (**AND, OR, XOR**) provide a result based on two operands.

As you can see from Figure 4.1, the **AND** operation will generate a value of true only if both operands are true, and will return false for all other conditions. The **OR** operation will generate a value of true if either input term is true, and will generate a false output only if both inputs are false. The final operator, **XOR,** stands for exclusive-or. It will generate a value of true only when the two inputs are dissimilar (one true and one false). If both inputs are the same state (either true or false), the output will be evaluated as false. These three operators are the building blocks of logic operations; all complex logic operations that do not require memory of past states can be modeled by using combinations of these three operators.

Table 4.3 The Basic Logical Operators

Operator	Description
AND	Performs a logical AND (conjunction)
NOT	Performs a logical NOT (negation)
OR	Performs a logical OR (disjunction)
XOR	Performs a logical XOR (exclusive OR)

Figure 4.1   The complete set of Boolean operators.

AND	False AND False → False False AND True → False True AND False → False True AND True → True	0 AND 0 → 0 0 AND 1 → 0 1 AND 0 → 0 1 AND 1 → 1
OR	False OR False → False False OR True → True True OR False → True True OR True → True	0 OR 0 → 0 0 OR 1 → 1 1 OR 0 → 1 1 OR 1 → 1
Exclusive OR (XOR)	False XOR False → False False XOR True → True True XOR False → True True XOR True → False	0 XOR 0 → 0 0 XOR 1 → 1 1 XOR 0 → 1 1 XOR 1 → 0
NOT	NOT False → True NOT True → False	NOT 0 → 1 NOT 1 → 0

One of the more useful features of Boolean operations is that you can group them together like normal arithmetic expressions. For example, if you want a section of code to be executed on a Tuesday with a full moon, you might write

```
IF (Fullmoon AND Today_tues) THEN
```

where it is implied that the variables **Fullmoon** and **Today_tues** have both been defined as **Boolean** and that they were set to true earlier in the program if a full moon was out and today was Tuesday, respectively. We can even combine **Boolean** variables with other types to have the same effect. Imagine that instead of having a **Boolean** defined as **Today_tues,** we have an enumerated variable defined as

```
TYPE Day_of_wk = (Monday, Tuesday, Wednesday, Thursday, Friday, Saturday,
                  Sunday );
  VAR Today_is : Day_of_wk;
```

so that we could convert the previous **IF** statement to:

```
IF (Fullmoon AND (Today_is = Tuesday) ) THEN
```

Before we go any further, you'll need to know that *enumerated variables* are ones whose valid values are defined by the *user* rather than by the language. (They will be covered in greater detail in Chapter 7.) All you need to understand for now is that **Monday** is a valid value for the variable **Today_is**, in the same way that 15 is a valid value to assign to an **Integer** variable. Also, notice that, by placing parentheses around the expression for the enumerated variable, we can guarantee that the compiler won't get confused and perform an **AND** operation on the contents of **Today_is** and **Fullmoon**. (Such an operation might give us a different answer from what we are expecting).

Later in this chapter, we'll explore operator precedence in more detail; these are the rules that TP uses to evaluate expressions when there aren't parentheses to force evaluation in a certain order. For now, it is sufficient to know that TP will always evaluate the contents of the innermost set of parentheses first, and then it will evaluate terms that are not nested as deeply.

Bitwise Operators

You haven't been told yet that the Boolean operators can also be used with integer operand types to perform Boolean operations on all of the bits in the operand. When an operator is used in this manner, it is called a *bitwise operator.* In addition to **AND**, **NOT**, **OR**, and **XOR**, TP provides two other operators, **SHR** and **SHL**, to serve as bitwise operators. What do these operators do? They shift the bits in an operand right or left by a specified number of positions.

To understand how bitwise operations are performed, we're going to take a slight detour to review how numbers are represented in a digital computer. Figure 4.2 shows a typical 16-bit integer and the "weight" of each bit in the number. As you can see, the rightmost bit can indicate a 1, the next bit to the left a 2, then 4, 8, 16, and so on. By placing 1s in the proper bits, we can represent any whole number within the range of the particular type of variable. Figure 4.3 illustrates what the bit pattern would look like for several small integers. The number 15 has all four lowest bits turned on, the number 12 has two bits turned on and the lowest two bits turned off, and so on.

Figure 4.2 These are the bit weights for a 16-bit number.

					Bit Number										
15	14	13	12	11	10	9	8	7	6	5	4	3	2	1	0
32768	16384	8192	4096	2048	1024	512	256	128	64	32	16	8	4	2	1
					Numerical Weight of Bit										

Figure 4.3   These are the positive values for a 4-bit number.

Decimal	Binary	Hexadecimal
0	0000	0
1	0001	1
2	0010	2
3	0011	3
4	0100	4
5	0101	5
6	0110	6
7	0111	7
8	1000	8
9	1001	9
10	1010	A
11	1011	B
12	1100	C
13	1101	D
14	1110	E
15	1111	F

Now look at Figure 4.4. If we **AND** together the numbers 13 and 11, the first and last bits will remain 1 because they were on in both numbers, but the two middle bits go to 0 because, in each case, only one of them was on.

We could also **OR** the same two numbers. Figure 4.4 shows that **OR**ing 13 and 11 results in a number where all four bits are on (15). If we decide to **XOR**

Figure 4.4   Boolean operators on small integers.

Decimal		Binary	
Operation	Result	Operation	Result
13 AND 11	9	1101 AND 1011	1001
13 OR 11	15	1101 OR 1011	1111
13 XOR 11	6	1101 XOR 1011	0110
NOT 13	2	NOT 1101	0010

these numbers, we get yet another answer, in which the end bits are 0 and the middle bits are 1. This happens because the output of the exclusive-or operation goes to 0 if both bits are the same state.

Finally, Figure 4.4 takes a look at what happens when the **NOT** operation is performed on the number 13. As you can see, the **NOT** operation flips the bits so that all the 1s turn to 0s, and vice versa; the number 13 becomes the number 2!

Figure 4.4 Using each of the four Boolean operators on the same operands produces four different results.

For the most part, performing these Boolean operations on numbers is rather meaningless and can result in some very strange answers if you don't know what you're doing.

Boolean operations can come in handy, though, in *masking* numbers. By masking we mean selecting certain digits of a number. For example, recall that the letters of the alphabet are represented in your computer in a code called ASCII. This code uses numbers in the range of 1 to 127 to represent all the lowercase and uppercase letters, as well as punctuation marks and control characters. One popular word-processing program uses a trick in its files to indicate special operations, such as blanks inserted by the program to "even out" the right side of paragraphs. It turns on the top bit of each character when it is computer generated.

Unfortunately, if you try to read such a file into your TP editor, it would get indigestion because it wouldn't know what to do with those funny characters that are greater than 127! However, you could write a small preprocessor program that would first read the file and would **AND** each byte with a mask of 01111111 (127 decimal). This would allow the lower bits to come through, but would guarantee that the top bit would always be 0 (thus keeping the number within the acceptable range 0 through 127). Such tricks are often useful when dealing directly with hardware such as communications chips or video memory.

Shifting Bits

In the previous section, you learned how the bits in an integer operand could be changed by using the **AND**, **OR**, **NOT**, and **XOR** operators. But what about the **SHR** and **SHL** operators? What do they do? These operators use the following format to shift the bits in an integer to the right or to the left:

```
<operand> <shift instruction> <number of bits to shift>
```

For example, assume that we assign a value to a variable:

```
X := 8;
```

The variable **X** would be stored in memory with the following bit setting:

```
00001000
```

Now, if we used the **SHR** operator

```
NewX := X SHR 1;
```

the variable **NewX** would be set to 4 (00000100). Just as you might guess, the **SHL** operator produces a result that's the opposite of the **SHR** operator. Assuming our variable **X** still holds the value 8, the following statement puts 16 in the variable **NewX:**

```
NewX := X SHL 1;
```

 Note

> The **SHR** and **SHL** operators provide a very efficient way of dividing and multiplying an integer by a power of two. You should consider using these operators to increase the performance of your code.

1. Which of the following are Boolean operators?
   a. AND
   b. WITH
   c. OR
   d. IN
   e. XOR
   f. <>
2. Which of the following are bitwise operators?
   a. SHR
   b. >>
   c. !
   d. NOT
3. What values do the following expressions produce?
   a. 200 SHR 4
   b. $AB SHL 2
   c. 16 AND 5
   d. NOT 8

1. Answers a, c, and e are the Boolean operators.
2. Answers a and d are the bitwise operators.
3. The expression in step 3 produces the following values:
   a. 12
   b. 684
   c. 0
   d. -9

Set Operators

Another important category of operator that TP provides is the set operators. These operators are used to process operands of the **SET** data type. To see how these operators work, we'll first need to briefly examine how sets are represented.

A set is simply a related collection of data elements. In TP, you can create sets by using ordinal data types such as **Char** and **Integer**. Here is an example of how a **SET** variable is declared:

```
VAR
   Letter : SET of Char;
```

The variable **Letter** could then be assigned any group of characters from the standard character set. For example, the following statement assigns the set of vowels to **Letter**:

```
Letter := ['A', 'E', 'I', 'O', 'U'];
```

With this in mind, we can now apply the set operators to process set operands.

The set union operator (+) combines the elements of two sets. For example, if we have the two sets

```
Letter := ['A', 'E', 'I', 'O', 'U'];
Resp := ['Y', 'N'];
```

the statement

```
NewSet := Letter + Resp;
```

creates the new set

```
['A', 'E', 'I', 'O', 'U', 'Y', 'N']
```

The set difference operator, (—), compares two sets and then creates a new set that consists of only the elements that remain after the common elements in both sets have been removed. For example, using the following two sets

```
Resp = ['Y', 'N', 'y', 'n', '?'];
Yes_Ans := ['Y', 'y', 'Yes'];
```

the expression

```
Resp - Yes_Ans
```

produces the set

```
['N', 'n', '?', 'Yes']
```

Another useful set operator is the set intersection (*). This operator compares two sets and then creates a new set that consists of only those elements shared by both sets. For example, using the following two sets

```
Codes := ['0', '1', '2', '3'];
OddCodes := ['1', '3', '5'];
```

the expression

```
Codes * OddCodes
```

produces the set

```
['1', '3']
```

The last type of set operator is **IN**, which tests a set to determine whether an element is a member of a set. Here are some examples that show how this operator is used:

```
'c' IN ['a', 'b', 'c']        { Returns True }
'A' IN ['a' .. 'z']           { Returns False }
'&' IN ['+', '-', '/', '*'] { Returns False }
```

String Operators

Only one operator works on strings: the + symbol. In the case of strings, this symbol is called a *concatenator* because it hooks, or concatenates, two strings together, end to end. For example, if

```
String_one := 'First part';
```

and

```
String_two := 'Second part';
```

then the statement

```
String_three := string_one + string_two;
```

assigns the string 'First partSecond part' to the variable **String_three**. Notice that if we want a space between the two parts, we'd have to either insert it in one of the strings or insert it in the third line. For example:

```
string_three := string_one + ' ' + string_two;
```

All other string operations are performed using functions supplied with TP. These functions allow us to search for a string inside another, and to extract characters from either the beginning or the end of a string.

Pointer Operators

As programs become more sophisticated, it sometimes becomes necessary to handle collections of information as a group. Pointer operators allow us to manipulate entire collections of information, called *data structures*, simply by passing a pointer to the beginning of the structure. I will be discussing the use of pointers and data structures in detail in Chapter 11.

Operator Precedence

It's important to know that TP follows certain rules in the evaluation of expressions that don't have parentheses to define the order of computation. These rules involving the priority of evaluation are called *operator precedence*. There are four levels of operator precedence in TP. If parts of an expression have operators with a higher priority than others, these subexpressions will be evaluated first. Subexpressions involving operators at the same level of priority are evaluated in the left-to-right order they appear in the program.

The highest-priority operators in TP are the **@** pointer operator and the **NOT** Boolean operator (the **@** operator is used with pointers to take the address of an object; see Chapter 11 for more information on using pointers.).

The next highest level of priority includes the following operators:

- * (multiplication)
- / (floating-point division)

- **DIV** (integer division)
- **MOD** (residue from integer division)
- **AND** (Boolean operator)
- **SHL** and **SHR** (bitwise operators)

Subexpressions involving these operators are evaluated (from left-to-right) after operations that involve the **@** and **NOT** operators.

The third level of precedence includes the **+** and **−** (addition and subtraction) operators, and the **OR** and **XOR** Boolean operators.

The lowest level of precedence includes all of the relational operators (**>, <, =, =>, <=, <>**) and the **IN** operator.

Earlier in this chapter you learned that the order in which terms are evaluated in an expression can be controlled by using parentheses. Using parentheses whenever a complex arithmetic expression is evaluated is a very good programming practice for two reasons. Not only does it ensure that the expression is evaluated in the manner in which you expect it to be, it also makes your program easier to understand.

Here is an example:

```
Avg : = First + Second / 2;
```

When TP encounters this program statement, it generates code that first divides **Second** by **2** and then adds **First** and assigns this value to **Avg**. This is because **/** has a higher precedent than **+**. If you wanted TP to take the average of the two numbers by performing the addition first, then the division, you could use parentheses to force a different order of evaluation:

```
Avg := (First + Second)/2;
```

A second example shows how to use parentheses for greater clarity:

```
IF NOT A AND NOT B THEN
  Writeln('neither one is TRUE');
```

If you look at the order of operator precedence above, you'll see that **NOT** takes precedence over **AND**. This means the compiler will evaluate the subexpression **NOT A**, then the subexpression **NOT B**, and finally will compare the results using the **AND** operator. You and the other users of your program might find it useful to add parentheses to clarify what your program is doing:

```
IF (NOT A) AND (NOT B) THEN
  Writeln('neither one is TRUE');
```

Summary

In this chapter, you've learned how to use the different operators to construct expressions. We began by discussing the basics of writing TP expressions, and then examined the operators from the seven categories—including arithmetic operators, relational operators, Boolean operators, bitwise operators, set operators, string operators, and pointer operators.

In Chapter 5, you'll learn how to put Boolean expressions to work as we explore program control and decision-making statements.

Exercises

1. Write a program that reads two strings and then joins the strings by placing a single space between them.

2. Explain what's wrong with the following program:

```
PROGRAM OpTest;
VAR
   X, Y : Integer;

BEGIN
   Writeln('Enter a number');
   Readln(Y);
   X := (312 > Y);
END.
```

3. What values are produced by the following expressions?

   a. 25 * 12 + 7 * 18

   b. 19 / 17 * 4 + (45 − 12)

   c. (200 > 120) AND (43 <> 12)

   d. 28 SHR 2

4. Explain why parentheses should be used to write complex expressions.

Answers

1. The program JOINSTRINGS reads two strings and then joins the strings by placing a single space between them.

```
PROGRAM JoinStrings;
Var
   Str1,Str2, ResultStr : String;

BEGIN
   Writeln('Enter the first string');
   Readln(Str1);
```

```
    Writeln('Enter the second string');
    Readln(Str2);
    ResultStr := Str1 + ' ' + Str2;
    Writeln('The new string is ', ResultStr);
END.
```

2. The statement **X := (312 > Y);** is invalid because the result of a relational expression like (312 > 4) is a Boolean value and cannot be assigned to a variable of type Integer.

3. The following values are produced by the expressions in step 3:

    a. 426

    b. 37.47

    c. True

    d. 7

4. Parentheses are important because they define the order in which the different parts of an expression should be evaluated.

Program Control:
Decision-Making and
Loop Statements

Sooner or later, you're going to write programs that need to make decisions on their own. Think about it. If you have a program that calculates an equation that produces an out-of-range value, or if the user of your program types in an incorrect response, you'll want to catch the error and perform a different action. What you need is a way to control the ability of your programs to make the correct decisions.

In addition to making decisions, your programs will also need a way to repeat selected sequences of statements. As an example, assume that you need to write a program that reads and sorts a list of names. If you have a long list of names, you certainly wouldn't want to include a **READ** statement in your program for each name that you must read. The best way to handle this type of problem is to use a *loop statement*, which will let you repeat a set of instructions a fixed number of times.

The goal of this chapter is to show you how to use all of the TP decision-making and looping statements. The cast of players is quite extensive; however, you'll quickly discover that decision-making and loop statements are easy to construct. Some of statements we'll be exploring include **IF-THEN**, **CASE**, **GOTO**, **FOR**, **WHILE-DO**, and **REPEAT-UNTIL**.

After you complete this chapter, you'll know how to:

• Write simple decision-making statements

• Nest decision-making statements

• Use loops

• Create Boolean expressions

• Exit from loops

Note

In Pascal, the term *Boolean expression* is used to refer to a logical expression that evaluates a true or false value.

Simple Decision-Making Statements

Our tour of decision-making statements will begin by examining the **IF-THEN** and **IF-THEN-ELSE** statements. These statements are called *conditional statements* because they test a specified logical expression (true or false) and direct a program to follow one of two alternative paths, depending on the outcome of the logical condition.

The IF-THEN Statement

Let's start by looking at the basic format of the **IF-THEN** statement:

```
IF <Boolean expression> THEN <statement>
```

For example:

```
IF Balance < 0 THEN Writeln('Your account is overdrawn');
```

In this case, **Balance < 0** is the Boolean expression and **Writeln(...)** is the statement that follows the **THEN** clause. This says that if the variable **Balance** is less than 0, then the "overdrawn" message is displayed. That's all there is to it. Here's the only requirement for writing the **IF-THEN** statement: The **IF** expression must *always* be a Boolean expression. Therefore, think about what might happen if you try to write a statement such as:

```
IF Readln(Balance) THEN Writeln('Your account is overdrawn');
```

The compiler will generate an error message.

You can combine multiple Boolean expressions in an **IF** clause if you use the **AND** or **OR** operators. For example:

```
IF (Balance < 0) AND (Withdraw > 0) THEN Writeln('Your account is overdrawn');
```

In this case, notice that parentheses were used to separate the two Boolean expressions.

Now that you've seen how simple **IF-THEN** statements are written, let's put together a short program that joins two strings:

```
PROGRAM JoinStrngs;
{Joins two strings if they are different}

VAR
  Str1, Str2 : STRING;

BEGIN
  Writeln('Input the first string');
  Readln(Str1);
  Writeln('Input the second string');
  Readln(Str2);
  IF Str1 <> Str2 THEN BEGIN
    Str1 := Str1 + Str2;
    Writeln('The new string is ', Str1);
  END;
END.
```

Type in this program and take it for a "test drive." It asks you to enter two strings, and if the strings are different, the program joins them. This time around, notice that we're using multiple statements in the body of the **IF-THEN**. You can think of the **BEGIN-END** block as a single statement.

Note

Remember that the **+** operator is used in TP to combine strings.

Adding the ELSE Clause

Thus far, we've only used **IF-THEN** statements that are capable of making a single decision. That means we're not using the full power of the **IF-THEN**. How can you make the **IF-THEN** an actual conditional statement? Add the **ELSE** clause. For example:

```
IF <Boolean expression> THEN <statement 1> ELSE<statement 2>
```

Note

Remember, *<statement 1>* and *<statement 2>* can be compound statements bracketed by **BEGIN-END** statement pairs.

In this case, if the Boolean expression evaluates to true, the first statement is executed; otherwise, the second statement is executed. Therefore, we are guaranteed that either statement 1 or statement 2 will be executed. Let's put this statement to work by modifying our previous program so that it will join two strings, using the shortest string first:

```
PROGRAM JoinStrngs;
{Joins two strings if they are different, version 2}
VAR
  Str1, Str2 : STRING;

BEGIN
  Writeln('Input the first string');
  Readln(Str1);
  Writeln('Input the second string');
  Readln(Str2);
  IF Str1 <> Str2 THEN BEGIN
    IF Length(Str1) < Length(Str2) THEN Str1 := Str1 + Str2
      ELSE Str1 := Str2 + Str1;
    Writeln('The new string is ', Str1);
  END;
END.
```

As Figure 5.1 illustrates, the program compares the two input strings and branches, depending on the outcome of the comparison. Notice that, in the second **IF** statement, we are using a built-in TP function called **Length**, which returns the length of a string.

1. What will happen if you omit the **THEN** keyword from an **IF-THEN** statement?
2. What is the difference between an **IF-THEN** and an **IF-THEN-ELSE** statement?

Figure 5.1   Use IF-THEN-ELSE to compare two input strings.

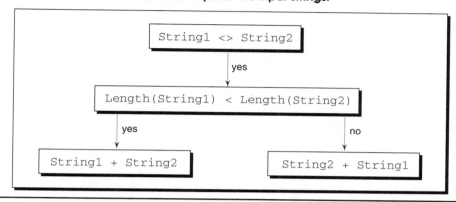

3. What will happen if you include a semicolon after the **END** statement as shown in the following program section?

```
IF Str1 <> Str2 THEN BEGIN
   Str1 := Str1 + Str2;
   Writeln('The new string is ', Str1);
   END;
ELSE Writeln('The strings cannot be joined');
```

1. The compiler will indicate that the **THEN** keyword is missing by displaying an error message.
2. The **IF-THEN** statement is a single-decision statement, while the **IF-THEN-ELSE** provides for two-way decisions (true or false).
3. The compiler will generate an error message because it won't be able to process the **ELSE** clause.

Nested IF Statements

In the previous program, a feature was introduced that hasn't really been explained yet. Consider the main **IF** statement again:

```
IF Str1 <> Str2 THEN BEGIN
   IF Length(Str1) < Length(Str2) THEN Str1 := Str1 + Str2
      ELSE Str1 := Str2 + Str1;
   ...
END;
```

Can you find the unexplained feature? One **IF** statement is included inside the body of another **IF** to allow us to make complex decisions. This technique is called *nesting*. The following format is used to nest **IF-THEN** statements:

```
IF <Boolean expression 1> THEN
  IF <Boolean expression 2> THEN
    IF <Boolean expression 3> THEN
      <statement>
```

As Figure 5.2 indicates, this type of statement sequence creates a chain of decisions in which each Boolean expression that evaluates to true leads to the next statement. With this in mind, we'll code the following expression:

```
IF X is larger than 200 and Y is greater than 75 and Z is equal to 50, then
print the sum X + Y.
```

The nested **IF** version is:

```
IF X > 200 THEN
  IF Y > 75 THEN
    IF Z = 50 THEN
      Writeln('The total is ', X+Y);
```

Note Nested **IF** statements can be difficult to read if they are nested too deeply. If you need to make a number of related decisions, the **CASE** statement, which we'll go over next, might be a better alternative.

The C A S E Statement

The major limitation of the **IF-THEN** statement is its "cut-and-dried" approach to decision making. A statement either evaluates as true or as false. However, the real world isn't quite so tidy. Some decisions require a number of different special cases. Fortunately, TP provides a statement for these purposes, called **CASE,** that allows us to make a decision based on a number of options. Here is the general format for this statement:

```
CASE <case selector> OF
  <case list 1> : <statement 1>;
  <case list 2> : <statement 2>;
  ...
  <case list n> : <statement n>
  ELSE <statement>
END;
```

Figure 5.2   A decision chain is created by using nested IF-THENs.

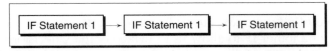

The case selector must be an *ordinal expression*—an expression that evaluates to a **Boolean**, **Char**, or **Integer** type. (Remember that a variable is also an expression.) Each case list component, or *case label*, must be a constant value or list of constants. When the **CASE** statement executes, the case selector is compared with each of the case labels until either a match is found or all of the case labels have been checked. If a match is not found, the statement following the **ELSE** clause is executed. Keep in mind, however, that the **ELSE** clause is optional. Here is an example of the **CASE** statement:

```
Read(Ch);     { Reads a character }
CASE Ch OF
  'A','E','I','O','U' : Writeln('Vowel');
  '0'..'9'            : Writeln('Digit');
  '+','-','*','/'     : Writeln('Operator');
  ' '                 : Writeln('Space');
ELSE Writeln('Other character')
END;
```

Here, every type of case label that is supported is used—including a list of constants, a range (one to ten), and a single constant (a blank).

Note

Remember that a case label must be a constant and not an expression. For example, the following case label would produce a compiler error:

```
CASE Ch OF
  UpCASE(CH) = 'A' : Writeln('This is an error');
  ...
END;
```

Now that we've explored the basic format of the **CASE** statement, let's write a program that uses the **CASE** statement to perform a set of string operations. The following program, called PROCESSSTRNGS, supports three types of string processing operations: inserting a substring, searching for a substring, and concatenating two strings.

```
PROGRAM ProcessStrngs;
{ Processes a set of strings }
VAR
  Str1, Str2 : String;
  ProcOpt    : Integer;
  StrPosn    : Integer;

BEGIN
  Writeln('Input the first string');
  Readln(Str1);
  Writeln('Input a string processing option');
  Writeln('1 Insert a substring in a string');
```

```
Writeln('2 Search for a substring');
Writeln('3 Concatenate two strings');
Readln(ProcOpt);
CASE ProcOpt OF
  1 : BEGIN
      Writeln('Input the string to insert');
      Readln(Str2);
      Writeln('Input the insertion position');
      Readln(StrPosn);
      Insert(Str2, Str1, StrPosn);
      Writeln('The new string is ', Str1);
  END;
  2 : BEGIN
      Writeln('Input the search substring');
      Readln(Str2);
      StrPosn := Pos(Str2, Str1);
      Writeln('The position of the substring is ', StrPosn);
  END;
  3 : BEGIN
      Writeln('Input the second string');
      Readln(Str2);
      Str1 := Str1 + Str2;
      Writeln('The new string is ', Str1);
  END;
   ELSE Writeln('Invalid string processing operation');
  END;
END.
```

The first thing you probably noticed is that the first three case conditions consist of **BEGIN-END** blocks because multiple statements are used with each case label. When a match occurs with one of these labels, all of the statements between **BEGIN** and **END** are executed.

We're also using the standard **Insert** procedure to insert a substring in another string and the **Pos** function to locate the position of a substring in a string. The basic formats for these built-in routines are:

```
PROCEDURE Insert(Source : String; VAR Target : String; Pos    : Integer);
FUNCTION Pos(SubStr : String; Source : String) : Integer;
```

With **Insert**, the **Source** string is inserted in the **Target** string at the location specified by **Pos**. The **Pos** routine, however, is a function and therefore returns a value—the position of the string **SubStr** in the string **Source**.

1. Why might the **CASE** statement be preferred over a complex or nested **IF-THEN** statement?

2. Explain how case selectors are used in the **CASE** statement. What are the requirements for specifying case selectors?

3. What happens if you omit the **ELSE** clause from the **CASE** statement?

1. The **CASE** statement is easier to read than heavily nested **IF-THEN** statements.
2. When a **CASE** statement executes, the case selector value is matched with each of the case items until a match is found or until all of the items have been tested. The case selector must be an ordinal expression.
3. The **CASE** statement is still valid without the **ELSE** clause; however, if the case selector does not match any of the case constants, no statement is executed.

A Little Bit of GOTO

If you have experience programming using a programming language such as BASIC, you've probably used **GOTO** statements. Normally, they are not used in Pascal because they violate the basic principles of structured programming.

The biggest problem in using **GOTO**s is that they make programs very difficult to read—especially if a program has a number of branches. However, in a few situations, it can make sense to use a **GOTO** statement in Pascal. For example, a **GOTO** can be used within a loop structure to help you get out of the loop.

The format for using a **GOTO** statement in TP is:

```
GOTO <label>
```

Here, the term *label* must be a numeric label that has been defined in the **LABEL** section of a program. The following program template illustrates the proper technique for using a **GOTO** statement:

```
PROGRAM Test_Goto;
LABEL
  210;
VAR
  X : Integer;

BEGIN
  ...
  IF X > 20 THEN GOTO 210;
  ...
  ...
  210 : Writeln('Jump to label');
END.
```

Controlling Programs with Loops

Now that decision-making statements are out of the way, we're ready to move on to explore the second feature of this chapter: looping statements. What exactly is a loop? It is simply a statement that repeats a set of one or more actions. You can use loops to perform a number of different tasks, including reading data from the keyboard, sorting data, performing computations, and so on.

FOR Loops

Let's start with the simplest type of loop: the **FOR** loop. This type of loop is used to repeat a section of a program a fixed number of times. Here's a program that calculates the factorial for each loop count:

```
PROGRAM TestFor;
VAR
  I      : Integer;
  Result : LongInt;

BEGIN
  Result := 1;
  FOR I := 1 TO 10 DO BEGIN
    Result := I * Result;
    Writeln('Loop count is ',I,', Result is ', Result);
  END;
  Writeln('The loop has finished')
END.
```

Type in the program and run it in the TP environment; you'll get the following output:

```
Loop count is 1, Result is 1
Loop count is 2, Result is 2
Loop count is 3, Result is 6
Loop count is 4, Result is 24
Loop count is 5, Result is 120
Loop count is 6, Result is 720
Loop count is 7, Result is 5040
Loop count is 8, Result is 40320
Loop count is 9, Result is 362880
Loop count is 10, Result is 3628800
The loop has finished
```

When the loop starts, the variable **I** is set to the value 1. Each time the loop repeats, this variable is incremented. At first, you might be wondering how this is done. After all, there isn't an increment statement in the body of the loop, as you could find with:

```
I := I + 1;
```

In our program, this variable is automatically incremented by the **FOR** statement each time the loop repeats. At the start of each loop iteration, the variable **I** is tested to ensure it is not greater than ten. When this occurs, the loop stops executing and program control is transferred to the statement that follows the loop body. This process is illustrated in Figure 5.3.

Now that you've seen the **FOR** loop in action, take a look at the general format of the **FOR** loop statement:

```
FOR <control variable> := <start> TO <end> DO <statement>
```

In comparing our previous example with this format, the variable **I** serves as the control variable, 1 is the start value, and 10 is the end value. The control variable can be any ordinal type (**Boolean, Char, Integer**) or a subrange of an ordinal type.

Warning: Don't change the contents of the control variable in the body of a loop because this variable is maintained by the **FOR** statement. The control variable should be treated as a "read-only" variable.

When you first start to work with **FOR** loops, you might not realize that you can use a control variable that is of an enumerated type. For example, if you have a type such as:

```
TYPE
   CarTypes = (Mercedes, Jaguar, Rolls, Porsche);
```

you can define a variable of this type

```
VAR
  Cars : CarTypes;
```

Figure 5.3 The FOR loop process.

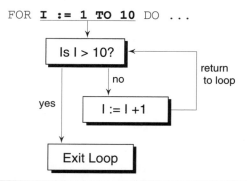

and use it as a loop control variable:

```
FOR Cars := Mercedes TO Porsche DO
   BEGIN
     IF Cars = Jaguar THEN ...
   END;
```

In this case, the control variable **Cars** is assigned to each car type until the end of the set has been reached.

The DOWNTO Option

Not every loop that you write has to count forward—that is, with the count increasing for each pass through the loop. TP allows you to use the **DOWNTO** keyword instead of the **TO** keyword to create a loop that works in the reverse order of the standard **FOR** loop. The general format is:

```
FOR <control variable> := <start> DOWNTO <end> DO <statement>
```

Using this style of loop, let's modify our program so that it counts backwards. Here's the new version:

```
PROGRAM TestFor2;
VAR
   I      : Integer;
   Result : LongInt;

BEGIN
   Result := 1;
   FOR I := 10 DOWNTO 1 DO BEGIN
     Result := I * Result;
     Writeln('Loop count is ',I,', Result is ', Result);
   END;
   Writeln('The loop has finished')
END.
```

Now the program produces this output:

```
Loop count is 10, Result is 10
Loop count is 9, Result is 90
Loop count is 8, Result is 720
Loop count is 7, Result is 5040
Loop count is 6, Result is 30240
Loop count is 5, Result is 151200
Loop count is 4, Result is 604800
Loop count is 3, Result is 1814400
Loop count is 2, Result is 3628800
```

```
Loop count is 1, Result is 3628800
The loop has finished
```

Nested FOR Loops

You've seen how to write simple **FOR** loops to serve as counters and perform calculations. Now let's put together a program that illustrates how **FOR** loops can be nested to create more complex loop structures. The following program uses a nested loop to draw an X on the screen:

```
PROGRAM DrawX;
USES Crt;
VAR
  Col, Row : Integer;
BEGIN
  ClrScr;
  FOR Row := 1 TO 25 DO
    FOR Col := 1 TO 25 DO
      IF (Row = Col) OR ((Row + Col) = 26) THEN BEGIN
        GotoXY(Row, Col);
        Write('X');
      END;
END.
```

The first loop is called the *outer loop* and the second loop is called the *inner loop*. Each time the outer loop starts a new cycle, the inner loop repeats 25 times. When the inner loop terminates, control is passed to the outer loop so that it can increment itself and start another cycle. To see how this works, you might want to use the built-in debugger and set breakpoints at the start of each loop statement. Of course, when you run the program, keep in mind that the two loop statements produce a total of 625 iterations—25 iterations (outer loop) * 25 iterations (inner loop) = 625 iterations.

1. Why is it dangerous to change the value of the loop control variable in the body of a **FOR** loop?

2. What will the variable **I** equal after the following code section executes?

```
FOR I := 1 TO 10 DO BEGIN
  Writeln('Loop count is ', I);
  ...
END;
Writeln('Loop count is ', I);
```

3. Specify the number of times the following loop will execute:

```
FOR I := 3 TO 3 DO
  Writeln('The value of I is ', I);
```

4. Why can't a variable of real type be used for a loop control variable?

1. The loop control variable is also changed by the **FOR** statement.
2. The value is undefined.
3. The loop will execute one time only.
4. The loop control variable serves as a counter and can be incremented only by a whole number.

WHILE-DO Loops

The key feature of the **FOR** statement we've just explored is that it guarantees a loop will repeat for a fixed number of times. But what happens if you need a loop to repeat until a condition you are testing fails? As an example, assume that we need a program to keep reading characters until the user presses the Enter key. If we use a **FOR** loop to do this, we would have to limit the number of characters that the user could type in.

Fortunately, TP provides two other statements for writing nonfixed-iteration loops, or *open loops*: the **WHILE-DO** and **REPEAT-UNTIL**. We'll examine the **WHILE-DO** first. Here's the general format required for this statement:

```
WHILE <loop control expression> DO <statement>
```

How does this loop work? Look at an example:

```
WHILE I < 10 DO Readln(I);
```

Here, the expression **I < 10** serves as the loop control expression, and **Readln(I);** serves as the loop statement, or loop body. This loop will continue to repeat as long as the variable **I** is less than 10. For the loop control expression, you can use any expression as long as it evaluates to a true or false value—the loop control expression must be a Boolean expression. After the loop body executes, the loop expression is tested and, as long as the expression evaluates as true, the loop body will continue to execute. The following examples illustrate the types of loop control expressions that are supported:

```
WHILE Ch <> ' ' DO Read(Ch);

WHILE SName IN NameSet DO
  BEGIN
    IF SName = Bob THEN ProcName
    ELSE DisplayName;
    Succ(SName);
  END;
```

Note | If the loop expression evaluates as false the first time it is tested, the loop body will never be executed.

Here is a sample program that shows how a **WHILE-DO** loop is used to count the number of words in an input string:

```
PROGRAM CountWords;
{ Counts the number of words in a string}
USES Crt;
VAR
  Ch : Char;
  WCount : Integer;

BEGIN
  WCount := 0;
  Writeln('Input a string');
  Ch := ReadKey;
  Write(Ch);
  WHILE Ch <> Chr(13) DO BEGIN
    IF Ch = ' ' THEN WCount := WCount + 1;
    Ch := ReadKey;
    Write(Ch);
  END;
  Writeln; { Just to add a spacer line}
  Writeln('The word count is ', WCount + 1);
END.
```

In this program, the **ReadKey** function from the **Crt** unit is used to read a single character at a time. Because **ReadKey** does not display the character that it reads, a **Write** statement is included after each **ReadKey** call so that you can see what character has been typed in. The initial loop statement

```
WHILE Ch <> Chr(13) DO BEGIN
```

tests the input character to see if the Enter key has been pressed by comparing the variable **Ch** to the character representation of ASCII 13 (the Enter key). Notice that the loop body consists of multiple statements placed in a **BEGIN-END** block. Each time a space character is found, the word count variable **WCount** is incremented by 1.

REPEAT-UNTIL Loops

The second type of open loop provided by TP is the **REPEAT-UNTIL**. How is this loop statement different from the **WHILE-DO**? It checks the loop control expression at the end of the loop instead of at the beginning. This approach ensures that the loop body will execute at least once. Here is the general form of the **REPEAT-UNTIL** loop:

```
REPEAT <statement> UNTIL <loop control expression>;
```

Again, the loop control expression must evaluate to a true or false value. The loop body executes before the loop control expression is tested. The important point to keep in mind is that, when a loop control expression evaluates to false, the loop continues to execute.

```
PROGRAM CountWords;
{ Counts the number of words and characters in a string}
USES Crt;
VAR
  Ch : Char;
  WCount, CCount : Integer;
BEGIN
  WCount := 0;
  CCount := 0;
  Writeln('Input a string');
  REPEAT
    Ch := ReadKey;
    Write(Ch);
    IF Ch = ' ' THEN WCount := WCount + 1;
    CCount := CCount + 1;
  UNTIL Ch = Chr(13);
  Writeln;
  Writeln('The word count is ', WCount + 1);
  Writeln('The character count is ', CCount - 1);
END.
```

▼ 1. Use the TP debugger to see if you can find the error in the following program. (Hint: Set a breakpoint at the **WHILE-DO** loop and set a watch value for the variable **I** used in the loop control expression.)

```
PROGRAM Loop_Check;
VAR
  I, Total : Integer;

BEGIN
  Total := 0;
  FOR I := 1 TO 200 DO
  BEGIN
    Total := I + Total
    IF Total > 100 THEN Total := Total - 10
    ELSE I := 10;
  END;
END.
```

2. Write a **FOR** loop to perform an integer power function. That is, the loop should compute where X and n are integers. Also, code this loop as a **WHILE-DO**. Which version is better? Why?

3. Explain the difference between **WHILE-DO** and **REPEAT-UNTIL** loops.

4. What is the minimum number of times that a **REPEAT-UNTIL** loop will execute?

1. The loop will never terminate because the **ELSE** clause keeps resetting the loop control variable **I** to 10.

2. The **FOR** loop version is:

```
Result := 1;
FOR I := 1 TO N-1 DO
    Result := Result * X;
```

The **WHILE** loop version is:

```
Result := 1;
WHILE N >= 2 DO BEGIN
  Result := Result * X;
  N := N - 1;
END;
```

The **WHILE** loop version is better because it can test the value of n before the loop starts.

3. A **WHILE-DO** loop tests the loop termination condition before the loop starts and the **REPEAT-UNTIL** loop tests the condition at the end of the loop.

4. A **REPEAT-UNTIL** loop will always execute at least once.

Exiting Loops

TP does not provide a break statement like other languages for jumping out of a loop. There is, however, an **Exit** statement you can use to terminate the execution of the program block that is currently executing.

Here is an example of a program that uses **Exit** to let you try your luck at guessing random numbers:

```
PROGRAM RandomGuess;
USES
    WinCRT;
VAR
  RNum, I, Guess : Integer;

BEGIN
  Randomize;  { Initializes the random number generator}
  RNum := Random(100);  { Creates a random number between 0 and 100}
  FOR I := 1 TO 10 DO BEGIN
```

```
      Writeln('Input a guess between 0 and 100');
      Readln(Guess);
      IF Guess = RNum THEN BEGIN
        Writeln('Your guess number ', I, ' is correct');
        EXIT
      END
      ELSE IF Guess > RNum THEN
          Writeln('Your guess number ', I, ' is too high')
      ELSE
          Writeln('Your guess number ', I, ' is too low')
   END;
END.
```

When the **Exit** statement is executed, program control is transferred from the current block to the next highest block. Because our example program only contains a main program, the only place to go is back to the TP environment. This means that the **FOR** loop will repeat for 10 iterations unless you guess the number that has been randomly generated. A correct guess will make the program stop.

Summary

In this chapter, you learned how to use program control statements to make decisions and to construct loops. We started with the basic **IF-THEN** and **IF-THEN-ELSE** statements, and then covered the flexible **CASE** statement. You saw how these basic decision-making statements can be used to control the execution flow of Pascal programs. In the second part of this chapter, we covered the loop statements, including **FOR**, **WHILE-DO**, and **REPEAT-UNTIL**. Here, you learned how to nest one loop inside another and how to use loop variables to control the number of loop iterations.

In Chapter 6 we'll shift gears and look at the console input and output features of TP. Here, you'll learn how to control how your programs communicate with the outside world.

Exercises

1. Write a program that uses **IF-THEN** statements to determine the category in which an input character belongs. The categories you should use include:

   a. vowel (a, e, i, o, u)

   b. letter (b, c, d, f, g, ...)

   c. digit (0, 1, 2, 3, ...)

   d. operator (+, –, *, /)

2. Change the program in step 1 so that it uses a **CASE** statement instead of **IF-THEN** statements.

3. Write a program that allows you to type in a set of numbers and then computes a total and average. The program should keep reading numbers until 0 is entered.

4. Explain the differences between the **FOR**, **WHILE-DO**, and **REPEAT-UNTIL** loops.

Answers

1. The LETTERCHK1 program uses **IF-THEN** statements to determine the category (listed in step 1) in which an input character belongs.

```
PROGRAM LetterChk1;
Const
   LCLetter  =  ['a'..'z'];
   Vowel  =  ['A', 'E', 'I', 'O', 'U'];
   Letter = ['B', 'C', 'D', 'F', 'G', 'H', 'J', 'K', 'L', 'M', 'N',
             'P', 'Q', 'R', 'S', 'T', 'V', 'W', 'X', 'Y', 'Z'];
   Digit   = ['0'..'9'];
   Operator = ['+','-','*','/'];
VAR
   InpChar : Char;

BEGIN
   Writeln('Input a character to test ');
   Readln(InpChar);
   IF InpChar IN LCLetter THEN
     InpChar := UpCase(InpChar); { Converts to uppercase}
   IF InpChar IN Vowel THEN
     Writeln('The character is a vowel')
   ELSE IF InpChar IN Letter THEN
     Writeln('The character is a letter')
   ELSE IF InpChar IN Digit THEN
     Writeln('The character is a digit')
   ELSE IF InpChar IN Operator THEN
     Writeln('The character is an operator')
   ELSE
     Writeln('No match found');
END.
```

2. The following program is a modified version of LETTERCHK that uses a **CASE** statement instead of **IF-THEN** statements.

```
PROGRAM LetterChk2;
CONST
   LCLetter = ['a'..'z'];
VAR
   InpChar : Char;

BEGIN
```

```
Writeln('Input a character to test ');
Readln(InpChar);
IF InpChar IN LCLetter THEN
   InpChar := UpCase(InpChar); { Convert to uppercase }
CASE InpChar OF
   'A','E','I','O','U' : Writeln('The character is a vowel');
   'B','C','D','F','G',
       'H','J','K','L',
       'M','N','P','Q',
       'R','S','T','V',
       'W','X','Y','Z' : Writeln('The character is a letter');
   '0'..'9'            : Writeln('The character is a digit');
   '+','-','*','/'     : Writeln('The character is an operator')
ELSE
   Writeln('No match found');
END;
END.
```

3. The AVGNUMS program allows you to type in a set of numbers and then computes a total and average:

```
PROGRAM  AvgNums;
VAR
   InpNum,Total,Count : Integer;
   Result             : Real;

BEGIN
   Total := 0;
   Count := 0;
   REPEAT
     Writeln('Input a number');
     Readln(InpNum);
     Total := Total + InpNum;
     Inc(Count);
   UNTIL InpNum = 0;
   IF Total > 0 THEN BEGIN
     Result := Total / (Count-1);
     Writeln('The average number is ', Result)
   END;
END.
```

4. The **FOR** loop is a fixed iteration loop—it always executes for a fixed number of times. This type of loop is normally used for counting operations. The **WHILE-DO** and **REPEAT-UNTIL** loops are called open loops because they will continue to execute until a terminating condition is met. The terminating condition for the **WHILE** loop is evaluated at the beginning of the loop and causes the loop to terminate when the condition evaluates as false. The terminating condition in the **REPEAT-UNTIL** loop is evaluated at the end of the loop and stops the loop when it evaluates as true.

6

Console Input/Output

n the early days of computers, performing I/O tasks was a real chore. Input devices consisted of keyboards built into awkward, metal boxes, and output devices were typically hard-to-read, black-and-white TV sets that could only display 40 lines of text. Fortunately, today's hardware and software systems provide much greater capabilities. In fact, TP—with its support of graphics, windows, and color—provides us with a truly state-of-the-art system for performing I/O tasks. All you have to do now is learn to harness this power.

In this chapter we're going to explore the basic TP screen and keyboard I/O features. The chapter begins by presenting the techniques available for inputting data from the keyboard, one keystroke at a time. Next, you'll learn how to use the **Read** and **Readln** statements to read numbers and strings, which provide enough flexibility to read data formatted in different ways.

After you complete this chapter, you'll know how to:

- Read a single keystroke with the **ReadKey** function
- Read numbers and strings with **Read** and **Readln**
- Handle input errors using the **$I–** option
- Write data using **Write** and **Writeln**
- Use the computer-specific I/O routines provided with the **Crt** unit.

Inputting Data from the Keyboard

The most basic unit of data that can be inputted from the keyboard is a single keystroke, which is usually represented as a single character (**CHAR** data type). Remember that a character can be regarded as either a letter (uppercase or lowercase), a digit (0 through 9), or a punctuation character (comma, period, percent symbol, and so on).

The easy way to read single keystroke is to use the function named **ReadKey**. When any of these standard character keys are pressed, the function **ReadKey** will return a byte containing the number corresponding to the ASCII code for the key pressed. For example, imagine that you want a question on the screen answered by either y or n. The section of code to wait for the answer might look like this:

```
Get_out := False;
REPEAT
  In_key := ReadKey;
  IF (In_key = 'y' OR In_key = 'n') THEN
    Get_out := True
UNTIL Get_out = True;
```

For this example, the variable **In_key** must be declared as a **CHAR** type. The code between the **REPEAT** and **UNTIL** statements will keep repeating until the lowercase y or n is pressed. Notice that all other keys will be ignored. Keep in mind that, when **ReadKey** reads a keystroke, the key entered is not echoed to the screen. Therefore, you won't be able to see what key you are entering.

One thing that hasn't been mentioned yet is that **ReadKey** is not an automatic feature of the TP I/O system, even though this function is supported by TP. A special set of routines for performing I/O operations has been packaged in a file called the **Crt** unit. To use any of these routines, you must include the unit by placing the following line immediately after the program's declaration statement:

```
USES Crt;
```

You might be wondering why the routines provided with the **Crt** unit aren't actually built into TP. After all, why should you have to worry about accessing other files to perform a simple operation such as reading a keystroke? The reason: These I/O routines are not included in the standard Pascal definition, but they are well-recognized I/O functions available in other languages that run on computers. With the exception of **Read, Readln, Write**, and **Writeln**, all of the functions and procedures discussed in this chapter are provided by the **Crt** unit. Thus, you should develop the habit of including the above **USES** statement in any program that performs different types of I/O operations.

Note

The routines provided with the **Crt** unit will be presented later in this chapter. (You can also explore the routines by choosing the Units option in the Contents help window and then selecting the **Crt** option.) If you have Turbo Pascal for Windows, you can use the routines in the **WinCrt** unit to perform these same actions while running your program in Windows.

You now know that **ReadKey** returns a single character that corresponds with the ASCII code for the key pressed. Now, what do you think **ReadKey** would do if you pressed one of the function keys or the Arrow keys? If the key pressed is not a normal typewriter symbol for which a standard ASCII code exists, **ReadKey** will first return a value of 0. A second call to **ReadKey** will then return a special value to identify the function key that was pressed. Thus, special keys require two successive **ReadKey** calls to determine which key has been pressed. Any program that uses **ReadKey** should test for a value of 0 in order to detect a number pair associated with a special key. Later in this chapter, I provide a program that shows how **ReadKey** can be used to detect the pressing of any key.

1. How would you modify the program presented earlier to also check for uppercase Y and N?
2. How can you display the key that a user types in? Why doesn't **ReadKey** display the key that it reads?

1. You could use the **UpCase** function to convert the input character to an uppercase letter before it is tested.
2. **ReadKey**, unlike the **Read** procedure, does not echo the key that is read. If you want to display the key pressed, you must use the **Write** procedure.

Reading Numbers

Thus far, you've seen how to read a single keystroke. Fortunately, we don't have to process all input data in this manner! Imagine that each time you wanted to input a real number you had to identify each keystroke as a sign-character (+ or –), the individual digits, a decimal point for a real number, and so on. Programming would quickly get very tedious. The good news is that most high-level languages provide better methods for reading an entire number at one time. TP provides the two functions **Read** and **Readln** for this purpose.

The first thing you need to know is that both of these routines can read data from either the keyboard or from a *data file*. To keep things simple in this chapter, we will only discuss the forms of commands associated with the keyboard and screen. (If you are curious about how the statements are used to read file data, turn to Chapter 10 after studying the discussion here.)

Here is the basic statement format for **Read** and **Readln**:

```
Read(argument_1, argument_2, ...);
Readln(argument_1, argument_2, ...);
```

The arguments in the parentheses can be simple variables, such as reals, integers, and so on. The variables are always assigned values in the order in which they appear in the argument list. For example, when this statement executes

```
Read (A, X, I);
```

and these numbers are typed in and the Enter key is pressed

```
27 13 4 128 <cr>
```

the number 27 is assigned to the variable **A**, 13 is assigned to **X**, and 4 is assigned to **I**, as shown in Figure 6.1. Notice that the data after the third number is ignored because only three arguments were provided in the **Read** function.

Figure 6.1 Use the Read function to read numbers inputted from the keyboard.

Note The symbol <cr> is used to represent a carriage return. This character is produced by pressing the Enter key on your keyboard.

When the **Read** statement is processed, TP must first determine the data type of the variable **A**. From the declaration, TP knows that **A** is an integer and, therefore, when it reads the data for this variable it scans the keyboard input, from left to right, looking for characters that could be part of a number. In our case, it reads a 2, then a 7, and then a blank. Because the blank character serves as a delimiter, TP knows when to stop reading the data for the variable **A**. (The **Read** statement also uses a tab and the <cr> as a delimiter.) After the characters are read, the necessary conversion operation is performed to store the input data as an integer. The same steps will then be followed for assigning values to the variables **X** and **I**. Because **Read** uses the carriage return as a delimiter, the same data could have been entered in the following format:

```
27 <cr>
13 <cr>
4 <cr>
```

The **Readln** statement is similar to **Read**, with one slight difference— **Readln** reads an entire line of data in one call. This distinction might not be obvious to you when reading from the keyboard because input data is not processed with either routine until the Enter key is pressed. The differences will become more apparent when we discuss techniques for reading data from files. If there aren't sufficient numbers on a line to satisfy the argument list for a **Readln** statement, TP will patiently wait for you to enter additional data on subsequent lines.

Checking for Errors

Thus far in our discussions, we've assumed that entered data is always of the correct data type. But how would you expect the TP input function to react if it encounters as input the number 27.0 rather than 27 when assigning a value to an integer? To us, 27 is 27, whether the decimal point is there or not, but as discussed in Chapter 3, the representation of the floating-point value for 27 is quite different from the way the integer version is represented. TP provides one of two responses to such a problem. The default response is to stop execution and display an error message. This is fine if you are debugging a program and want to know immediately that something went wrong. The second option is more benign and is extremely useful when writing programs to be used by nontechnical users. By using the **$I–** option, you can disable I/O checking. Using this option doesn't make the problem go away; it simply keeps the program from halting in mid-session. It now becomes your responsibility to check the result of your I/O operations for errors. To disable I/O checking, you must place

```
{$I-};
```

immediately after the program definition line.

Here is a program template that illustrates the correct format for using this option:

```
PROGRAM Read_Data;
{$I-}
VAR
   ...

BEGIN
   ...
END.
```

Note

> TP provides a built-in function called **IOResult** that allows you to test the outcome of your I/O operations. Typically, this function is used with file I/O commands. You'll learn how it is used when we explore file I/O in Chapter 10.

Another way to prevent TP from halting your program is to use floating-point numbers to read in numeric data, and then convert them to integers if necessary (following the rules presented in Chapter 3).

Reading Strings

Reading string input is relatively foolproof. Whether you use **Read** or **Readln**, strings entered from the keyboard are only delimited by the end-of-line character <cr>. This can create some interesting problems. For example, imagine you are writing a program that asks for the user's last name as part of a password. If the user accidentally enters a blank at the end of the name before pressing the Enter key, the character string read from the keyboard will be one character longer than would be expected, and the last character in the string will be a blank. To prevent this sort of problem, you might want to process the input data to remove common "human errors." For example, the following program fragment removes trailing blanks from a last name:

```
Readln(Last_name);
L := Length(Last_name);
WHILE L > 0;
BEGIN
  IF (Copy(Last_name, L, 1) = ' ') THEN
    BEGIN
    Last_name := Delete(Last_name, L, 1);
    L := Length(Last_name);
    END
  ELSE
    L := 0;
END;
```

On the first line, the code reads a string and stuffs it in the variable **Last_name**. The second line invokes a built-in function called **Length** that returns the length of the string, which is a value corresponding to the number of characters in the string. Because TP allows string variables to be up to 255 characters long, it is recommended that the variable **L** be defined as an **Integer** or larger type to avoid any possibility of overflow when manipulating string lengths. The third and fourth lines simply define the top of a **WHILE** loop that will execute as long as the string length is greater than 0 (you must plan for the case in which the user types in one space and then presses the Enter key).

The fifth line uses another built-in function, **Copy**, to isolate the last character of the string so that it can be compared with a blank. What does **Copy** do? It simply extracts a substring from another string. The first argument tells the function which string to extract from (**Last_name**, in this case). The second argument, **L**, tells **Copy** where in the string to start the extraction. The third character indicates how many characters to extract. Since we pointed at the last character by setting the second argument to the length of the string, and we told TP to copy only one character, the entire operation will extract only the last character of the string. If the character is a blank, another built-in function, **Delete**, is invoked to delete the blank character (which we happen to know is the last character because the entire string is of length **L**). In this function, the third argument tells **Delete** that we want to delete only one character. At this point, we re-evaluate the length of the string **Last_name** (although we could just as easily have decremented the value of **L** by one).

The entire program segment is in a **WHILE-DO** loop to cope with the case in which multiple blanks appear at the end of the string. This set of instructions will therefore remove all trailing blanks. When the **IF** statement encounters a trailing character that is not a blank, we set the value of **L** to 0 in order to force an end to the **WHILE-DO** loop.

1. Explain the differences between **Readln** and **Read**.
2. You need to press the Enter key after typing data in order to get **Read** to input the data. True or False?
3. Given the following variable declarations and **Readln** statement:

```
VAR
  I, J : Integer;
  Ch   : Char;
  F    : Real;
Readln(I, J, Ch, F);
```

describe the contents of the four variables after the following line of data is read:

```
200 72 3 A 73.9
```

1. The **Read** procedure reads one or more data elements into the specified variables. **Readln** does the same, but then skips to the next line of input, ignoring any extra input data.
2. True
3. The variable **I** is set to 200, **J** is set to 72, **Ch** is set to '3', and **F** is undefined.

Screen Output

Now that you've been exposed to the basics of input, you'll want to learn how to control screen output. Computer screen hardware can be divided into two general categories: (1) those capable of some form of graphics and (2) those limited strictly to alphanumeric characters. The existence of this limitation depends on the design of the *display card* within the computer.

TP provides two basic output statements to display alphanumeric data: **Write** and **Writeln**. The **Write** statement generates output starting at the current cursor position. This cursor position can be moved around under program control, as we'll explain later in the chapter. If the next message generated tries to write characters past the eightieth character of the bottom line, the entire display contents will be scrolled up by one line and the new data will be displayed at the vacant bottom line.

The **Write** statement leaves the cursor at the position immediately after the last character written. The **Writeln** statement also displays data at the current cursor position, but always forces the cursor to column 1 of the next line after completing the current output. The **Write** statement is, therefore, useful for question-and-answer situations in which the program may ask a question and expect the answer to be entered on the same line as the question. (This is accomplished by using a **Read** statement to read one variable, beginning from the current cursor position.) **Writeln**, however, is used to display left-justified text (such as instructions to a user). You can also use **Writeln** to insert blank lines by simply coding:

```
Writeln;
```

Since no arguments are passed to the procedure, it simply generates a carriage return (which, in effect, creates a blank line if the previous output command had left the cursor at column 1).

Using Write and Writeln

The **Write** and **Writeln** procedures both require the following general format:

```
Writeln(<variable> [:<width> [:<decimals>] ]);
```

Here, *variable* stands for the name of the particular variable or constant data to be output. The square brackets in the example indicate optional fields. (Keep in mind that the brackets aren't actually used in a statement.) The first optional parameter is *width*, which specifies the total number of spaces to be allocated for the contents of the variable.

Note

> If you specify a width that is too small to properly display the contents of output data, TP will override your specification in favor of a *default width*. This default specification is guaranteed to be large enough to display all necessary digits or characters.

The other optional parameter is used only with floating-point variable output. It specifies the number of digits behind the decimal point that you wish to have displayed. Obviously, the *decimals* specification must be smaller than the entire *width* field for the specification to make sense. If *decimals* is greater than *width*, TP will always honor the *decimals* specification and will override *width*. For example, if a variable **Cost** contains data in which the integer part represents dollars and the fractional part represents cents, you could use the following statement to place the data on the screen:

```
Write(Cost:9:2);
```

Note that this would allow for the display of positive numbers as large as 999999.99. (Remember, you lose two digits for the cents, plus one digit for the decimal point.) The maximum for negative values would be −99999.99. (The negative sign also eats up a digit.) TP never inserts commas for numbers greater than 1000, so these extra spaces need not be taken into consideration.

Both **Write** and **Writeln** can also be used to output constant data to the screen. For example, the instructions

```
Writeln;
Writeln('Welcome to the Air Ace correspondence course!');
```

would move the cursor to column 1 of the line below its original location, would display the message between the single quotation marks, and would move the cursor to column 1 of the next line. You can also combine constants and variable data. For example,

```
Stb := 2000;
Writeln('The number of suntan booths in Arizona is ', Stb);
```

will print out the message between quotation marks and will then print out the contents of the variable **Stb**.

There is another interesting feature about the *width* specification discussed earlier. If the value for *width* is positive, the output will be right justified within the output field. If the value of *width* is negative, the output will be left justified within the field. Thus, for example, if the suntan booth example is changed to

```
Stb := 2000;
Writeln('The number of suntan booths in Arizona is ', Stb:6);
```

then the screen output would consist of the message, three spaces (one space between the "is" and the single quotation mark) plus two blanks for the unused part of the output field of width 6. Since this would look unprofessional, you might want to modify the statement as follows:

```
Stb := 2000;
Writeln('The number of suntan booths in Arizona is ', Stb:-6);
```

This still allows for the display of a number up to 999999, but now the output on the screen will always consist of the message, one separating blank after the "is" included in the literal string, and the left-justified number (2000 in this case).

Note

You should develop a habit of including a trailing blank at the end of string literals to be printed on the screen. By doing so, you can avoid output "traffic jams" such as:

```
The number of suntan booths in Arizona is2000
```

1. What are the differences between the **Write** and **Writeln** statements?
2. The **Write** and **Writeln** routines are part of the **Crt** unit. True or False?

3. Assuming the cursor is positioned at the fifth row and the seventieth column, specify where the cursor will be after the following statement executes:

```
Write('Please enter your name');
```

4. Describe the format of data output by the following **Writeln** statements:
   a. Writeln(X:2);
   b. Writeln('Please enter your name ', Y:4);
   c. Writeln(X:10);
   d. Writeln(X:–10);

For these examples, assume that X contains the value 275 and Y contains 3001.

1. The **Write** procedure outputs data without advancing the cursor to the next line, whereas **Writeln** advances the cursor after data is output.
2. False.
3. The sixth row, twelfth column
4. The format of the data output from each **Writeln** statement in step 4 is shown here:
   a. The output is right justified in a two-column width.
   b. The data in variable **Y** is right justified in four columns.
   c. The data is right justified in 10 columns.
   d. The data is left justified in 10 columns.

TP Screen and Keyboard Extensions

Thus far, we've explored the routines provided with the standard Pascal I/O library. These commands aren't "tailor-made" for the computer. However, TP also provides flexible text I/O routines, such as color output and window control, that do take advantage of the unique features of the computer. Remember that these routines are contained in the **Crt** unit and are used primarily for DOS programs. Windows doesn't directly support text-oriented I/O, and although many of the variables and routines in the **Crt** unit can also be found in the **WinCrt** unit, others cannot. Let's now explore the commands contained in this unit, making note of those that appear only in the **Crt** unit. Then we'll write a brief example program that illustrates how to use several of these commands.

At this point, we'll need to return to our discussion on display hardware to explain a few important details. Recall that monochrome display cards and cards capable of displaying colors are available with computers. But it is also possible (and not unusual) for a monochrome display to be connected to a color display card. For example, most CGA (color graphics adapter) cards generate a signal called *composite video*, which meets standards for video signals used between home video cameras and video recorders. Just as you can view a tape of *The Wizard of Oz* on either a black-and-white or color TV, you can connect either a black-and-white or color display to the composite video output on your computer.

Unfortunately, there's a bit of a catch—the electronic commands for certain colors look terrible on monochrome displays; the signals are fully compatible, but the visual perception isn't. Here's what usually happens: Certain colors will display letters on the monochrome monitor as if they are being shown through a heavy netting; the general outline of the letter is there, but it's very difficult to read.

We mention these peculiarities of output devices to help you understand how to foresee and overcome display problems so that your program outputs will look their best. If you're writing a program for an application that guarantees that the display card/monitor combination will always be able to display color, then you may safely use all of the functions provided with the **Crt** unit. The use of color can make a dramatic difference in the visual impact of your package. For example, it's possible for you to customize the TP display window so that reserved words appear in one color, comments in another, strings in a third color, and so on.

Back to Basics

For the remainder of this chapter, we'll assume that you have at least CGA color capability in order to explore the full range of display capabilities of TP. If you have a monochrome system, you may wish to skip the description of the commands associated with colors.

The Window Procedure (Crt Only)

Even though it is last alphabetically, let's look at the **Window** procedure first because it impacts many other commands in the **Crt** unit. The **Window** command allows you to define an active area within the normal CRT screen. If we assume the usual 80-column by 25-line screen, **Window** allows you to create a smaller screen within this region. Once a window has been defined, the other commands act only on the area of the screen that is taken up by the window. For example, assume that your program contains this command:

```
Window(20, 5, 60, 20);
```

Figure 6.2 illustrates how this area would look on an 80-column by 25-line screen. As we'll later explain in detail, the **ClrScr** command clears the active window and moves the cursor to the top-left corner of the window. If no window has been defined for TP output (so that the default window is in effect), the **ClrScr** procedure performs the same task as the DOS CLS command. However, if a window has been defined, the **ClrScr** command will reinitialize only the area inside the window, leaving the other areas of the screen unaltered. This window also interacts with such commands as **Write** and **Writeln**.

Figure 6.2 A window within an 80-column by 25-line screen.

Note

In the standard text mode, the upper-left corner of the screen is addressed as location (1,1) and the lower-right corner is addressed as location (25,80). If you have a high-resolution monitor (EGA or VGA), you can access up to 43 rows. (See *The TextMode(Mode) Procedure Crt Only* for more details.)

Our sample command defined a window 41 characters wide (from column 20 through column 60 is 41 character positions). Normally, if a TP output command reaches column 80 and still needs to print additional information to the screen, the data is sent to the next line. This means any information that would have been assigned logically to columns 81, 82, and so on will appear on the next line in columns 1, 2, and so on. Thus, no information is lost (although the screen may be difficult to read). If you attempt to write (output) a 60-character line in a window that's only 41 characters wide, the additional 19 characters will wrap to the next line within the smaller window! The text in column 61 of the CRT screen will not be affected. This is an extremely powerful technique for creating professional-looking displays with relatively little effort.

The AssignCrt Command

This powerful command is used to redirect keyboard input and/or screen output to a disk data file. Normally, when the **Crt** unit is used, I/O redirection is inhibited by TP. I/O redirection means that instead of looking for input from a keyboard, redirected input will read a disk file. When output is redirected in this way, messages are sent to a file rather than a screen. To re-enable I/O redirection, you must use the **Assign** function. After you've specified this function, the keyboard and screen will be ignored unless you use the **AssignCrt** command. You'll have an opportunity to work with this procedure in Chapter 10 when we explore file I/O.

The ClrEol Procedure

This procedure clears the screen from the current cursor position to the rightmost edge of the current window, but leaves the cursor at its original position. If the current window is smaller than the screen area, the remainder of the screen will not be affected. This command comes in handy when you want to produce professional-looking output. For example, imagine that you've written a program that takes a TP file as input and generates a list of all variables and constants used in the file. When the user enters the name of the input file, the program will search for the file. If the file doesn't exist, the program will print a message at the bottom of the screen describing the problem to the user.

After your program has displayed this message, it certainly would be convenient to return to the point in your program at which the screen asks for the filename, then have the mistaken name erased, with the cursor returned to a position that follows the initial question. In this way, the user could try again to enter a filename correctly. Such visual gymnastics can be accomplished by using the **GotoXY** command (discussed a little later) to move the cursor to the spot immediately after the question, and by using the **ClrEol** command to erase the previous answer.

The ClrScr Procedure

The **ClrScr** procedure performs a task similar to the DOS CLS command. That is, **ClrScr** clears the current screen (or window) and places the cursor at the top-left corner. However, note that **ClrScr** clears only the *current* window. If you've defined a window smaller than the entire screen, only that part in the active window will be cleared. Since **ClrScr** clears the screen by writing blanks (which use the currently defined background color), this command is an effective way to color a window. The **ClrScr** procedure accomplishes this by forcing all locations within the window to display blanks of a predetermined background color. However, if no window has been defined, the **ClrScr** command will clear the entire screen.

1. Explain why windows are useful for formatting data.
2. Specify the actual screen location used to display the text output by the following commands. Where will the cursor be after the text is displayed?

```
Window(10, 5, 50, 20);
Writeln('Enter a single character');
```

3. What happens if you try to create a window that is larger than the size of the computer's screen?

1. Windows are useful because they allow you to partition the screen into a smaller region.
2. The text is displayed at column 10, row 5. After the text is displayed, the cursor will be positioned at column 34, row 5.
3. You will get a run-time error.

The Delay(Time) Procedure (Crt Only)

This procedure delays program execution for a specified length of time. The argument, Time, must be an integer in the range 0 .. 65535 and must specify the number of milliseconds (thousandths of a second) that the program is to wait before continuing. (If the argument is set at 1000, the program will delay for 1 second since there are 1,000 milliseconds in 1 second.) Thus, one call to this routine can delay for as long as 65 seconds. Understand that when TP says **Delay**, it means just that—for the specified period of time, the computer will do nothing except count time in fractions of a second, "holding its breath" in effect. TP will not allow input from the keyboard or output to the screen during the delay period. Since the procedure uses the internal computer clock to determine when to "return to life," there is no reason to prevent successive calls to this procedure if delays longer than 65 seconds are required.

Another nice feature of **Delay** can be described by a brief slice of computer history. In the early years of programming, delays were often implemented by performing a floating-point division within a loop. Under this approach, the delay would vary with the speed of the processor performing the division, so that a delay of 1 second on one machine might be only .5 second on a machine that ran twice as fast. By comparison, the **Delay** function of TP specifies all wait periods in milliseconds. As a result, this function will always delay for the appropriate amount of time—regardless of whether it is running on a 4 MHz XT machine or on a 33 MHz 80386 system.

The DelLine Procedure

The **DelLine** procedure deletes the entire line on which the cursor resides. This function only deletes the line in the active window so that text outside the window is unaffected. When the line is deleted, the lines below it move up by one, leaving the last line of the active window blank. The cursor does not move from its original position. In turn, the deleted line is discarded and *cannot* be recovered. This command inserts a full line of blanks of the current background color at the bottom of the window.

The GotoXY(Column,Line) Command (Crt Only)

This command allows you to control the location of the cursor on the screen. The first argument is the column number of the desired position relative to the top-left corner of the current window. For a typical display with only the default window in use, this number will range from 1 to 80. The second argument passed to the function is the line number of the desired cursor position. This value will typically range from 1 to 25 for a normal default window. It's important to stress that the valid ranges for these numbers are defined by the size of the current window. Position (1,1) is always located at the top-left corner of the window. Thus, if the program decides to move the cursor to the fourth column from the left of the window and on the second row, the statement would be:

```
GotoXY(4,2);
```

Keep in mind that it doesn't matter where on the screen the window is located; the cursor position is always identified relative to the top-left corner of the window itself.

Note

> Since the **GotoXY** command ignores commands for values that are out of range, we recommend that you make it a habit to define integer constants that contain the maximum dimensions of each window.

The HighVideo and LowVideo Procedures (Crt Only)

The **HighVideo** procedure changes the foreground color by turning on the high-intensity bit. The information currently on display is not affected, but any new information written to the screen after this command will be bright (high intensity) rather than normal intensity. The **LowVideo** procedure has exactly the opposite effect. That is, **LowVideo** doesn't affect what is currently on the screen, although any new information will be displayed at normal intensity. The previous state of the intensity prior to the called procedure doesn't really matter; each procedure sets the attribute unequivocally for future output.

The InsLine Procedure (Crt Only)

The **InsLine** procedure works in a manner exactly the opposite of the **DelLine** procedure explained earlier. That is, the line containing the cursor is pushed down by one line (as are the lines below this initial line) and a blank line (of the current background color) appears across the full width of the current window at the location of the cursor. The bottom line of the active window is pushed out of sight so that its contents are lost. The cursor remains at the same position relative to the window.

The KeyPressed Procedure

The **KeyPressed** procedure returns a boolean value of true if a key code is currently being held in the keyboard buffer. Most computers have a storage area, called a *keyboard buffer*, used to hold keystrokes pressed while the machine is busy doing something else—calculating, printing, and so on. When a TP program is executing, any keys pressed while the program is not specifically asking for input are simply stored in the buffer until later. This feature can be very useful when you want to type in advance some information that you know a program will request. This can be a disadvantage, however, if a key is accidentally pressed before your program is ready. Here's a way to guarantee that this kind of accidental storage to the keyboard buffer won't happen: Insert some code at the beginning of your program (or at any spot where you wish to "flush" the keyboard buffer) similar to the following line:

```
WHILE KeyPressed DO Dummy_char := ReadKey;
```

This one-line **WHILE** loop repeatedly reads a key from the keyboard buffer into a dummy character variable (**Dummy_char**) until the buffer is empty.

Note

In the example, you don't need to define a new dummy variable just for this operation. Instead, specify an existing character variable—one that will actually be used for input. In this way, you can avoid making your program any larger than is absolutely necessary.

The NormVideo Procedure (Crt Only)

When TP begins execution, it saves the values of current screen attributes in internal variables. By invoking the **NormVideo** procedure at the end of a program, you can return attributes to their original values, that is, to their values before program execution began. This may not sound important, but it is an element vital to elegant programming. If you don't invoke **NormVideo** at the end of a program that redefines colors, intensity, and blinking, you may end up with a blinking blue prompt on a red background after program termination. This can be very annoying to users. If you haven't specified **NormVideo**, the only way to undo such a mess in DOS is to perform a CLS command and then reset the screen attributes to default values.

The NoSound Procedure (Crt Only)

This procedure turns off any sound currently emanating from the computer speaker. If the speaker isn't making any noise at the time **NoSound** is invoked, nothing happens. Thus, it's safe to call this procedure any time you suspect that the speaker is on.

The ReadKey Function

This function, introduced at the beginning of the chapter, returns one character at a time from the keyboard buffer.

The Sound (Frequency) Procedure (Crt Only)

This procedure is used to turn on the sound from the computer's speaker and also to select the pitch of the note. The argument passed to it is an integer value that corresponds with the frequency of the desired tone in Hertz (cycles per second). Table 6.1 shows the frequency values of musical notes. The main thing to remember about **Sound** is that, once invoked, the sound stays on until a **NoSound** command is issued—even if the program terminates. For this reason, you should always group these three commands together:

```
Sound(Tone_freq);
Delay(Duration);
NoSound;
```

This technique will always cause the length of the tone to be the duration defined by the **Delay** command.

The TextBackground (Color) Procedure (Crt Only)

This procedure defines the background color for future output commands. Typically, the default background color for computer output is **Black**. With this command, it is possible to change the background color to create very lively displays. Table 6.2 contains a list of integer color constants that TP has defined for use anywhere that a color must be specified.

An important detail to remember about **TextBackground**: It defines the background color to be used as soon as an output command is executed and then maintains that color from that time forward. Thus, if you define

Table 6.1   Frequency Values of Musical Notes

Note	Frequencies for Each Octave								
C	33	65	131	262	523	1046	2093	4186	8392
C#	34	69	139	277	554	1109	2218	4435	8870
D	37	73	147	294	587	1175	2349	4699	9397
D#	39	78	156	311	622	1244	2489	4978	9956
E	41	82	165	330	659	1318	2637	5274	10548
F	44	87	175	349	698	1397	2794	5588	11175
F#	46	98	196	392	784	1568	3136	6272	12544
G	49	98	196	392	784	1568	3136	6272	12544
G#	52	104	208	415	831	1661	3322	6645	13290
A	55	110	220	440	880	1760	3520	7040	14080
A#	58	116	233	466	932	1865	3729	7459	14917
B	62	123	247	494	988	1976	3951	7902	15804

Table 6.2 Background Colors and Codes

Color	Code	Color	Code
Black	0	Dark gray	8
Blue	1	Bright blue	9
Green	2	Bright green	10
Cyan	3	Bright cyan	11
Red	4	Bright red	12
Magenta	5	Bright magenta	13
Brown	6	Yellow	14
Dim gray	7	White	15
Blink	128		

TextBackground for one of several windows that you've defined on the screen, the same background color will also be used in the other windows. To avoid this problem, you should define integer variables or constants to hold background and character colors for each active window. Thus, as you switch from window to window on the screen, you'll need only one call to **TextBackground** and a call to **TextColor** (described next) to reset these attributes to their previous values for that window.

You can use the **Blink** constant to create a flashing character or background. For instance, to define a blue background that blinks, you can use this command:

```
TextBackground(Blue + Blink);
```

TP will perform the addition operation at compile time in order to pass a value of 129 to the procedure (1 +128).

TextColor (Color) Procedure (Crt only)

The **TextColor** procedure operates the same way as **TextBackground**, but defines the color and blink status of the character rather than the background. The same cautions that we made earlier about **TextBackground** apply here: A new **TextColor** definition applies to all output commands from that point forward, even if the commands are outside of the window that **TextColor** defines.

The TextMode (Mode) Procedure (Crt Only)

This procedure uses the integer argument to set the video-display card to a selected mode (if possible). Table 6.3 contains a set of constants defined by TP for use in setting the screen mode. Obviously, if you select **Font8x8** for use

Table 6.3 Constants for Setting Screen Modes

Constant	Value	Action
BW40	0	Set screen to 40 by 25 monochrome text
BW80	2	Set screen to 80 by 25 monochrome text
Mono	7	Set screen to 80 by 25 monochrome set
CO40	1	Set screen to 40 by 25 color text
CO80	3	Set screen to 80 by 25 color text
Font8x8	256	EGA/VGA 43-line color text

with a CGA display card, unpredictable things will occur. The TP default mode is **CO80** when any color card is present.

LastMode is an interesting word variable defined by the **Crt** unit to be used with **TextMode.** This variable always contains the video mode data previous to the current setting (or the default setting if video mode has never been changed). To return the screen to the previously defined mode, use:

```
TextMode(LastMode);
```

Since this variable is updated each time a mode change is made, you may wish to save the content of this variable at various points by simply assigning it to another word variable:

```
Mode_on_tuesday := LastMode;
```

This will allow you to restore the video mode at some future time by using:

```
TextMode(Mode_on_tuesday);
```

The WhereX and WhereY Functions

These two functions return the X and Y coordinates, respectively, of the current cursor location relative to the active window. Thus, the integer values returned by these functions can be saved and later used with the **GotoXY** procedure to reposition the cursor at the same location.

Variables Defined by the Crt Unit

You know from our discussion of **TextMode** that the **Crt** unit defines a word variable called **LastMode** to retain the previous mode data. However, **Crt** also defines several other variables that you might find useful. Let's explore these variables next.

The CheckBreak Variable

This boolean is used by TP to decide whether to monitor the Ctrl+Break command key combination. When in the default state (true), program execution will stop at the next invocation of **Read**, **Readln**, **Write,** or **Writeln** after Ctrl+Break is pressed by the user. If this boolean is set to false, the Ctrl+Break key sequence will be ignored by the program and execution will continue. You should leave this variable in the default state when debugging software since it can be quite useful for stopping runaway programs, such as infinite loops.

The CheckEof Variable

When this boolean is set to true, pressing Ctrl+Z ends input for the particular command being executed. All input variables that had not yet been assigned values will be set to 0. If this variable is set to false (the default state), then Ctrl+Z will only assign an ASCII(26) to the input variable.

The CheckSnow Variable (Crt Only)

This variable is used to cope with hardware limitations of older video-display boards. You'll need to consider this variable only if **DirectVideo** (discussed next) is set to true. If a program is generating a large amount of output to the screen, it's probable that a collision will occur between the microprocessor trying to write to video RAM and the video hardware wanting to read the same RAM location. When this happens, you may notice "garbage" characters or a momentary blinking of the screen. Modern hardware uses arbitration circuitry (an electronic traffic cop) to prevent these problems, but there are still a lot of older video boards in use. So TP provides this variable as a way to prevent problems encountered with older boards.

In the default state of true, TP output routines will write to the hardware only during the horizontal retrace interval. This is a time when the electron beam on the display is moving from the right side of the screen back to the left to start painting the next line. During this time period, the video hardware can't possibly access video RAM, so no collision can occur. Unfortunately, this limits screen output to only a fraction of the total time available, thus slowing down screen updates. If you can be certain that your program will not run on "old" video circuitry, set this boolean to false to increase your screen update speed.

The DirectVideo Variable (Crt Only)

This boolean tells TP to ignore the built-in video output routines in your computer in favor of direct writes to video RAM. In the default state of false, TP uses the routines provided by the operating system to generate all output to the screen. If the variable is set to true, TP will directly access the video RAM (thus bypassing many limitations in the built-in software that tend to slow down screen output). The risk is that output may occasionally be garbled if an older video board is driving the display.

The LastMode Variable (Crt Only)

As mentioned previously in this chapter, the word contents of this variable can be used with the **TextMode** command to preserve the characteristics of a previous screen.

The TextAttr Variable (Crt Only)

This bytewide variable contains the current foreground and background color information as well as the blink state. When you call **TextBackground** or **TextColor**, these routines actually set parts of **TextAttr**. Thus, if you understand the details, it is possible to change future screen output by simply changing the value of this variable directly. Figure 6.3 shows how the bits are allocated.

The WindMin and WindMax Variables (Crt Only)

These two-word variables hold the beginning and ending coordinates of the current window, respectively. **WindMin** holds the x-value of the top-left corner of the window in the lower byte and the y-value of the same corner in the upper byte. **WindMax** holds the x-value of the lower-right corner of the window in the lower byte and the y-value of this point in the upper byte. A note of caution: The values held by these variables are *zero relative*. This means that if **WindMin** is pointing to the top-left corner of the screen it holds a value of (0,0), whereas **GotoXY** wants a value of (1,1) for this same physical point. Thus, exercise caution when you use the contents of these two variables.

Figure 6.3   The bit assignment in TextAttr.

B l i n k	Background Color		Foreground Color			
7	6	5	4	3	2	1	0

Summary

In this chapter we've covered basic techniques for performing console I/O operations. You learned how to use the standard **Readln** and **Writeln** family of procedures to read and write characters, strings, and numbers. In the second part of this chapter, we examined the **Crt** unit, which provides a set of useful procedures and functions for handling I/O tasks that are fine-tuned for the IBM PC.

Exercises

1. Using the **ReadKey** function, write a program to read the function keys (F1, F2, and so on). Display a message to indicate which function key has been entered.

2. The **Window** command defines a screen region for screen output, but it does not draw a border around the window. Write a program to display a window that includes a border. (Hint: You can create a border by using the extended ASCII characters.)

3. Write a program that allows the user to input and edit a string by using the Arrow keys. When the Left Arrow key is pressed, the character to the left of the cursor should be erased. (Hint: Use **ReadKey** to read the user inputs.)

4. Use the **GotoXY** procedure to write a program that allows the user to display an input string at a user-specified screen location.

Answers

1. The program GETKEY reads the function keys and displays a message to indicate which function key has been entered:

```
PROGRAM GetFKey;
USES Crt;
CONST
  F1  = #59;
  F2  = #60;
  F3  = #61;
  F4  = #62;
  F5  = #63;
  F6  = #64;
  F7  = #65;
  F8  = #66;
  F9  = #67;
  F10 = #68;
VAR
  InpChar : Char;
```

```
BEGIN
Writeln('Input a function key');
InpChar := ReadKey;
IF InpChar <> #0 THEN BEGIN { Checks for extended key code }
  Writeln('Invalid key pressed');
  Exit;
END;
InpChar := ReadKey;
CASE InpChar OF
  F1  : Writeln('Function key 1 pressed');
  F2  : Writeln('Function key 2 pressed');
  F3  : Writeln('Function key 3 pressed');
  F4  : Writeln('Function key 4 pressed');
  F5  : Writeln('Function key 5 pressed');
  F6  : Writeln('Function key 6 pressed');
  F7  : Writeln('Function key 7 pressed');
  F8  : Writeln('Function key 8 pressed');
  F9  : Writeln('Function key 9 pressed');
  F10 : Writeln('Function key 10 pressed');
  ELSE
      Writeln('Invalid key pressed');
  END;
END.
```

2. The program DOSBOX displays a window with a border.

```
PROGRAM DOSBox;
{ Makes a DOS window with a simple box using ASCII characters }
USES Crt;
VAR
  I, J               : Integer;
  DrawChar           : Char;
  Bheight, BWidth  : Integer;
  X1, Y1, X2, Y2   : Integer;

BEGIN
  Writeln('Enter the window coordinates');
  Readln(X1, Y1, X2, Y2);
  BHeight := Y2 - Y1;
  BWidth := X2 - X1;
  ClrScr;
  Window(X1, Y1, X2, Y2); { Makes the window }
  GotoXY(1, 1);
  DrawChar := #201;          { Upper-left corner }
  Write(DrawChar);
  DrawChar := #205;          { Straight line }
  For I := 1 TO BWidth - 2 DO
    Write(DrawChar);
```

```
    DrawChar := #187;           { Upper-right corner }
    Writeln(DrawChar);
    FOR I := 1 TO BHeight - 2 DO
      BEGIN
      DrawChar:= #186;          { Side character }
      Write(DrawChar);
      FOR J := 1 TO BWidth - 2 DO
        Write(' ');
      DrawChar := #186;
      Writeln(DrawChar);
    END;
    DrawChar := #200;           { Bottom-left corner }
    Write(DrawChar);
    DrawChar := #205;           { Straight line }
    For I := 1 TO BWidth - 2 DO
      Write(DrawChar);
    DrawChar := #188;           { Bottom-right corner }
    Writeln(DrawChar);
END.
```

3. The program STRINGEDIT allows the user to input and edit a string with the Arrow keys. When the Left Arrow key is pressed, the character to the left of the cursor is erased.

```
PROGRAM StringEdit;
USES Crt;
CONST
  LeftArrow = #75;
  BackSp    = #8;
  EnterKey  = #13;
  ExtendKey = #0;
  Bell      = #7;
  Space     = #32;
VAR
  InpChar : Char;
  Done    : Boolean;

BEGIN
  Done := False;
  Writeln('Input a string');
  REPEAT
    InpChar := ReadKey;
    CASE InpChar OF
      ExtendKey : BEGIN
        InpChar := ReadKey;
        IF InpChar = LeftArrow THEN BEGIN
          Write(BackSp); { Moves to the left }
          Write(Space);
```

```
            Write(BackSp);
         END
         ELSE Write(Bell); { Makes a beep sound }
      END;
      EnterKey : Done := True;
      ELSE
         Write(InpChar);
   END;
  UNTIL Done;
END.
```

4. The program STRINGEDIT allows the user to display an input string at a user-specified screen location.

```
PROGRAM StringEdit;
USES Crt;
VAR
  InpStr  : String;
  X, Y    : Integer;

BEGIN
  Writeln('Input a string');
  Readln(InpStr);
  Writeln('Input the column and row position');
  Readln(X, Y);
  Clrscr;
  GotoXY(X, Y);
  Write(Inpstr);
  Readln; { Waits for user to press Enter key }
END.
```

7

Static Data Structures

n the early years of programming, data was represented in two ways: a 1 or a 0. Fortunately, a lot of programming advancements have been made since then. In fact, the Pascal language provides an assortment of helpful devices for representing data. The lowest-level data storage components are the data types, such as **Integer**, **Real**, **Char**, and so on. As we begin to write more complex programs, we'll need other ways to represent data. To make it easier for you to manipulate many similar data elements, TP supports data structures such as *arrays*, *enumerated data types*, and *records*, which are built from the basic data types. We can also represent nonnumeric collections of data by using *sets* and *strings*.

In this chapter, you'll learn how to use the static data structure components that TP provides to help you write more useful programs. We'll start by exploring sets, then move on to a related topic—enumerated types. Our third stop will be strings. Although you've seen and used strings in earlier chapters, you haven't yet had the opportunity to look closely at the ways strings are represented. We'll follow up our discussion on strings with an introduction to arrays, then close the chapter with a look at record data structures.

After you complete this chapter, you'll know how to:

• Define and use sets

• Define and use enumerated types

• Work with strings

• Use single- and multi-dimensional arrays

• Define and use records

Sets

In mathematics, a set is defined as a collection of unique elements. For example, if you have a bag of marbles containing one blue, one yellow, and one red marble, you can call this collection of marbles a set. The order of the elements in the set is not important, that is; the two lists of marbles shown below both represent the same set:

```
red marble, blue marble, yellow marble
blue marble, yellow marble, red marble
```

Sets are easy to use in TP. However, you should be aware of one major limitation: The value of each element in a set must be in the range 0 to 255.

The following statement illustrates the standard format you use to define a set:

```
Decimal_char : SET OF Char = ['0'..'9'];
```

In this case, the quotation marks around the digits tell TP that we want to assign the ASCII characters 0 through 9 to the set. The two periods indicate that we wish to have the values between ASCII 0 and ASCII 9 also included in the set. If we had only wanted to define odd digits, we could have used:

```
Odd_decimal_char : SET OF Char = ['1','3','5','7','9'];
```

Here, the commas are used to separate the elements in the set.

These set definition statements are placed in the **CONST** section of a program.Our next task is to assign set values to a variable.

When you assign values to each set variable, you must use brackets to enclose the list of elements. Some examples are:

```
Even_digits   := ['0','2','4','6','8'];
Upper_letters := ['A'..'Z'];
All_letters   := ['a'..'z', 'A'..'Z'];
Empty_one     := [];
```

These are all valid set assignment statements. Notice that, for the case of **All_letters**, we had to define both lowercase a through z and uppercase A through Z in order to include all possible letters. Also note that the two brackets with nothing in between are also legal; these brackets form an *empty set*. An empty set is similar to an empty glass; it's not usually of much use in that state, but it can be filled at a later time. The empty set is also used in comparison expressions to determine whether a set has any elements.

Declaring Set Variables

Thus far, you've seen how to define simple set constants and assign values to set variables. It makes sense now to examine how set variables are declared. The easiest approach is to define set data types first. For example:

```
TYPE
  Digits  = SET OF '0'..'9';
  UpChar  = SET OF 'A'..'Z';
  AllChar = SET OF Char;
```

With these definitions in place, we can now use the data types to declare variables:

```
VAR
  Numb1, Numb2 : Digits;
  Initials     : UpChar;
  Resp         : AllChar;
```

Notice that the keyword **TYPE** is used to create our own data types. If you don't want to define a data type, you can also declare a set variable directly by using the following format:

```
VAR
  <Variable name> : SET OF <Set data type>;
```

Some examples are:

```
VAR
  Resp : SET OF Char;
  Numb1: SET OF Byte;
```

After a set variable has been declared, it can be assigned only values that correspond with its set data type. For example, the following assignment statement would not be allowed because the **Numb1** variable is declared as a set variable to hold digits only:

```
Numb1 := ['A','B','C'];   { Can't do this! }
```

You can use only the ordinal types **Boolean**, **Char**, and **Byte** to define a set data type. The **Integer** data type cannot be used because a set can store only up to 256 elements. With this storage limitation, using an **Integer** data type to declare a set variable would be like trying to stuff 42 giant pandas into a Volkswagen.

1. What's wrong with the following set variable declaration?

```
TYPE
  Orders   = 1..712;
VAR
  SalesNo : SET OF Orders;
```

2. Declare a set variable to store the following character input responses:

```
'Y', 'y', 'N', 'n'.
```

3. Declare a set constant to store all even numbers from 1 to 20.

1. The range of the data type Orders is too large to represent a set.
2. Here is the set variable that will store the character input responses from step 2:

```
VAR
  ChResp : SET OF Char;
```

3. Here is the set constant to store all even numbers from 1 to 20:

```
CONST
  Even_Num : SET OF Byte = [2,4,6,8,10,12,14,16,18,20];
```

Enumerated Data Types

Many of the things that we deal with in day-to-day life are members of sets. For example, the days of the week, the months of the year, and the colors of the rainbow are all items of sets that most people recognize. Computers aren't intuitive enough to handle such direct relationships between the name of a set and its abstract items. (Imagine trying to define the word *color* or *rainbow* to a computer so that it will understand these concepts as well as people do.)

At their lowest level, computers can understand only numbers. Many programming languages still in use today tend to accommodate this limitation. Fortunately, TP is an advanced language that allows us to represent nonnumerical sets in intuitive ways. For example, the statement

```
TYPE
   Days = (Sunday, Monday. Tuesday, Wednesday, Thursday, Friday, Saturday);
```

identifies a variable type called **Days** that contains seven ordered elements from **Sunday** through **Saturday**. We say *ordered* because this definition establishes a sequence in which **Monday** occurs before **Tuesday**, and so on. Definition statements like the one for **Days** always appear in a **TYPE** section of a procedure or program since, in effect, we are defining a unique new variable type that didn't exist when TP was created. This isn't going to be of much use, however, if we can't figure out a way to define variables to be of the same type. This can be done by including such statements as

```
NormalDay : Workdays;
```

in the **VAR** section following the **TYPE** section that defined **Workdays**. Now we can assign values to the variable by using assignment statements in the body of the program, such as:

```
NormalDay := Tuesday;
```

Here is another example of a definition of an enumerated type:

```
TYPE
   Languages = (English, German, French, Spanish, Italian);
```

In addition to standard enumerated types, you can create enumerated *subranges*. For example, we could use the previous enumerated type definitions to create the following enumerated subranges:

```
Workdays = Monday..Friday;
RomanceLanguages = French..Italian;
```

The type **RomanceLanguages** is a subrange of type **Languages**. A variable declared from this type could be assigned either French, Spanish, or Italian.

An enumerated type can contain up to 65,535 members. Each label in the enumerated type is stored as a unique integer. The first label in an enumerated type is represented as the value 0, the second label is represented as the value 1, and so on.

Processing Enumerated Types

TP provides a set of functions, shown in Table 7.1, to help you process enumerated type variables. To demonstrate how these functions work, let's use the following enumerated type definition and variable declaration:

```
TYPE
   Options = (edit,list,view,save,help,quit);
VAR
   Select : Options;
```

Now, you can obtain the first element in the enumerated type by writing

```
Select := First(Options);  { Returns edit }
```

And likewise, you can obtain the last element with

```
Select := Last(Options);  { Returns quit }
```

You can also retrieve an element by using the **Succ** and **Pred** functions. For example:

```
Select := Succ(list);  { Returns view }
Select := Pred(list);  { Returns edit }
```

The final function, **Ord**, returns the integer value of the enumerated label. For example, consider this statement:

```
Value := Ord(view);  { Returns ? }
```

Table 7.1 Functions for Processing Enumerated Types

Function	Description
First	Returns the first element of an enumerated type element
Last	Returns the last element of an enumerated type element
Succ	Returns the successor of an enumerated type element
Pred	Returns the predecessor of an enumerated type element
Ord	Returns the value of an enumerated type element

At first, you might think that the value 3 is returned because **view** is the third element in the enumerated list. Actually, this function returns a value of 2 because the first element in a list is assigned to 0. The following statement shows a trick you can use to ensure that the first element in an enumerated list is represented with the value 1:

```
Options = (dummy,edit,list,view,save,help,quit);
```

In this case, the label **dummy** is represented as element 0, **edit** is represented as element 1, and so on.

When working with enumerated types, you may want to include the {$R+} compiler directive so that TP will activate its run-time checking feature. This approach can help make sure you don't try to access an element that precedes or follows an enumerated list.

1. Define a subrange type to represent lowercase letters.
2. Given the following definition and variable declaration

```
TYPE
   Colors = (red,blue,green,cyan);
VAR
   Paint : Colors;
```

   explain what is wrong with the following assignment statement:

```
Paint := (red,blue);
```

3. Using the **Options** enumerated type described in the preceding text, determine which values are returned by the following functions:
   a. Ord(quit);
   b. Succ(quit);
   c. Pred(edit);

1. The following subrange type represents lowercase letters:

```
LCLetters = 'a'..'z';
```

2. Only one enumerated type value can be assigned to a variable.
3. These are the values returned by the functions in step 3:
   a. 5
   b. an undefined value
   c. an undefined value

Strings

Strings are extremely useful data storage components for manipulating groups of characters. For example, if we are writing a program to perform the electronic equivalent of a personal telephone book, we would need to read in groups of characters associated with the name, address, and telephone number of each person. Strings allow us to hold each piece of information in a separate variable until we are ready to store, print, or otherwise manipulate the information.

TP can hold strings up to 255 characters in length. TP also allows strings to be either variables or constants. In fact, you've actually been using constant strings in early chapters. For instance, statements such as

```
Writeln('This is a constant string');
```

employ unnamed constant strings. The same effect could have been achieved by using:

```
CONST
  Message = 'This is a constant string';
```

And later in the program you could use this string constant:

```
Writeln(Message);
```

Constant strings can improve memory use since programs that generate fancy screens usually use similar titles or messages in several places. Using our telephone book program as an example, if we were to put these messages within quotation marks in **Write** statements, all copies of the string must be kept in memory. However, if one string variable is assigned the value and then referenced by several **Write** statements, only one copy needs to be stored in memory.

TP also allows you to define string variables. Some examples are:

```
VAR
  Name  : String;
  Alias : String;
```

A string variable can only be assigned a string constant or used in a procedure or function, such as **Readln**, that assigns a string to the variable. For example, if both **Name** and **Alias** are strings, then the statement

```
Alias := Name;
```

is valid.

A string variable can be cleared by using the following format:

```
Alias := '';
```

Notice that the two single quotation marks (no, they're not a double quotation mark) do not contain a space or blank between them. This type of string is called a *null string* and has a length of 0. If we insert a space between the single quotation marks, the string would no longer be a null string. Instead, TP would treat it as a single space character having a length of 1. Also, strings can be combined by using the string concatenation symbol: the plus sign. Thus, if we write

```
String1 := 'Greetings';
String2 := 'Earthling';
```

then this concatenation

```
Alias := String1+String2;
```

will create the following string in **Alias** (with length 18):

```
Alias := 'GreetingsEarthling';
```

By now, you should detect a pattern: After each assignment statement, the length of the string variable is readjusted. Also notice that the strings are literally attached end-to-end, with no space between *Greetings* and *Earthling*. One way to solve this problem is to modify either **String1** or **String2** by adding a space. Another way to solve this is to include the space in the assignment expression:

```
Alias := String1 + ' ' + String2;
```

This line inserts a string constant consisting of a single blank between the two strings. Keep in mind that any valid character or groups of characters can be inserted between strings—letters, numbers, punctuation marks, and so on.

Processing Strings

As with enumerated types, TP also provides a set of useful functions for processing strings. These procedures and functions are listed in Table 7.2. As the table indicates, you can perform a number of different string processing operations with these routines. We'll briefly explain some of these routines.

To determine the length of a string, use the following function:

```
FUNCTION Length(Str : String) : Integer;
```

Table 7.2   String Processing Routines

Routine	Description
Length	Returns the length of a string
Concat	Joins two strings
Delete	Deletes one or more characters in a string
Pos	Locates the position of a substring in a string
Copy	Extracts a substring from a string
Insert	Inserts a substring in a string
Str	Converts a number to a string
Val	Converts a string formatted number to a number

If a string is empty, this function returns 0; otherwise, it returns the number of characters in the string, including spaces. For example, the statement

```
Size := Length('Pascal is a structured language');
```

assigns the value 31 to the variable **Size**.

Another useful function is **Pos**, which allows you to locate a substring within another string. The format for this function is:

```
FUNCTION Pos(Search : <char or string>; Str : String) : Integer;
```

Notice that the first argument can be either a character or a string. If a character is used, such as

```
Loc := Pos('p', 'apple');
```

the function will return the position of the first occurrence of the character *p*—in this case, position 2. The other type of search involves using a substring:

```
Loc := Pos('man', 'Postman');
```

Here, **Pos** returns the starting position of the substring *man* in the main string *Postman*, which is 5.

In addition to these routines, TP provides three routines to edit strings:

```
PROCEDURE Insert(Source : String; VAR Target : String; Pos : Integer);
PROCEDURE Delete(VAR Target : String; Pos, Num : Integer);
FUNCTION Copy(Str : String; Index, Size : Integer) : String;
```

The first procedure, **Insert**, inserts a string immediately before a specified position of another string. For example,

```
Str1 := 'Object Programming';
Str2 := '-Oriented ';
Insert(Str2,Str1,7);
```

produces the new string *Object-Oriented Programming*. But where is this string stored? It is placed in the target variable **Str1**. The **Source** string is inserted at the position **Pos** in the string **Target**.

Another useful string processing operation supported by TP involves removing a set of characters from a string. For this task, you use the **Delete** procedure. For example:

```
Str1 := 'Please enter your last name';
Delete(Str1,19,5);
```

After the **Delete** procedure is called, the variable **Str1** will contain the string *Please enter your name*.

The last routine in our category of string editing routines is **Copy**. This function extracts one or more characters from a string. Keep in mind, however, that the original string is not altered. The following function copies the substring *ball* to the string variable **Str1**:

```
Str1 := Copy('Baseball',5,4);
```

To show you how some of these string processing procedures and functions work, the following program, STRINGEXAMPLE, manipulates and provides information about an entered string:

```
PROGRAM StringExample;
VAR
  Str1, Str2 : String;

BEGIN
  Writeln('Enter a string');
  Readln(Str1);
  Writeln('The length of the string is ', Length(Str1));
  Str2 := Copy(Str1,1,2);
  Writeln('The first two characters in the string are ', Str2);
  Str2 := Str1;
  Delete(Str2,1,2);
  Writeln('The string without the first two characters is ', Str2);
END.
```

▼ 1. What is wrong with the following string constant?

```
CONST
  Msg = "Press a key to continue";
```

2. What is the length of the string variable after the assignment statement:

```
NewStr := 'One' + ' '+ 'Two' + ' ' + 'Three'
```

3. What results are returned by the following functions:
   a. `Length('What is my length');`
   b. `Pos('Pascal','Turbo Pascal');`
   c. `Copy('one two three', 5,9);`

1. Double quotation marks instead of single quotation marks are used as delimiter characters.
2. 13
3. Here are the results returned by the functions in step 3:
   a. 17
   b. 7
   c. 'two three'

Arrays

An array is conceptually like a plastic ice-cube tray; it's basically a group of identical little bins attached to each other in a fixed position so they can be moved as a group. Arrays can be defined to be of any simple variable type such as integers, reals, and even strings. In fact, as Figure 7.1 illustrates, a string is stored as an array. Notice that the first element of the array (element 0) contains the size of the string. When a string variable is defined using the standard declaration:

```
VAR
  Str : String;
```

TP reserves 255 storage locations for the string. Each character is stored in its own compartment, so to speak. Of course, you don't have to use them all.

For general arrays, TP allows us to declare arrays of any type—even data types that are user-defined. The values in individual elements of an array are

Figure 7.1 TP stores strings as arrays.

size					string data													
19	T	u	r	b	o		P	a	s	c	a	l		S	t	r	i	n	g
[0]	[1]	[2]	[3]	. . .														[19]

accessed in two basic steps: (1) by referring to the name of the array, and (2) by providing an index within brackets to tell the program which element you wish to use. Thus, the statement:

```
Cars_out := Daily_volume[Day_index];
```

assigns the value contained in a specific element of the array **Daily_volume** to the variable **Cars_out**. To access this array, the index variable **Day_index** must be some type of ordinal value for the statement to compile properly. If you think about our analogy with the ice-cube tray, this requirement should be fairly intuitive. After all, it wouldn't make much sense to "access" the contents of ice-cube bin number 3.5. Thus, array indexes must always be of types that represent only whole numbers (**Integer**, **Word**, **Char**, **Byte**, and enumerated types).

When you attempt to access an array element by assigning its value to a variable, you must also ensure that the data type of the variable you are using is the same as that of the array.

Declaring Arrays

By now, you might be wondering how arrays are actually declared. Well, an array is defined in TP with the following general statement:

```
Variable_name : ARRAY[Index_range] OF Data_type;
```

The keyword **ARRAY** tells the compiler that you are declaring an array, while **Index_range** identifies the range of storage compartments needed for the array. The last part of the statement, **Data_type**, identifies the type of the array (such as **Integer**, **Char**, and so on). Notice that **Index_range** specifies the range of array elements, rather than just the number of elements in the array. This is an important point to keep in mind. In other programming languages, an array is defined simply by stating the number of elements that the array will hold. These types of arrays always start with index values of either 0 or 1, depending on the language.

Fortunately, TP provides more flexible arrays. You can actually use your own indexing system, with the compiler performing the necessary translations for you. To see how this works, let's revisit the ice-cube tray analogy for a moment. Figure 7.2 illustrates three possible ways to number the compartments of the same tray. As you can see from the figure, TP allows you to use different indexing systems. Notice that even negative index values are allowed. This could be useful if your array will hold the results of a survey that correlates average time outside without a coat versus winter temperatures in degrees Fahrenheit.

Figure 7.2 TP allows you to index arrays in many ways.

1	2	3	4	5	6
7	8	9	10	11	12

-6	-5	-4	-3	-2	-1
0	1	2	3	4	5

1980	1981	1982	1983	1984	1985
1986	1987	1988	1989	1990	1991

Some examples of valid array declarations are:

```
VAR
   Employes  : ARRAY[1..100] OF String;
   Numbers   : ARRAY[-100..100] OF Integer;
   Scores    : ARRAY[200..300] OF Real;
```

Recall the earlier statement that an array index can be any valid ordinal value. This means you can use enumerated types and subranges as array indices. The main advantage of this technique: Array elements can be accessed with symbolic names. For example, assume that you have the following enumerated type and subrange:

```
TYPE
   Flavors = (vanilla, strawberry, lime, orange, peach);
   Letters = 'A'..'Z';
```

You could then use these types to declare arrays; for example:

```
VAR
   Ice_cream_sales : ARRAY[Flavors] OF Real;
   Codes           : ARRAY[Letters] OF Char;
```

Some examples to show how values can be assigned to these arrays are:

```
Ice_cream_sales[strawberry]  := 200.99;
Ice_cream_sales[lime]  := 0;
Codes['B']  := 'D';
Codes['Z']  := '9';
```

1. Declare an array to store 100 strings.
2. Assume that you have the following array variable declared in a program:

```
VAR
    Nums : ARRAY[1..20] OF Integer;
```

Explain what the TP compiler will do if your program uses the following assignment statement:

```
Cost := Nums[25];
```

3. True or False: Arrays can be defined with any standard or user-defined data types.

1. This array will store 100 strings:

```
TYPE
    StrList : ARRAY[1..100] OF String;
```

2. The compiler will not detect this type of array index error; however, your program will generate a run-time error if you try to execute this statement.
3. True

Multi-Dimensional Arrays

Thus far, we've defined only single-dimensional arrays; that is, an array that has only one index value for each position in the array. TP also supports multi-dimensional arrays, which can have two or more index values for each position in the array. To illustrate, imagine that you want to use a two-dimensional array to track monthly paper-clip expenditures for the Engulf and Devour Corporation over several years (a great way to get noticed if you aspire to a fast-track corporate career!). This array could be declared with the following statement:

```
ARRAY[1980..1992, 1..12] OF Integer;
```

Figure 7.3 shows what this two-dimensional array looks like. Note that even though the array uses the years 1980 through 1992 as index elements, a second index is provided to identify the months for each year. Thus, the actual array consists of 156 integers (13 years by 12 months).

Figure 7.3 Calculating monthly paper clip consumption is easy with a two-dimensional array.

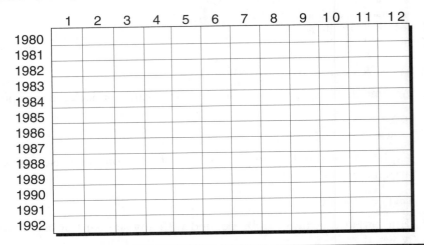

To show you how to use both indices, take a look at the following program segment, which calculates all of the paper clip units purchased by Engulf and Devour in 1987:

```
PROGRAM Clips;
TYPE
   Paper_clips = ARRAY[1980..1992, 1..12] OF Integer;
VAR
   Clips_bought   : Paper_clips;
   I, Total_clips : Integer;

BEGIN
   FOR I := 1 TO 12 DO BEGIN { Fills array with data }
     Writeln('Enter the amount for paper clips ', I);
     Readln(Clips_bought[1987,I]);
   END;
   Total_clips := 0;
   FOR I := 1 TO 12 DO
     Total_clips := Clips_bought[1987, I] + Total_clips;
   Writeln('The total of paper clip sales ', Total_clips);
END.
```

The first part of the program consists of a **FOR** loop that asks you to enter the number of paper clips purchased for each month. The second **FOR** loop computes the total number of paper clips purchased.

Copying Arrays

You've now seen how to place data in arrays, but what happens when you want to copy one array into another? The most frequently used approach is to use a simple loop. For example, given the two arrays

```
VAR
   Group1, Group2 : ARRAY[1..20] OF Integer;
```

you can write a loop that will copy the arrays, as follows:

```
FOR I := 1 TO 20 DO
  Group2[I] := Group1[I];
```

This example is convenient because we assume that both arrays are the same size. But what happens if you have different-sized arrays and you want to copy data from the smaller to the larger? The following example will copy the smaller array into the larger one, starting with the fifth element:

```
VAR
   Group1 : ARRAY[1..20] OF Integer;
   Group2 : ARRAY[1..10] OF Integer;

FOR I := 1 TO 10 DO
BEGIN
  J := I + 4;  { The first element of Group2 will wind up in element 5 of
                 Group1 }
  Group1[J] := Group2[I];
```

The result produced by this code segment is illustrated in Figure 7.4. The same types of tricks can be done with multi-dimensional arrays. The main thing

---

Figure 7.4 TP allows you to copy one array into another, providing both arrays are of the same data type.

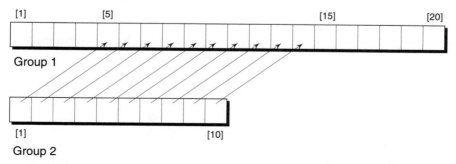

to remember is that, if the arrays are not both of the same type (**Integer**, **Real**, **LongInt**, and so on), then it won't be possible to assign elements from one array to the other.

When developing programs that use arrays, you can include the {**$R+**} compiler directive to instruct the compiler to generate run-time range-checking code. With this option, the program will automatically halt execution if you exceed the boundaries of the array.

Records

Imagine that you have a distribution business that sells products to small companies. You might have hundreds of transactions each day. Even though your operation cannot be easily automated, you would like to have an online system so that your telephone salespeople can look up basic customer information, such as names and addresses. This will prevent the costly delays that occur when your delivery people go to the wrong addresses. In order to keep the program simple, you would like to somehow package several types of variables, such as integers, reals, and strings, into one structure that can be manipulated easily. Does TP provide such a feature? Yes; what you need is a *record*.

Defining a Record

Records are defined by placing the variables that you wish to group between the statements **RECORD** and **END**. Figure 7.5 illustrates the definition of a record that could be used for our customer database system. The first line identifies the name of the record, in this case, **Customer**. In other words, we'll use this name to declare record variables. The second line is the first element within the record, which we have called **Company_name** and have defined as a string of 50 characters. The third line is an integer that we intend to use as an

---

Figure 7.5 Create your own database using this sample record definition as a guide.

```
      record name
        │
Type    ↓
  Customer = RECORD◄─────────── start of record definition
    Company_name : String[50];
    Account_number : Integer;
    Address : ARRAY[1..3] OF String[60];
    Telephone : String[12];
    Credit_line : Real;
  END; ◄─────────── end of record definition
```

---

account number for billing purposes. (Perhaps we should make it a **LongInt** in the hope that our business will grow over time!) The fourth line is more interesting; it is a three-row array in which each element is a 60-character string. We will use this array to print the mailing label or invoice for the order. We will use one string per line of address. The last two lines define elements for a telephone number and a credit limit. (We may want the operator to know when a particular customer hasn't paid his or her bills in several months!)

At this point, you might be thinking, "Okay, you've got a record, but a record does not a database make!" This is true. We must either build an array of records to hold the information or we must build a disk data file to hold and access each individual record. Since we haven't explained how data files work yet, we'd better stay with arrays of records!

Continuing the customer database example, we can define our key data structures and variables as follows:

```
TYPE
  Customer = RECORD
    Company_name    : String[50];
    Account_number  : Integer;
    Address         : ARRAY[1..3] OF String[60];
    Telephone       : String[12];
    Credit_line     : Real;
  END;
CONST
  Max_num_cust = 100;
VAR
  Cust_list : ARRAY[1..Max_num_cust] OF Customer;
```

As you can see from this code segment, an array called **Cust_list** has now been defined, which consists of 100 separate customer records.

Accessing Record Elements

Now that the record is defined, we need to figure out how to get to the individual elements. Let's first try to get to the **Company_name** field, since this is the most likely way for a telephone salesperson to find a particular record. Since we also need to identify which record within the array is to be accessed, we'll need an index of some sort. Finally, we need to identify which element within the record we wish to access (**Company_name** in this case). The result is:

```
Temporary_string := Cust_list[index].Company_name;
```

As Figure 7.6 illustrates, the record variable and field name are separated by a period. Note that we don't have to mention the label **Customer** in this

Figure 7.6   Use this format to access a record's field.

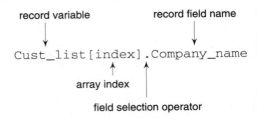

statement because the declaration of **Cust_list** explicitly identifies that the records are of type **Customer**. It is important to keep in mind that this type of format can be used wherever a regular variable can be used.

For example, the program could print out the credit limit data in a different color if the proposed purchase exceeds the allowable value. (This would make it easy for the person processing the order to figure out whether the order should be filled.) To do this, we could use a statement such as:

```
IF ( Order_cost > Cust_list[index].Credit_line ) THEN
BEGIN   {We have a problem, so change color, etc. }
  TextColor(Red);
  ...
END;
```

This technique allows us to use the data without first having to transfer it to temporary variables.

1. What is wrong with the following record?

```
TYPE
   Customer = RECORD
      Name    : String;
      Address : String;
      Balance : Real;
```

2. True or False: Records can contain only fields of the same data type.

3. Assume that the following declarations have been made:

```
TYPE
   Screen = RECORD
      X,Y   : Integer;
      Color : Byte;
VAR
   Display1 : Screen;
```

Write an assignment statement that will set the screen coordinates **X** and **Y** to 50, 5.

4. What are the differences between an array and a record?

1. The record is missing an **END** statement.
2. False
3. This assignment statement will set the screen coordinates **X** and **Y** to the screen coordinates 50, 5:

```
Display1.X := 50;
   Display1.Y := 5;
```

4. A record is a data structure that allows you to combine data components that are of different types. An array, however, can be used only to store data of the same type. Records are also accessed differently than arrays: the elements in a record are accessed using the name of the record, whereas array elements are accessed using an index value.

Records in Action

Let's now put together a working program that uses records. The program shown next operates much like an electronic version of index cards. Each record consists of a title field and of an array of strings that correspond with five lines of data. When the program is executed, it clears the screen and allows you to enter the data for each field of all six cards (each field is terminated when the user presses Enter). After the last card has been entered, the program enters a loop to ask for a card number and then displays the contents of the selected record. Notice that the record elements are read and written directly, without the need for us to use intermediate variables.

```
PROGRAM IndexCard;
USES
  Crt;
CONST
  Num_of_cards = 6;
  Max_row = 70;
TYPE
  Card = RECORD
    Title : String[20];
    Entry : ARRAY [1..5] OF String[Max_row];
  END;
VAR
  Deck : ARRAY [1..Num_of_cards] OF Card; { Deck of six }
  Crd_num, I : Integer;
```

```
BEGIN
  TextBackground(Blue);
  TextColor(LightGray);
  { Here, we begin by defaulting to ENTER mode }
  FOR Crd_num := 1 TO Num_of_cards DO
  BEGIN
    ClrScr;
    GotoXY(35, 2);
    Write ('Card Number ', Crd_num : 2 );
    GotoXY(21, 5 );
    Write('TITLE: ');
     Readln(Deck[Crd_num].Title);
    GotoXY(1, 8 );
    Write('Line 1: ');
     Readln(Deck[Crd_num].Entry[1]);
    GotoXY(1, 9);
    Write('Line 2: ');
     Readln(Deck[Crd_num].Entry[2]);
    GotoXY(1, 10);
    Write('Line 3: ');
     Readln(Deck[Crd_num].Entry[3]);
    GotoXY(1, 11);
    Write('Line 4: ');
     Readln(Deck[Crd_num].Entry[4]);
    GotoXY(1, 12);
    Write('Line 5: ');
     Readln(Deck[Crd_num].Entry[5]);
  END;
  GotoXY(20, 20);
  Write('Select card number to be viewed ');
  Readln(Crd_num);
  WHILE ((Crd_num > 0) AND (Crd_num <= Num_of_cards)) DO
  BEGIN
    ClrScr;
    GotoXY(35, 2);
    Write ('Card Number ', Crd_num : 2);
    GotoXY(21, 5);
    Write('TITLE: ');
     Writeln(Deck[Crd_num].Title);
    GotoXY(1, 8);
    Write('Line 1: ');
     Writeln(Deck[Crd_num].Entry[1]);
    GotoXY(1, 9);
    Write('Line 2: ');
     Writeln(Deck[Crd_num].Entry[2]);
    GotoXY(1, 10);
    Write('Line 3: ');
     Writeln(Deck[Crd_num].Entry[3]);
    GotoXY(1, 11);
    Write('Line 4: ');
```

```
       Writeln(Deck[Crd_num].Entry[4]);
       GotoXY(1, 12);
       Write('Line 5: ');
       Writeln(Deck[Crd_num].Entry[5]);
       GotoXY(20, 20);
       Write('Select card number to be viewed ');
       Readln(Crd_num);
    END;
 END.
```

Using the W I T H Statement

If you begin to build arrays or records that contain other arrays or records, you can quickly get confused by all the lengthy variable identifiers. However, TP provides an elegant solution for this problem—the **WITH** statement—which allows you to identify a particular record so that only the elements of the record need to be used in subsequent statements. The general form consists of the keyword **WITH**, followed by the detailed specification of the name of the record. This specification is followed by the keyword **DO** and the statement affected by the **WITH** statement. (If you want the effect of the **WITH** to apply to a group of statements, use **BEGIN-END** blocks to bracket the statements affected.)

To show how the **WITH** statement is used, we've modified some of the code in the **IndexCard** program presented earlier.

```
WITH Deck[Crd_num] DO
BEGIN
   Writeln(Title);
   GotoXY(1, 8);
   Write('Line 1: ');
   Writeln(Entry[1]);
   GotoXY(1, 9);
   Write('Line 2: ');
   Writeln(Entry[2]);
   GotoXY(1, 10);
   Write('Line 3: ');
   Writeln(Entry[3]);
   GotoXY(1, 11);
   Write('Line 4: ');
   Writeln(Entry[4]);
   GotoXY(1, 12);
   Write('Line 5: ');
   Writeln(Entry[5]);
END;
```

In this code section, the **WITH** statement is used only in the output section to show you the difference. It is definitely much easier to read the record information in the output section than in the input part.

Summary

This chapter presented the static data structures that TP provides. In the first part of the chapter, you learned how to work with sets and use the basic set operators to process set data. We also explored techniques for defining and using enumerated types and subranges. Our next stop was strings. Here you learned how strings are represented in TP and how the basic built-in string processing procedures and functions work. In the second half of this chapter, arrays and records were covered. Arrays are useful structures for storing sequential lists of related data. Records, however, provide useful structures for combining different types of data elements.

Exercises

1. What is wrong with the following enumerated type declaration?

```
TYPE
   Keywords = (BEGIN, END, IF, ELSE, REPEAT, UNTIL);
```

2. Declare a set variable **LCLetters** to store the lowercase letters from a to g.

3. Declare an enumerated type to represent five major U.S. cities.

4. Write a program that converts a string from lowercase letters to uppercase letters. (Hint: Remember that you can access the elements in a string by using array notation.)

5. Using an array, write a program to reverse a string.

Answers

1. TP keywords cannot be used as identifiers in a enumerated type.

2. Here is set variable **LCLetters** which will store the lowercase letters from a to g:

```
TYPE
   SubChars = 'a'..'g';

VAR
   LCLetters : SET OF SubChars;
```

3. Here is an enumerated type that will represent five major U.S. cities.

```
TYPE
   Cities = (L_A, New_York, San_Francisco, Chicago, Atlanta);
```

4. The program TOUPPER converts a string from lowercase letters to uppercase letters.

```
PROGRAM ToUpper;
CONST
  LCLetters : SET OF Char = ['a'..'z'];
VAR
  InpStr     : String;
  Size, I    : Integer;

BEGIN
  Writeln('Input a string');
  Readln(InpStr);
  Size := Length(InpStr);
  FOR I := 1 TO Size DO BEGIN
    IF InpStr[I] IN LCLetters THEN { Convert to uppercase }
      InpStr[I] := UpCase(InpStr[I]);
  END;
  Writeln('The converted string is ', InpStr);
END.
```

5. The program STRREV uses an array to reverse a string.

```
PROGRAM StrRev;
VAR
  InpStr    : String;
  OutStr    : String;
  Size, I   : Integer;

BEGIN
  Writeln('Input a string');
  Readln(InpStr);
  Size := Length(InpStr);
  FOR I := 1 TO Size DO
    OutStr[I] := InpStr[Size - (I - 1)];
  OutStr[0] := Chr(Size); { Stores size of string }
  Writeln('The reversed string is ', OutStr);
END.
```

User-Defined Functions and Procedures

User-defined functions and procedures can help you to improve the organization of your programs. Additionally, once a particular function or procedure has been successfully tested, you can use it in many different programs, thus minimizing the work of writing applications. This is one of those rare win-win scenarios—not only can you streamline your work by organizing code into separate routines, but other programmers can use the routines that you write to help them develop their own applications.

In TP, procedures and functions serve as the basic building blocks for writing structured programs. They allow us to package code that is written to perform a specific task. This feature is important because it can help us hide the details required to perform tasks and eliminate the need to write duplicate code for recurring processing situations.

We'll start this chapter by reviewing the techniques for calling functions and procedures. Next, you'll learn how to define your own functions and procedures. Then, we'll explore the two methods supported for passing arguments: pass by reference and pass by value. Finally, we'll look at ways procedure and function definitions can be nested to help create modular programs.

After you complete this chapter, you'll know how to:

- Call procedures and functions
- Define functions and procedures
- Pass arguments to procedures and functions
- Use the pass-by-reference and pass-by-value methods
- Nest the definitions of procedures and functions

Calling Procedures

Before we get into the details involved in defining functions and procedures, let's review the points we've made earlier about functions and procedures. In Chapter 4, you learned how to use the functions and procedures provided with the **Crt** unit. You might recall, for instance, that you invoke the clear screen procedure by executing the statement

```
ClrScr;
```

Thus, you've already learned that you invoke a procedure by using its name. This is an example of the simplest type of procedure call because **ClrScr** is self-contained. That is, no information will be passed to the procedure.

When you need to pass information to a procedure, you use components called *arguments*. So what, precisely, is an argument? In most cases, an argument can be a variable that has been assigned data or a constant. For example, the required format for calling another procedure in the **Crt** unit is:

```
TextColor(Green);
```

The argument **Green** tells TP to use a value that has been defined by the **Crt** unit to identify this particular color. When this procedure is called, TP expects the argument to match the parameter that has been defined for the **TextColor** procedure. If we attempt to call **TextColor** with an argument of the wrong data type, such as

```
TextColor('Green');
```

the compiler would display an error message. In this chapter, you'll discover how to define your own procedures that can be invoked in this same way.

Note

Parentheses are included with a procedure call only when one or more arguments are passed. A statement such as

```
ClrScr();
```

would generate a compiler error.

Calling Functions

The only practical difference between a procedure and a function is that a function always returns a value. This means that a function must appear either on the right side of an assignment statement or in some other context that will use the returned value (such as a **Write** statement or a relational expression). Returning to the **Crt** unit, the simplest example of a function is **ReadKey**. Whenever this function is invoked, it returns the next character in the keyboard buffer. It doesn't require an argument because it reads data directly from a buffer built into the computer.

A common example of a function that requires an argument is **Sqrt**. This function accepts as input a **Real** argument and returns a **Real** value that is the square root of the argument. Thus, the statement

```
A := Sqrt(4.5);
```

will assign to **A** the square root of 4.5 (assuming that **A** is a **Real**). Some other examples that illustrate how functions can be called are:

```
Len := Length('Hello');
IF Length('Pascal') <> 10 THEN Write('Size is ok');
Sum := 25 + Sqrt(25) / 2;
```

When using a function call in an expression, remember that the return value *must* match the data type of the other data components in the expression.

1. Which of the following routines are procedures and which are functions?
   a. **Write**
   b. **Sin**
   c. **GotoXY**
   d. **Ord**
2. Explain the difference between a function and a procedure.
3. True or False: Functions can return only ordinal values.
4. True or False: Functions can be used in standard Pascal expressions.

1. **Write** and **GotoXY** are procedures, and **Sin** and **Ord** are functions.
2. A function returns a value, whereas a procedure cannot return a value.
3. False
4. True

Defining Your Own Functions and Procedures

Although we've been using many of the built-in Pascal procedures and functions, such as **Writeln** and **ReadKey**, you haven't yet learned how to write your own routines. This is a good place to discuss user-defined functions and procedures.

Procedures and functions are defined in a similar manner. Each begins with a statement that consists of either the keyword **PROCEDURE** or **FUNCTION**, which is then followed by the name of the procedure or function. The name used in a procedure or function definition is the same name that we use to call the routine. If the procedure or function requires arguments, the argument declarations are also listed in the first line of the procedure or function definition. Some examples are:

```
PROCEDURE Count;
FUNCTION Total : Boolean;
PROCEDURE DisplayString(X,Y : Integer; Str : String);
FUNCTION GetString(X,Y : Integer) : String;
```

Figure 8.1 shows the components of a sample function and procedure. Notice that the format for the function declaration is different from that of the procedure declaration. This difference exists because the function requires a data type description for its return value. If you omit the return value, such as

```
FUNCTION GetString(X,Y : Integer);
```

the compiler will return an error message.

Figure 8.1   Use these formatting guidelines when you declare a function or procedure.

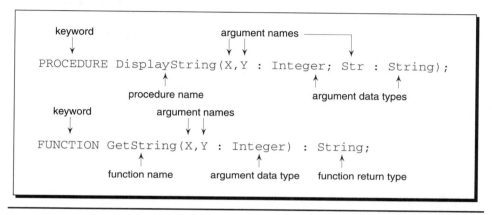

The actual code for a function or procedure is placed between **BEGIN** and **END** statements—just like a main program. The basic format of a user-defined routine is illustrated in Figure 8.2. Notice that variables, constants, and data types are defined before the **BEGIN** statement.

Figure 8.2   The format of a user-defined routine is similar to the format of a TP program.

FUNCTION or PROCEDURE **header**
CONST **declarations**
TYPE **declarations**
VAR **declarations**
function and procedure definitions
BEGIN
function or procedure body
END;

At this point you might have noticed that each user-defined routine is modeled after the format of a Pascal program. The major difference is that the keyword **FUNCTION** or **PROCEDURE** replaces the **PROGRAM** keyword.

The simplest types of functions have no input—only an output. As we've discussed previously, the **ReadKey** function of the **Crt** unit is one such function; an example of a procedure that requires no input is **ClrScr**.

About now, you might be wondering how a return value is controlled by the code within the function. The technique is extremely simple: You simply place the function name on the left side of an assignment statement (**:=**) and set it to whatever you wish the returned value to be. Since the function has been defined to be of a particular type, make sure that you assign values to the function name that are valid for that type. For example, if the function **Tiny** is defined as

```
FUNCTION Tiny : Byte;
```

then the following line within the function would yield, at best, unpredictable results:

```
Tiny := 32767; { This number is too big for a byte! }
```

Note

For the safety of your program, you should guarantee that the return variable of a function is always assigned a valid value. If you want to avoid the unnecessary gray hairs you get from late-night debugging sessions, *never* count on a language default to handle uninitialized variables.

Defining Your First Function or Procedure

With the exception of the return value, the following discussion applies equally to both procedures and functions.

Let's begin with a rather simple numeric function that calculates the square root of a **Real**, then returns an integer that is the whole number part of the square root:

```
PROGRAM Sample_func;
{ Asks the user to enter a real number, and will return
  the largest integer whose square is less than or equal
  to the entered number; if the entered number is too large
  or is negative, an appropriate message will be generated }
USES
  Crt;
VAR
  R_in     : Real; { Number can go up to 10**38 }
  Intg_out : Integer;
```

```pascal
FUNCTION Int_sqrt(x : Real) : Integer;
{ Input is a Real, but the answer is an Integer }
VAR
  I : LongInt; { Need for the result of the Trunc function }
  Z : Real;

BEGIN
  IF X >= 0 THEN
  BEGIN
    Z := Sqrt(X); { Takes the square root of X, returns a real }
    I := Trunc(Z); { Extracts the whole number part }
    IF (I <= 32767) THEN { Valid range for integer }
      Int_sqrt := I { IF statement guarantees this is safe }
    ELSE { Too big }
      Int_sqrt := -1; { Protects against the unreasonable }
  END
  ELSE { Number is negative—illegal for normal square root }
    Int_sqrt := -1; {Sets output to indicate illegal value }
END;

BEGIN { Main body of the program starts here }
  TextBackground(Blue);
  TextColor(LightGray);
  ClrScr;
  GotoXY(10, 5); { Places the cursor }
  Write('Welcome to the Integer Square Root Program.');
  GotoXY(10, 7);
  Write('Please enter a real number now: ');
  Read(R_in);
  Intg_out := Int_sqrt(R_in);
  GotoXY(10, 9);
  IF Intg_out < 0 THEN {Something went wrong }
    Write('The entered number was too big or negative!')
  ELSE
    Write('Largest integer square root is ', Intg_out :5);
  GotoXY(1, 12);  Write('Type CLS at prompt to clear screen and reset colors');
END.
```

As you can see, this program consists of a relatively brief main program that calls a single user-defined function (**Int_sqrt**). The user-defined function is specified to be of type **Integer** and defines two internal variables, **I** and **Z,** which will be used to hold intermediate values. When defining algorithms, always be aware that an overflow possibility can exist; in this case, the input is a **Real**, which can represent numbers as large as 10^{38}. However, the allowed result of our subroutine can be a maximum of 32767. (See Chapter 2 if you need to review the characteristics of **Real** and **Integer** data types.)

The **Int_sqrt** function first tests for a positive input. (The square root of negative numbers generally exists only in the minds of mathematicians and inside radar equipment; TP does not support this concept.) If the input is positive or 0, TP invokes the **Sqrt** function (a built-in function of the **SYSTEM** unit automatically included in all programs). The output of this function is also a **Real**, which is saved in the variable **Z**.

From the definition of the square root function, we know that **Z** must contain a positive number or 0. Thus, we next test for the magnitude of the number to make certain it isn't going to exceed the maximum value of an **Integer**. If the number is small enough, it is converted to a **LongInt** by the built-in function **Trunc**. The last step is to assign to the **Integer** represented by the function name the value contained by the intermediate **LongInt**. If the result of the square root is too large, or if the original input is negative, we assign a value of -1 to the function variable to indicate to the calling program that we could not perform the requested task. The value -1 is legal for an **Integer**, but it is outside of the acceptable range for this function. This makes for a convenient way to indicate an error condition.

Forward Declarations

One characteristic that differentiates Pascal from many other languages is the requirement that all elements (variables, constants, functions, procedures, and so on) *must* be defined before they are used. In the case of functions and procedures, it may sometimes be undesirable or impossible to satisfy this requirement because their definition might appear in a file before they are called. In order to provide an elegant solution to this dilemma, TP allows you to include *forward declarations* of both procedures or functions. This category of declarations is accomplished by providing the **PROCEDURE** or **FUNCTION** statement line as it will appear later, followed by a second line that contains only the word **FORWARD,** followed by a semicolon. Two examples are:

```
FUNCTION XYZ(Count : Integer) : Real;
FORWARD;
```

and

```
PROCEDURE ABC(X_position, Y_position : Real);
FORWARD;
```

Both of these statements are valid examples of forward definitions. The procedure and function still have to be defined later, but the forward declaration provides the compiler with enough information to satisfy the first pass. We recommend that forward declarations all be grouped together—near the beginning of the program, if possible—since this provides for maximum flexibility.

1. Write a short function to compare two values and to return the largest number.

2. True or False: A procedure or function must be declared with the **FORWARD** keyword if it is called by another routine before the procedure or function is defined.

3. True or False: Procedures and functions declared as forward must be placed in the **TYPE** section of a program.

1. This function compares two values and returns the largest number.

```
FUNCTION MaxNum(X,Y : Integer) : Integer;
BEGIN
  IF X >= Y THEN MaxNum := X
  ELSE MaxNum := Y;
END;
```

2. True

3. False

Global Variables

In the previous section, you learned how to define a simple function that used only two local variables. A local variable is a variable that can be used only inside the body of the function or procedure in which it is defined. In that example, the single parameter passed is a simple type (a **Real**). Fortunately, TP allows data to be shared between the program that calls a procedure (or function) and the routine itself. How is this done? We can use *global variables*. A global variable can be used by any of the functions or procedures defined in a main program. Before we show you how to use this type of variable, we should examine some of the advantages and possible pitfalls of this information-sharing technique.

If you take a close look at the program we presented in the previous section, you will notice that variables are declared in three different places. The first location is in the **VAR** section, located between the **PROGRAM** statement and the **FUNCTION** statement. Although this section declares variables for the main program, it also has an interesting side effect. Because the variable declarations are placed before the function definition, as Figure 8.3 illustrates, the variables become global, which means that they can be accessed by any procedure or function that follows the declaration.

One problem with global variables lies in the ease with which they can be modified by any program section, including a function or a procedure. Needless to say, you can waste a great deal of time trying to locate a problem that occurs when one function accidentally modifies a global variable!

Figure 8.3   In this example, the variables are declared before the function is defined.

```
   . . .
   VAR
    R_in : Real;  ←─────────────┐   ── variables declared before function
    Intg_out : Integer; ←───────┘

   Function Int_sqrt(X : Real) : Integer;
     . . .
     . . .
   BEGIN
     . . .
     . . .
   END;
```

On the other side of the coin, the advantage of global variables lies in their ease of access, which can greatly simplify data passing between functions and procedures. Nevertheless, one of the secrets to intelligent Pascal programming is to use as few global variables as possible.

Returning to the **Int_sqrt** program, the location of the **VAR** group before the **FUNCTION** definition is legal, but undesirable since none of the variables defined there are actually used as global variables. The following program illustrates where the **VAR** definitions should have been placed to define variables that can be accessed only by the main program.

```
PROGRAM Sample_func;
{ Asks the user to enter a real number, then returns the
  largest integer whose square is less than or equal to
  the entered number; if the entered number is too large
  or is negative, an appropriate message will be generated }
USES
  Crt;

FUNCTION Int_sqrt(x : Real) : Integer;
{ Input is a Real, but the answer is an Integer }
VAR
  I : LongInt; { Need for the result of the Trunc function }
  Z : Real;

BEGIN
  IF X >= 0 THEN
  BEGIN
    Z := Sqrt(X); { Takes square root of X, returns a real }
```

```
    I := Trunc(Z); { Extracts the whole number part }
    IF (I <= 32767) THEN { Valid range for integer }
       Int_sqrt := I { IF statement guarantees this is safe }
    ELSE { Too big }
      Int_sqrt := -1; { Protects against the unreasonable }
    END
    ELSE { Number's negative, illegal for square root }
    Int_sqrt := -1; { Sets output to indicate illegal value }
END;

VAR
  R_in      : Real; { Number can go up to 10**38 }
  Intg_out  : Integer;

BEGIN   { <Main body of the program starts here }
  TextBackground(Blue);
  TextColor(LightGray);
  ClrScr;
  GotoXY(10, 5); { Places the cursor }
  Write('Welcome to the Integer Square Root Program.');
  GotoXY(10, 7);
  Write('Please enter a real number now: ');
  Read(R_in);
  Intg_out := Int_sqrt(R_in);
    GotoXY(10, 9);
  IF Intg_out < 0 THEN { Something went wrong }
    Write('The entered number was too big or negative!')
  ELSE
    Write('Largest integer square root is ', Intg_out : 5);
  GotoXY(1, 12);
  Write('Type CLS at prompt to clear screen and reset colors');
END.
```

Local Variables

In looking at the modified version of the **Int_sqrt** function, you can see that the function also has a **VAR** group of its own. Variables defined within the body of a function or procedure in this way are known only within the procedure itself; these are called *local variables*. Local variables are useful because they cannot be modified by other procedures and assignment statements. This means it isn't possible for a local variable to corrupt similarly named variables in other procedures or in the main program. Thus, if you use the variable **I** in five different procedures or functions, but always define the variable as local, the first function cannot affect the contents of **I** in any of the other functions. In fact, **I** could be a **Byte** in the first function, a **Real** in the second, and even a **String** array in the third.

Using local variables is like erecting walls between different sections of your program; processing that affects variables in one procedure or function will not affect variables in any other procedures or functions. We strongly recommend that you use local variables whenever they are practical.

1. What is the difference between local and global variables?
2. List the local and global variables in the **Sample_func** program.
3. True or False: A program can assign the same name to a local and a global variable.

1. Local variables can only be used inside the body of the program block or section in which they are declared. Global variables can be accessed by any procedure or function defined within a program.
2. The global variables are **R_in** and **Intg_out**. The local variables in the function **Int_sqrt** are **I** and **Z**.
3. True

Arguments

By this point you may be wondering if Pascal supports any other types of variables. The answer? Yes—arguments. An argument plays an extremely important role since it acts as a data messenger between functions and procedures and the statements that call them.

For example, imagine that you want to prove, by repetitive numeric evaluation, that the sine of angle x is the same as the sine of the quantity 180.0 - x for values of x between 0 and 90 degrees. The code might look something like this:

```
FOR I := 0 TO 90 DO
  BEGIN
    X := I; {Converts to Real for trig routine}
    Compl_X := 180.0 - X; {Calculate complement of X}
    IF (Sin(X) <> Sin(Compl_X)) THEN
      Writeln('OOPS, found a nonmatch!!');
  END;
Writeln('End of loop reached.');
```

Notice that, in the **IF** statement, we invoke the built-in **Sin** function twice, but with different variables as arguments each time. If we can't pass information by using an argument, we are forced to use a global variable. What a mess it would be to reassign the value of a global variable each time we want to invoke the function!

Now, take one last look at the **Int_sqrt** function introduced in the **Sample_func** program presented earlier. Notice that the local variable **X** is defined as a **Real** within the parentheses in the **FUNCTION** statement. If this function had several arguments, they would all be defined as

```
FUNCTION funct_name(var1 : type, var2 : type, ...) : type;
```

where each group of *varx : type* identifies the local variable name and the type of that specific variable. Notice that the variables must appear in the same order in which the data will be passed when the function is invoked. If several arguments are of the same type and in order, it is possible to define them as follows to save typing:

```
FUNCTION funct_name(var1, var2, var3 : type, ...) : type;
```

The only rule here is that, again, the variables must appear in the order in which the data will be passed. By the way, this technique for declaring function arguments also applies to procedure definitions.

Passing Arguments by Value

Thus far in this chapter, the procedures and functions that have been defined illustrated a form of parameter passing called *passing by value*. The program shown next illustrates this concept:

```
PROGRAM Arg_no_mod;
USES Crt;

PROCEDURE Test_div(Inp : Integer);
BEGIN
  Writeln('We are now in the procedure Test_div');
  Inp := Inp DIV 2;
  Writeln(Inp);
END;

VAR
  M : Integer;

BEGIN
  M := 27;
  ClrScr;
  Writeln(M);
  Test_div(M);
  Writeln('We have now returned to the main program');
  Writeln(M);
END.
```

This program consists of a simple main program that passes an integer argument to a procedure. The procedure then divides the value by 2 and prints out the new value. Upon returning execution from the procedure, the main program also prints the value of the variable passed to the procedure.

If you were to execute this program, you would see the following answers on the screen:

```
27
We are now in the procedure Test_div
13
We have now returned to the main program
27
```

Notice that, even though we changed the contents of the variable that was defined as the argument of the procedure, the contents of the variable remained unchanged at the section of the program that had called the procedure. Why is this? Well, normally TP passes the *value* of an argument from the calling program to the lower-level routine. This method acts like a trap door; data can flow down from the calling portion of the program, but alterations of the arguments in the procedure or function can't flow back up. Thus, if you avoid using global variables in a function or procedure, you can guarantee that the called unit will not corrupt data in other functions and procedures.

Passing Arguments by Reference

Great, so you can't hurt yourself by modifying the values of arguments within a function or procedure. You also can't hurt yourself if you're wearing a strait-jacket! What happens if you intentionally want to modify data? Imagine that you decide to write a small procedure that will clear an array by setting all of the elements to 0. Ideally, you would like to perform this operation by executing a line such as:

```
Array_clear(My_array);
```

The problem: As stated, it won't do any good to go through the motions of zeroing out all of the elements within **Array_clear**. But, TP has left us an option called *pass by reference*. This means TP actually passes the *address* of the variable to be modified, and does not create a local variable for that parameter within the called procedure or function. This pass-by-reference option can be selected for each (or all) parameters of a function or procedure. The following program illustrates how the pass-by-reference method works:

```
PROGRAM Pass_by_ref;
USES Crt;
{ The following definition does not reserve any memory space; it simply
```

```
      defines the attributes for a particular type of array }
TYPE
   Template = ARRAY[1..6] OF Integer;

PROCEDURE Array_clear(VAR Inp : Template);
VAR
   K : Integer;

BEGIN
   FOR K := 1 TO 6 DO
   Inp [K] := 0;
END;

VAR
   Test_set : Template;
   M        : Integer;

BEGIN
   FOR M := 1 TO 6 DO
     Test_set [M] := M * 2;
   ClrScr;
   FOR M := 1 TO 6 DO
     Writeln(Test_set[M]);
   Array_clear(Test_set);
   FOR M := 1 TO 6 DO
     Writeln(Test_set[M]);
END.
```

The previous example shows how you can declare a single argument to be of type pass by reference. In this case, an array is passed to a procedure, which then clears a fixed number of elements and returns the modified array to the main program. Now imagine that we wish to create a procedure that will search an array and zero out the first element that it finds that is 10 or greater.

To illustrate multiple variables in a **FUNCTION** or **PROCEDURE** definition, we've written the next program, in which we define a second argument that will also be of type pass by reference. This variable will indicate to us the index position of the changed element in the array. Notice that we do not initialize this variable before we use it in the procedure call.

```
PROGRAM Pass_by_ref;
USES Crt;

{ The following definition does not reserve any memory space; it simply
  defines the attributes for a particular type of array }
TYPE
   Template = ARRAY[1..6] OF Integer;

PROCEDURE Less_than_ten(VAR Inp : Template ; VAR I : Integer);
```

```
{ This procedure will look for the first value
  10 or greater and will set it to 0 and
  return in I the index of the zeroed item }
VAR
  K : Integer;

BEGIN
  I := 0;
  K := 0;
  WHILE I = 0 DO BEGIN
    K := K + 1;
    IF Inp[K] > 9 THEN
      BEGIN
        np[K] := 0;
        I := K;
      END;
  END;
END;

VAR
  Test_set : Template;
  M, L     : Integer;

BEGIN
  FOR M := 1 TO 6 DO
    Test_set[M] := M * 2;
  ClrScr;
  FOR M := 1 TO 6 DO
    Writeln(Test_set[M]);
  Writeln(' ');
  Less_than_ten(Test_set, L);
  FOR M := 1 TO 6 DO
    Writeln(Test_set[M]);
  Writeln(' ');
  Writeln('The index element is ', L : 1);
END.
```

1. Explain how you could rewrite the **Less_than_ten** procedure in the PASS_BY_REF program as a function.

2. Explain the difference between passing arguments by reference and passing arguments by value.

3. Specify which of the following built-in TP procedures and functions use the pass-by-reference and pass-by-value methods of parameter passing:

   a. **Write**

   b. **Readln**

   c. **Pred**

   d. **Inc**

1. To convert the procedure to a function, the index of the modified element must be provided as a return value, rather than as a pass-by-reference argument.
2. When an argument is passed by value, the actual contents of the argument are passed to the procedure or function. When an argument is passed by reference, the address of the argument's storage location is passed.
3. **Write** and **Pred** pass parameters by value, and **ReadIn** and **Inc** pass parameters by reference.

Nesting Procedures and Functions

You've seen earlier that variables defined locally within a procedure or function are unknown and unreachable by the program entities that call them. If you look at any of the programs in this chapter, a structural pattern emerges where the functions or procedures are always defined following the **PROGRAM** statement. Technically, a function or procedure must be defined before it is used. It turns out that TP allows the definition of "local" functions or procedures defined *within* other functions or procedures; this concept is known as *nesting*.

A nested procedure or function can be invoked only by the procedure or function in which it is defined and by others that are at an equal or deeper level than the routine to be called. At first, this technique may sound rather useless. However, it can be very important when attempting to merge programs while modifying them as little as possible.

The next program illustrates nesting by performing two variants of the integer square root program developed earlier in this chapter. First, we have a function called **Int_sqrt,** which calls an embedded function named **Inside_fn**. This section will provide the largest integer less than the square root of the entered number. The second section consists of the procedure **Sqrt_plus_one**, which calls a different internal function called **Inside_fn**, and obtains the integer that is closest to but greater than the square root of the entered number. The order of procedure and function calls is illustrated in Figure 8.4.

Figure 8.4 The order of procedure and function calls in the program HIDDEN_FUCTIONS.

If we had defined both of the **Inside_fn** functions at the same level as the other functions and procedures, the compiler would have complained about a duplicate name. Thanks to nesting, the compiler is satisfied and the program works as intended.

```
PROGRAM Hidden_functions;
{ Asks the user to enter a real number, then calls two separate functions
  or procedures to provide the nearest integer that is less than the
  square root of the number and the nearest integer that is greater than
  the square root of the number }
USES
  Crt;

FUNCTION Int_sqrt(D : Real) : Integer;
{ Input is a Real, but the answer is an Integer }

  FUNCTION Inside_fn(X : Real) : Integer;
  VAR
    I : LongInt; { Needed for result of Trunc function }
    Z : Real;

  BEGIN
    IF X >= 0 THEN
      BEGIN
        Z  := Sqrt(X); { Takes square root of X, returns real }
        I := Trunc(Z); { Extracts the whole number part }
        IF (I <= 32767) THEN { Valid range for integer }
          Inside_fn := I {IF statement guarantees this safe }
        ELSE { Too big }
          Inside_fn := -1; { Guards against the unreasonable }
      END
    ELSE
      { Negative number, illegal for square root }
      Inside_fn:= -1; {Sets output to indicate illegal value}
  END; { Terminates the definition of Inside_fn }

BEGIN { Starts the function Int_sqrt; notice the absence of a VAR section
        in this function because the only variables being used are defined
        in the FUNCTION statement }
  Int_sqrt := Inside_fn(D);
END; { Ends the procedure Int_sqrt, which contains Inside_fn }

PROCEDURE Sqrt_plus_one(T : Real; VAR Answer : Integer);

  FUNCTION Inside_fn(X : Real) : Integer;
  VAR
    I : LongInt; { Needed for the result of the Trunc function }
    Z : Real;
```

```
    BEGIN
      IF X >= 0 THEN
        BEGIN
          Z := Sqrt(X);
          I := Trunc(Z) + 1; { Changed this line!! }
          IF (I <= 32767) THEN
            Inside_fn := I
          ELSE
            Inside_fn := -1;
        END
      ELSE
        Inside_fn := -1;
    END; { Terminates the second definition of Inside_fn }

BEGIN { Starts the procedure Sqrt_plus_one }
  Answer := Inside_fn(T);
END;

{ Main body of the program starts here }
VAR
  R_in : Real; { This number can go up to 10**38 }
  Intg_first, Intg_second : Integer;

BEGIN
  TextBackground(Blue);
  TextColor(LightGray);
  ClrScr;
  GotoXY(10, 5); { Places the cursor }
  Write('Welcome to the Integer Square Root Program.');
  GotoXY(10, 7);
  Write('Please enter a real number now: ');
  Read(R_in);
  Intg_first := Int_sqrt(R_in);
  GotoXY(10, 9);
  IF Intg_first < 0 THEN { Something went wrong }
    Write('The entered number was too big or negative!')
  ELSE
    Write('Largest integer square root is ', Intg_first : 5);
  Sqrt_plus_one(R_in, Intg_second);
  GotoXY(10, 12);
  IF Intg_second< 0 THEN {Something went wrong }
    Write('The entered number was too big or negative!')
  ELSE
    Write('Next larger integer square root is ', Intg_second:5);
  GotoXY(1, 14);
  Write('Type CLS at prompt to clear screen and reset colors');
END.
```

Summary

You've seen how to use and define procedures and functions and how to pass arguments to advantage without jeopardizing the traditional "data hiding" that makes programming in Pascal so desirable. This chapter started by showing you how to call procedures and functions. Then, we explored the basics of defining our own functions and procedures. Along the way, you learned how to use the two types of parameter passing techniques: pass by value and pass by reference.

In Chapter 9 you'll learn how to use the built-in units that TP provides and you'll get some practice writing your own units.

Exercises

1. What is wrong with the following function definition?

```
FUNCTION GetString(X,Y : Integer);
Var
  Str : String;

BEGIN
  GotoXY(X, Y);
  Readln(Str);
END;
```

Change the function so that it will work.

2. Convert the following procedure to a function:

```
PROCEDURE MaxString(Str1, Str2 : String; VAR Str3 : String);
BEGIN
  IF Length(Str1) <= Length(Str2) THEN
    Str3 := Str1
  ELSE
    Str3 := Str2;
END;
```

3. Write a function called **AddNums** to return the sum of a list of values stored as an integer array. Assume that the array has 10 elements and is defined as:

```
TYPE
  NumList = ARRAY[1..10] OF Integer;
```

4. Write a function that displays a prompt message at a specified cursor position and asks the user to enter a "Yes" or "No" response. If the user enters a "Yes" response, the function returns true; otherwise, it returns false.

Answers

1. The first line of the function definition is missing a return type. Also, the function does not return a value. The correct version of this function is:

```
FUNCTION GetString(X,Y : Integer) : String;
Var
  Str : String;

BEGIN
  GotoXY(X, Y);
  Readln(Str);
  GetString := Str;
END;
```

2. Here is the converted function:

```
FUNCTION MaxString(Str1, Str2 : String) : String;
BEGIN
  IF Length(Str1) <= Length(Str2) THEN
    MaxString := Str1
  ELSE
    MaxString := Str2;
END;
```

3. The function **AddNums** returns the sum of a list of values stored as an integer array:

```
FUNCTION AddNums(Nums : NumList) : Integer;
VAR
  I, Total : Integer;

BEGIN
  Total := 0;
  FOR I := 1 TO 10 DO
    Total := Total + Nums[I];
  AddNums := Total;
END;
```

4. The function **GetResp** displays a prompt message at a specified cursor position and asks the user to enter a "Yes" or "No" response. If the user enters a "Yes" response, the function returns true; otherwise, it returns false.

```
FUNCTION GetResp(X, Y : Integer; Msg : String) : Boolean;
VAR
  Ans : String;

BEGIN
  GotoXY(X, Y);
```

```
      Write(Msg);
      Readln(Ans);
      IF Ans = "Yes" THEN GetResp := True
      ELSE GetResp := False;
   END;
```

Working with Units

n Chapter 6, we presented the functions and procedures contained in the **Crt** unit. If you recall, this unit provides certain variables that can be read or modified to set screen attributes. The **Crt** unit also contains predefined constants to help you work with the screen I/O routines. It's almost as though this unit works like a separate program that can be attached to your applications to provide certain services. In fact, you can improve your TP performance in similar ways by creating your own units.

In this chapter, you'll learn how to create custom units to perform specialized tasks. The chapter starts by showing you how to write the interface and implementation sections of a unit. Next, you'll see how a unit is compiled and used with a main program. You'll learn that units follow the framework of a TP program; that is, they can be composed of data types, constants, local and global variables, and procedures and functions. In the last part of the chapter we'll look at some of the other units provided by TP that haven't been mentioned yet.

After you complete this chapter, you'll know how to:

- Define the implementation and interface section of a unit
- Use the keywords **INTERFACE**, **IMPLEMENTATION**, **UNIT**, and **USES**
- Initialize the internal and public variables used in a unit
- Use some of the routines from the **Dos** unit

Putting Units to Work

As you've seen in the TP programs we've been using throughout this book, there's nothing difficult about using a unit. The only requirement is to include the following statement after the **PROGRAM** statement in your program:

```
USES
   Crt,ScTools;
```

Here, the labels **Crt** and **ScTools** refer to unit filenames. When the TP compiler encounters the **USES** statement, it attempts to read the unit files listed. (Unit files are stored with the extension .TPU.)

Basics of Creating a Unit

Let's start by exploring how a simple unit is created. Three new statements are needed to define a unit: **UNIT, INTERFACE**, and **IMPLEMENTATION**. Figure 9.1 provides the general format for a unit. Each unit definition must always contain these three keywords, in addition to an **END** statement. Notice that the **UNIT** statement is always the first line in the unit file. The basic format for using this statement is:

Figure 9.1 Follow this general format to create a unit file.

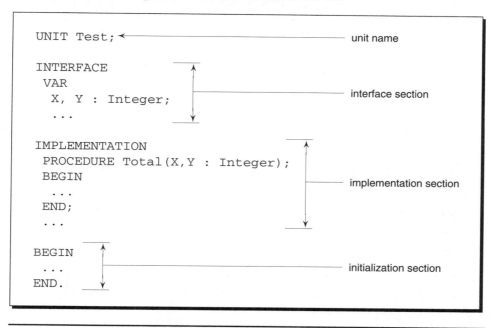

UNIT ScTools;

What does this keyword do? It tells the TP compiler to generate a file of type .TPU rather than the standard .EXE file type generated for programs. In a unit definition, the **UNIT** keyword plays a role similar to that of the **PROGRAM** statement. The name **ScTools** is the label assigned to the unit. Normally, this name is also used as the name for the .PAS file that contains the source code for the unit. Therefore, you may want to limit your unit names to eight characters or less and avoid special characters so that the unit name can be used as the filename.

Note

The name you specify to create the unit file is the same name that is later used with the **USES** statement to access the unit.

The second keyword, **INTERFACE**, tells the compiler that the definitions located between this keyword and the **IMPLEMENTATION** keyword should be made public to the user program. This section also contains the function and procedure declarations for the user-defined routines that are to be made public. These declarations consist of **PROCEDURE** or **FUNCTION** statements, similar to the ones we've used up until now. The only difference is that here, they are not followed by the customary **BEGIN-END** blocks containing the code for the routine. Instead, the actual definition of the routine is placed in the **IMPLEMENTATION** section. The intent is really quite simple; the only statements that appear in the **INTERFACE** section are definitions that will be accessed by the user program.

The **IMPLEMENTATION** section holds all function and procedure definitions as well as the private constant and variable definitions. The term "private" simply means that these constants and variables can be accessed only by the unit. All of the rules concerning the scope of variables apply here, just as they applied in using regular program definitions. You must also ensure that the functions and procedures declared in the **INTERFACE** section are defined in the **IMPLEMENTATION** section. Refer back to Figure 9.1 to see the placement of the private and public members.

If you forget to define a procedure or function that is identified in the **INTERFACE** section (or if you happen to incorrectly enter the name), TP will respond at compile time with an unsatisfied forward-reference error. One important caution: The data type of the parameters and the function return type used in the **IMPLEMENTATION** section should match the declaration in the **INTERFACE** section. Although you don't have to list the procedure and function parameters in the **IMPLEMENTATION** section, you should consider repeating the entire argument list for program clarity. The safest way to avoid problems is to copy the **PROCEDURE** or **FUNCTION** definition line from one place to the other by using the cut and paste editing features; this technique is quite reliable.

Note ▼

Units are standalone program modules, and are usually compiled separately from the programs that use them. Although TP can compile both the unit and the program that uses the unit at the same time, we will start by examining how to compile units separately.

At this point, you should be aware of one other unique feature of the **IMPLEMENTATION** section of a unit definition. Remember that, in a TP program, the last section always consists of a **BEGIN-END** block, which contains the code for the main program. TP uses this same technique to define a section of code that is executed when a unit is initialized. For example, assume you have the following initialization code in a unit you've created:

```
UNIT ScTools;
INTERFACE
VAR
   I, J : Integer;
   { Other public declarations go here }
IMPLEMENTATION
   { Private definitions go here }
```

```
BEGIN
  I := 1;
  J := 212;
END.
```

Now, if you include the following statement in your main program:

```
USES
  ScTools;
```

the code within the **BEGIN-END** block listed in the **ScTools** unit will be automatically executed. By supporting initialization code within a unit, TP allows variables to be initialized to known states. For example, when we invoke the **Crt** unit, we can assume that variables like **TextAttr** contain some valid value.

Note

> If a unit does not contain an initialization section, it must be terminated with an **END** statement, followed by a period. A unit containing an initialization section, however, always follows this format:
>
> ```
> BEGIN
>   <initialization statements>
> END.
> ```

Writing a Unit

Now that the basic format of a unit has been covered, we can look at how one is written. Our unit, **Tool2**, defines a single function named **Command**. It doesn't define any public variables or constants, nor does it use an initialization section.

```
UNIT Tool2;
INTERFACE
USES Crt;
FUNCTION Command(Explan, Options : String) : Byte;
IMPLEMENTATION

FUNCTION Command(Explan, Options : String) : Byte;
VAR
  Key_stroke, Letr : CHAR;
  I, J, L          : Integer;

BEGIN
{ Begins by emptying the input buffer }
  WHILE KeyPressed = TRUE DO Key_stroke := ReadKey;
  GotoXY(1, 25); { Locates explanation string }
```

```
ClrEol;
Write(Explan);
Write('(',Options,'): ');
L := Length(Options);
WHILE KeyPressed <> TRUE DO; { Waits for a key }
Key_stroke := ReadKey;
IF((Key_stroke <= 'z') AND (Key_stroke >= 'a')) THEN
  Key_stroke := UpCase(Key_stroke);
Command :=0; { Initializes to default }
I := 0;
WHILE I <= L DO
BEGIN
  I := I + 1;
  Letr := Options[I];
  IF((Letr <= 'z') AND (Letr >= 'a')) THEN
    Letr := UpCase(Letr);
  IF Letr = Key_stroke THEN { Identifies a match }
  BEGIN
    Command := I;
    I := L + 1; { Stops the WHILE loop }
  END; { IF statement terminates }
END; { While loop terminates }
END; { Function terminates }
END.
```

The function **Command** operates as a simple command-line processor and takes two string arguments. Figure 9.2 shows that the first string passed is displayed at column 1 of line 25 on the screen. The second string is then displayed on the same line, between parentheses. Next, the keyboard input

---

Figure 9.2. The output produced by Command.

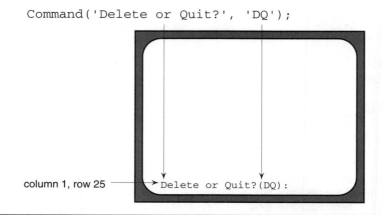

Command('Delete or Quit?', 'DQ');

column 1, row 25 ──────→ Delete or Quit?(DQ):

---

buffer is cleared to allow a response from the user. When a key is pressed, it is converted to uppercase to ensure that the search algorithm always compares letters of the same case.

At this point, a loop begins to search the contents of the second string for a match. If a match is found, the function returns the relative position of the pressed letter in the second string. If the user presses a key that isn't contained in the second string, the function returns a 0.

You may have noticed that we're using array notation to extract each character from the string. It turns out that the string functions, such as **Copy**, return a string. Thus, even if we specify a length of 1, the returned string will still be a type mismatch if we try to assign the result to a character. Also, there is no direct command to convert a string of length 1 to a character. To avoid this problem, we use the notation

```
Options[<index>]
```

to access the individual element of the string. We must begin with the element [1] because TP strings hold the string length in location [0].

1. What three keywords are used to define a unit?
2. What is the difference between the **INTERFACE** and the **IMPLEMENTA-TION** section of a unit?
3. True or False: Units must contain an initialization section.
4. What is wrong with the following unit definition?

```
UNIT TestSet
IMPLEMENTATION
FUNCTION GetResp: Boolean;
VAR
  Str : String;

BEGIN
  Readln(Str);
  IF Str = 'YES' THEN GetResp := True
  ELSE GetResp := False;
END;

INTERFACE
FUNCTION GetResp : Boolean;
END.
```

1. **UNIT**, **INTERFACE**, and **IMPLEMENTATION**
2. The **INTERFACE** section contains the declarations for the public variables, constants, data types, and routines for a unit, while the **IMPLEMENTATION** section contains the code for the private variables, constants, data types, and the routines used in a unit.

3. False
4. A semicolon is missing from the **UNIT** statement line, and the **INTERFACE** and **IMPLE-MENTATION** sections are in the wrong order.

Compiling a Unit

We've now created a unit that's ready to be compiled by TP. It turns out that you compile a unit in the same way you compile a regular TP program; that is, by using the Compile File option under the Make menu. Since TP encounters the keyword **UNIT** rather than **PROGRAM**, it generates a file with the same name as the source file, but of type .TPU rather than of type .EXE (used for normal TP programs).

Using the Example Unit

The example unit we've created is now ready to be used in a program. So how do we do this? Easy. We include the **USES** statement in our program, then include the name of the unit. The following program shows how we put our unit to work:

```
PROGRAM Unit_test;
USES Crt, Tool2;
VAR
   Let_pos, Turn_off : Byte;
CONST
   STR_1 = 'Delete, New, neXt, Quit';
   STR_2 = 'DNXQ';
   STR_3 = 'Do you really want to quit (Yes, No)?';
   STR_4 = 'yn';

BEGIN
   ClrScr;
   GotoXY(1, 5);
   Write('You will stay in an infinite loop until you press Q');
   Turn_off := 0; { Initializes loop control variable }
   REPEAT
     Let_pos := Command(Str_1, Str_2);
     IF Let_pos <> 0 THEN
     BEGIN
       GotoXY (10, 10);
       ClrEol;
       Write('Command = ', Let_pos : 2);
       IF Let_pos = 4 THEN
          IF Command(Str_3, Str_4) = 1 THEN Turn_off := 1;
     END
     ELSE { Let_pos must be 0 to select invalid code }
```

```
    BEGIN
      Sound(500);
      Delay(300);
      NoSound;
      GotoXY(10, 10);
      ClrEol;
      Write('Not a valid selection');
    END;
  UNTIL Turn_off = 1; {end of REPEAT loop}
END.
```

As you can see from this program, the custom unit is included in the same way as other units, such as **Crt**. The **Command** function is invoked just as if it were a TP built-in function.

Adding Initialization Code

The previous unit did not provide access to any variables or perform any initialization. We'll add these features to our sample unit, then show you how the main program can be modified to use the unit. The following program shows the new unit:

```
UNIT Tool4;

INTERFACE
USES Crt;
VAR
  Xpos, Ypos : Byte;

FUNCTION Command(Explan, Options : String) : Byte;

IMPLEMENTATION
FUNCTION Command(Explan, Options : String) : Byte;
VAR
  Key_stroke, Letr : Char;
  I, J, L          : Integer;

BEGIN
  { Empties the input buffer }
  WHILE KeyPressed = TRUE DO Key_stroke := ReadKey;
  GotoXY(Xpos, Ypos); { Finds explanation string }
  ClrEol;
  Write(Explan);
  Write('(',Options,'): ');
  L := Length(Options);
  WHILE KeyPressed <> TRUE DO; { Waits for a key }
  Key_stroke := ReadKey;
```

```
    IF ((Key_stroke <= 'z') AND (Key_stroke >= 'a')) THEN
      Key_stroke := UpCase(Key_stroke);
    Command := 0;  {Initializes to default}
    I := 0;
    WHILE I <= L DO
    BEGIN
      I := I + 1;
      Letr := Options[I];
      IF ((Letr <= 'z') AND (Letr >= 'a')) THEN
        Letr := UpCase(Letr);
      IF Letr = Key_stroke THEN { Identifies a match }
      BEGIN
        Command := I;
        I := L + 1; { Stops the WHILE loop }
      END; { Ends IF statement }
    END; { Ends While loop }
END; { Terminates function}

BEGIN { Initialization section }
  Xpos := 1;
  Ypos := 25;
END.
```

As you can see, there are few differences between the **Tool2** and **Tool4** units. In the new unit defined, two **Byte** variables (in the **INTERFACE** section of the unit) are included to allow the user program to define the beginning position of the query line. At the end of the unit, note that an additional **BEGIN** section initializes the position variables to valid values. If we now compile and use **Tool4,** rather than the original **Tool2**, the program will perform the same because the unit initializes the query line position at the same location.

Now consider a program that assigns discrete values to **Xpos** and **Ypos**. Note that since the two variables are defined in the unit **Tool4**, no **VAR** definition is required in the main program. When this program is executed, the query line appears near the center of the screen, rather than at the bottom.

```
PROGRAM Unit_test;
USES Crt, Tool4;
VAR
  Let_pos, Turn_off : Byte;
CONST
  STR_1 = 'Delete, New, neXt, Quit';
  STR_2 = 'DNXQ';
  STR_3 = 'Do you really want to quit (Yes, No)?';
  STR_4 = 'yn';

BEGIN
  Xpos := 5; { Move the query line around }
```

```
    Ypos := 16;
    ClrScr;
    GotoXY(1, 5);
    Write('You will stay in an infinite loop until you press Q');
    Turn_off := 0; { Initializes loop control variable }
    REPEAT
      Let_pos := Command(Str_1, Str_2);
      IF Let_pos <> 0 THEN
      BEGIN
        GotoXY(10, 10);
        ClrEol;
        Write('Command = ', Let_pos : 2);
        IF Let_pos = 4 THEN
           IF Command(Str_3, Str_4) = 1 THEN Turn_off := 1;
      END
      ELSE { Let_pos must be 0 to select invalid code }
      BEGIN
        Sound(500);
        Delay(300);
        NoSound;
        GotoXY(10, 10);
        ClrEol;
        Write('Not a valid selection');
      END;
    UNTIL Turn_off = 1; { Ends REPEAT loop }
END.
```

Tips on Initializing Units

Some final thoughts about initialization: In defining several units, you might inadvertently allow two or more units to set the same variable or perform a similar function (for example, by both calling **TextColor**). In such a situation, the operations will be performed in the order in which the names of the units appear in the **USES** statement. As a result, the last unit that affects the given variable will have the last word; however, the effects could be cumulative—with unintended and undesirable results. Take care not to paint yourself into such corners; these kinds of ambiguous interactions can take some time to locate and correct.

1. What statement is required to access a unit in a program?
2. True or False: A unit can be compiled like a standalone program.
3. What file extension is assigned to a compiled unit?
4. What keywords define an initialization section?
5. True or False: A unit can include another unit.

1. **USES**
2. True
3. .TPU
4. **BEGIN** and **END**
5. True

Working with Units

At the beginning of the chapter, you learned that you can compile a unit in more than one way. The alternative method to compiling a unit separately is to compile the **PROGRAM** file that includes the unit by using the Rebuild Main File option of the Make menu (or the /M option when compiling from the DOS command line using the TPC command). If TP discovers any problems, it will stop at the first encountered error, as you might expect. Also, remember that once you've compiled the unit successfully, it need not be recompiled as long as the unit hasn't been changed.

Thus, if you compile the previous sample program, the **Tool4** unit need not be recompiled each time the main program is changed. However, if you change the unit, you must recompile the unit and all programs that use it.

Another interesting problem can arise when two separate units define a function, procedure, or variable with the same name. As you might imagine, this can be the source of some serious problems. TP takes a logical approach: The version most recently defined is the one used. The processing occurs from left to right, in the order in which the units appear in the **USES** statement. Thus, if both of the units in the following statement define the same procedure **Scr_fmt**, the procedure in **Tool2** will be the default for the program:

```
USES Tool1, Tool2;
```

Interestingly enough, both versions are actually accessible. The way to access a specific one is by preceding the variable, function, or procedure reference with the name of the unit in which it is defined. Thus

```
Tool1.Scr_fmt
```

will invoke the procedure defined in the first unit, rather than the procedure defined in the second unit. In general, we recommend that you avoid this type of conflict whenever possible.

One last problem associated with custom units is called *circular referencing*. This occurs when one unit uses a second, which in turn uses a third, which then uses the first one. Dependency of one unit on another is perfectly legal—as long as a "wraparound" doesn't occur. Such "dog chasing tail" situations can generally be avoided or eliminated by carefully partitioning the different units.

TP Provided Units

TP provides several ready-made units for general programming use. These include **Crt**, **Dos**, **Graph**, **Graph3**, **Overlay**, **Printer**, **Strings**, **System**, **Turbo3**, **Win31**, **WinAPI**, **WinCrt**, **WinDos**, **WinPrn**, **WinProcs**, and **WinTypes**. Many of these are intended for use in programming in Microsoft Windows, and may not be included in your version of Turbo Pascal. Also, **Graph3** and **Turbo3** are units that provide backward compatibility for Turbo Pascal version 3.0, and shouldn't be used in any new programs you write.

We've already seen the **Crt** unit in operation in Chapter 6. For the most part, the functions and procedures available with the **Dos** unit can be tricky to use and can cause damage to disk files if used improperly. To use these functions and procedures effectively, you'll need to understand how DOS works. If you are inquisitive, you should experiment with such functions as the **Getxxx** series. These routines only retrieve data from DOS; they cannot cause any damage to existing files.

The **Overlay** unit provides support for TP's built-in overlay system. This is an advanced programming mechanism that allows a program to load code and data from disk during run-time.

The **Printer** unit is an extremely simple one, and provides no user-callable functions or procedures. It simply provides the linkage for the **Lst** file variable so that **Write** and **Writeln** statements pointing to **Lst** will be forwarded to the LPT1 port (usually reserved for a printer). When the **Printer** unit is included in a program, the following commands will send their output directly to the printer:

```
Write(Lst,'This should wind up on paper.');
Writeln(Lst,'This should be right behind...');
```

The details of the **Graph** unit and other basic graphics programming techniques are presented in Chapter 13.

The **Strings** unit contains functions that allow you to program using C-style *null terminated* strings. Again, this is primarily of interest to programmers working with Microsoft Windows.

The **System** unit provides the standard set of TP procedures and functions. Because this unit is automatically loaded when you run a TP program, you don't have to include it with a **USES** statement.

Summary

In this chapter you learned how to define and use units. We covered the three main components of a unit: the **INTERFACE**, **IMPLEMENTATION**, and **INITIALIZATION** sections. You also learned how units are compiled and included in programs with the **USES** statement. The more you work with units, the more readily you'll see how they can help you create complex TP programs by organizing your code into separate packages.

Exercises

1. Create a unit that defines an array to hold 250 integers. Does the unit need an implementation section?

2. Explain the differences between a unit and a user-defined routine (such as a procedure).

3. Correct the following unit so that it will compile correctly. What changes need to be made so that the constants **MaxColumns** and **MaxRows** can be used by programs that access this unit?

```
UNIT TestSet;
INTERFACE
FUNCTION CheckRange(X1, Y1 : Integer);

IMPLEMENTATION
CONST
  MaxColumns = 80;
  MaxRows    = 25;

FUNCTION CheckRange(X1, Y1, X2, Y2 : Integer) : Boolean;
VAR
  BEGIN
    IF (X1 < 0) OR (Y1 < 0) OR
       (X2 > MaxColumns) OR (Y2 > MaxRows) THEN
      CheckRange := False;
    ELSE
      CheckRange := True;
END;

BEGIN
END.
```

Answers

1. Here is an array that will hold 250 integers:

```
UNIT ArrayDef;
INTERFACE
VAR
  Numbers : ARRAY[1..250] OF Integer;

IMPLEMENTATION
END.
```

Notice that an **IMPLEMENTATION** section is required, although it contains no statements.

2. Units are different than routines (such as procedures) because units allow you to package variables, constants, data types, and user-defined routines in a separate file.

3. Here is the corrected version of the unit presented in step 3. To set up **MaxColumns** and **MaxRows** so that they can be used by programs that access this unit, they are now defined in the **INTERFACE** section of the unit.

```
UNIT TestSet;
INTERFACE
CONST
  MaxColumns = 80;
  MaxRows    = 25;
FUNCTION CheckRange(X1, Y1, X2, Y2 : Integer) : Boolean;

IMPLEMENTATION
FUNCTION CheckRange(X1, Y1, X2, Y2 : Integer) : Boolean;
  BEGIN
    IF (X1 < 0) OR (Y1 < 0) OR (X2 > MaxColumns) OR (Y2 > MaxRows) THEN
      CheckRange := False
    ELSE
      CheckRange := True;
  END;
END.
```

10

An Introduction
to File Input/Output

To increase the usefulness of the programs that you write, you'll need a way to store data permanently and to retrieve the data later. With TP, you can accomplish this by using disk files.

In this chapter, you'll learn how to work with TP's file system. The chapter starts by examining the types of files that TP supports. Next, we'll explore techniques for opening, closing, reading, and writing text files. In the second part of this chapter, you'll learn techniques for working with binary files—including typed and untyped files. As you'll discover, typed files can be defined by using standard data types, such as **Integer** and **Real**, and by using user-defined data types, such as records.

After you complete this chapter, you'll know how to:

- Open, close, read, and write files
- Handle file processing errors
- Use I/O redirection
- Process random access files
- Use the TP file processing procedures and functions

The File System

Because you've been writing TP files and using DOS, you should already be familiar with disk files to some degree. When you create a Pascal program, you must open a new file, type in the program statements in the TP editor, and save the file so that you can access it later. Your programs can even create and use files that contain program data.

For example, assume that you're writing a program to process information about the vendors that supply products and services for your company. Each time you add information about a new vendor, you'll want to save the data so that it can be used later. If the data is only stored in a program structure, such as an array or a record, it would be lost after the program terminates.

Our exploration of TP files starts by looking at how the file I/O system is organized. Two types of files are available to you: *text* and *binary*. The difference between these file types lies in the way data is stored. In text files, data is represented as a set of ASCII characters. As Figure 10.1 shows, each line is terminated with a carriage return (end-of-line marker). With this format, lines can vary in length. To display a text file, you can use the DOS **TYPE** command. Binary files, however, store data in a packed binary representation, much in the way a TP program stores its data. For example, assume that you need to store the following numbers in a file:

103, 111, 87

Figure 10.1 This figure illustrates the format of a text file.

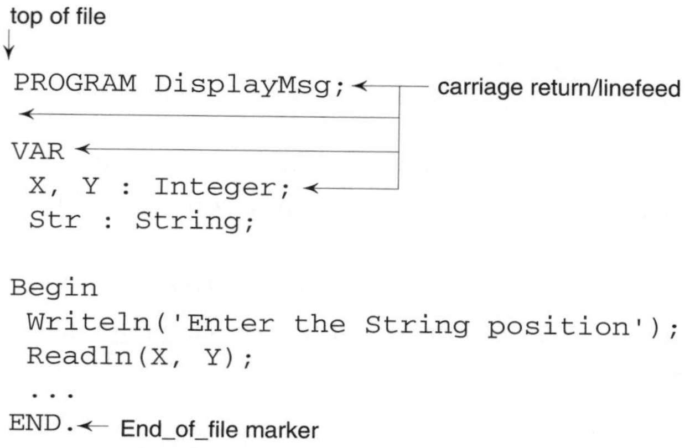

```
top of file
↓
PROGRAM DisplayMsg;  ←——————  carriage return/linefeed
←—————————————————————
VAR ←————————————————
 X, Y : Integer; ←——————
 Str : String;

Begin
 Writeln('Enter the String position');
 Readln(X, Y);
 . . .
END.←— End_of_file marker
```

In a binary file, the numbers would be stored exactly as they are represented— as three integers. In a text file, these numbers would be stored as ASCII characters. For example:

'1''0''3' '1''1''1' '8''7

This means that 8 bytes are used to store the three numbers.

Binary files actually come in two "flavors": *typed* and *untyped*. A typed file stores only data of a specified data type. To create a typed file, you can use any of the standard data types, such as **Integer**, **Boolean**, **Real**, or any user-defined data type that can be represented as a record. Some examples are:

```
FILE OF Integer;
FILE OF Real;
File OF Employees;
```

An untyped file provides more flexibility than a typed file because it stores data in sequences of untyped bytes. As you'll see later, files are typically accessed as untyped files to perform major file manipulation operations, such as file copying. Although an untyped file is processed as a sequence of unformatted data, you can open any file as untyped, including a text file.

File Processing Routines

Before examining how different types of files are created and used, you'll need to know about the built-in file processing routines that TP makes available.

Table 10.1 lists all the procedures and functions that are provided for processing text and binary files. Because these routines are provided with the standard TP library, you don't have to include units to use any of these procedures or functions. Notice in Table 10.1 that the routines are labeled to help you determine the type or types of files that each routine supports.

1. What are the differences between binary and text files?
2. True or False: Text files store data in a compressed format and cannot be displayed or viewed by an editor.
3. What is the format of .PAS files? How are .EXE files stored?
4. How many bytes are needed to store the following numbers in a text file and in a binary file? (Assume that the numbers are stored as reals in the binary file.)

   21.36   38.56432   29.001234

1. Binary files are stored in a compressed format, while text files are stored as ASCII characters.
2. False
3. .PAS files are stored as text files, while .EXE files are stored as binary files.
4. You need 22 bytes to store the numbers in a text file, and 18 bytes to store the numbers in a binary file.

Using Text Files

Because a text file stores data as sequences of ASCII characters, it is very easy to manipulate. However, you do need to be aware of two major limitations. First, text files can store only *printable* and *whitespace* characters. Of course, printable characters are those that can be output on a screen or printer. Whitespace characters include the carriage return, linefeed, tab, and so on. A rule of thumb: *Any character that can be displayed on the screen with the* **Write** *procedure can be written to a text file*.

The second major limitation of text files: They cannot be randomly accessed. To read data in a text file, you must always start at the beginning of the file. In writing data, you can start either at the beginning or the end of the file.

Table 10.1   File processing routines.

Routine	File Type Supported	Description
Append	Text	Opens a text file for appending text
Assign	Both	Assigns a filename to a file buffer
BlockRead	Binary	Reads a block of data from a file
BlockWrite	Binary	Writes a block of data to a file

Working with File Variables

To access a text or binary file, you must declare a file variable. For now, let's focus on text file variables. Later, we'll explore how binary file variables are declared.

A text file variable is declared in the **VAR** section of a program, with the following general format:

```
VAR
   <variable-name> : Text;
```

Here, **Text** is a keyword that tells the compiler that the variable will be used to access a text file. Now, you might be wondering how a file variable can be assigned to the name of a text file so that the file can be accessed. To do this, you'll need to use the **Assign** procedure:

```
PROCEDURE Assign(FileVar : <filetype>; FileName : String);
```

The first argument consists of the file variable, while the second argument specifies the DOS filename of the file you wish to access. For example, the following code segment shows how a file named SALES.DAT is assigned to the variable **TxtFile**:

```
VAR
   TxtFile : Text; { Declares a file variable }

BEGIN
   Assign(TxtFile,'Sales.dat'); {Assigns filename to variable}
```

After these two tasks have been completed, you can use the file processing procedures and functions to open, read, and write the file.

Keep in mind that the **FileName** argument can be specified using any valid DOS file-naming format. Some examples are:

```
'A:Scores.txt'       { Uses the file in drive A }
'C:\TP\samples.pas'  { Uses drive C and directory \TP }
'New.doc'            { Uses current drive and directory }
```

Note

The **Assign** procedure does not actually open a file; it creates a *File Information Block* so that the file can then be opened and accessed. If you try to open a file before issuing the **Assign** procedure, you'll get a run-time error.

Opening and Closing Files

Now that you've seen how a file variable is initialized, you are ready to learn how to open and close files. For opening a file, TP provides the following three procedures:

```
PROCEDURE  Rewrite(FileVar : <filetype>);
PROCEDURE  Reset(FileVar : <filetype>);
PROCEDURE  Append(FileVar : <filetype>);
```

The first procedure, **Rewrite**, is used to open a new file. For example, the statement

```
Rewrite(TxtFile);
```

opens the file assigned to the variable **TxtFile** as a new DOS file. When you use **Rewrite** to open a file, try to avoid opening a file that already exists. Because **Rewrite** clears the contents of an existing file, you could easily lose valuable data. For example, assume that you have a file named SCORES.DAT in the current directory. After you issue the commands

```
Assign(TxtFile,'Scores.dat');
Rewrite(TxtFile);
```

the data stored in SCORES.DAT will be erased.

Note

> Before opening a file, you can test to see if the file exists by using the **FindFirst** procedure provided with the **Dos** unit.

The other two file-opening procedures allow you to open files that already exist. The **Reset** procedure opens a file and sets the file pointer at the beginning of the file. **Append**, however, sets the file pointer at the end of the file so that you can add data. (A pointer is simply a memory address that your program uses to locate the starting point for data to be processed.)

After a file has been opened, you can use procedures such as **Read** and **Write** to, well, read and write data. When you're done using a file, you should remember to close the file to ensure that all the data written to the file is actually transferred to disk. This task is accomplished using the following procedure:

```
PROCEDURE  Close(FileVar : <filetype>);
```

Although TP will automatically close all open text files when a program terminates, you shouldn't rely on TP to close your files.

Now, let's put the techniques we've explored to work by writing a program that creates a new text file. The program first asks you to enter the name of a new text file, then allows you to type in text at the keyboard. The text is then written to the file. To close the file and quit the program, press the Esc key. The complete program is:

```
PROGRAM WriteData;
{ Writes characters to a text file }
USES
  Crt;
CONST
  EscKey = #27;
  ValidKeys : SET OF Char = ['0'..'9','A'..'z', #13, #32];
VAR
  TxtFile : Text;
  FName   : String;
  Ch      : Char;

BEGIN
  Writeln('Enter a filename');
  Readln(FName);
  Assign(TxtFile,FName); { Initializes the file variable }
  Rewrite(TxtFile);      { Opens a new text file }
  Writeln('Enter data to write to the file.');
  Writeln('Press the Esc key when you are done.');
  Ch := ReadKey;
  WHILE Ch <> EscKey DO BEGIN
  { Outputs only alphanumeric characters }
    IF Ch IN ValidKeys THEN BEGIN
      IF Ch = #13 THEN BEGIN
        Writeln(Ch);             { Displays the character }
        Writeln(TxtFile,Ch); { Writes a character to the file }
      END
      ELSE BEGIN
        Write(Ch);
        Write(TxtFile,Ch);
      END;
    END;
    Ch := ReadKey;
  END;
  Close(TxtFile); { Closes the text file }
END.
```

 1. What is wrong with the following program segment?

```
PROGRAM File1
VAR
  TxtFile : Text;
```

```
BEGIN
  Writeln('Enter a filename');
  Readln(FName);
  Rewrite(TxtFile);
  Assign(TxtFile,FName);
  Rewrite(TxtFile);
  ...
END;
```

2. What three steps are required to open a new text file?
3. Which procedure should be used to open an existing file to read?

1. The file is accessed before the **Assign** procedure is called.
2. You must declare a file variable of type **Text**, initialize the file variable with the **Assign** procedure, and then open the file with the **Rewrite** procedure.
3. **Reset**

Reading and Writing Data

In our first program, notice that the **Write** and **Writeln** procedures were used to write data to the text file. As with screen output, **Write** outputs a single character and **Writeln** outputs a line of text. Thus, how do the **Write** and **Writeln** procedures know when data should be written to the screen rather than to a file? Well, recall that the **Write** statement in our sample program was formatted as:

```
Write(TxtFile, Ch);
```

Here, the first argument specifies the file variable, while the second argument contains the data to be written to the file. When you omit the first argument, as in

```
Write(Ch);
```

the data is written directly to the screen.

In reading data, the **Read** and **Readln** procedures follow the same format as **Write** and **Writeln**. That is, the statement

```
Read(TxtFile, Ch);
```

reads a character from the file assigned to the variable **TxtFile**. When you use the **Readln** procedure, TP reads an entire line of text. Because a text file is stored as a sequence of characters, the data type of the variable used with **Read** or **Readln** line must be of type **Char** or **String**. If you have a file that contains numeric data, you must first read the data as a string, then convert the string to a number. (You will be able to try this task out first-hand in Exercise 1 at the end of the chapter.)

In the following program, **Read** and **Write** are used to show how a file can be copied one character at a time:

```
PROGRAM CopyFile;
{ Sample program to copy a file }
VAR
  TxtFile1,TxtFile2 : Text;
  FName             : String;
  Ch                : Char;

BEGIN
  Writeln('Enter the filename of the file to copy');
  Readln(FName);
  Assign(TxtFile1, FName); { Initialize the file variable }
  Reset(TxtFile1);         { Open the text file to copy }
  Writeln('Enter the filename of the file to create');
  Readln(FName);
  Assign(TxtFile2, FName);
  Rewrite(TxtFile2); { Open the new text file }
  REPEAT
    Read(TxtFile1, Ch);
    Write(TxtFile2, Ch);
  UNTIL Eof(TxtFile1);
  Close(TxtFile1); { Close the text file }
  Close(TxtFile2); { Close the text file }
END.
```

Notice that the **Rewrite** procedure is used to initialize the new file and **Reset** is used to initialize the existing file. The **REPEAT-UNTIL** loop performs the work of copying the file. The trick here is to keep copying data until the program arrives at the end of the file. The following is a statement that identifies this end-of-file condition:

```
UNTIL Eof(TxtFile1);
```

Eof tests the input file and returns true when the file pointer reaches the end of the file referenced by the variable **TxtFile**. Unfortunately, the read/write loop, the way it is written, contains a major problem. Consider what will happen if the input text file is empty. The **REPEAT-UNTIL** loop will still execute one time, which means the **Read** procedure will attempt to read data from an empty file and no data will be returned.

To correct this problem, the **REPEAT-UNTIL** loop can be written as a **WHILE** loop:

```
WHILE NOT Eof(TxtFile1) DO BEGIN
  Read(TxtFile1, Ch);
  Write(TxtFile2, Ch);
END;
```

In this case, the end-of-file marker is tested before the loop starts. With this **WHILE** loop in place, we provide a more reliable statement for reading a file.

In addition to the **Eof** function, TP provides the **Eoln** function so that you can test for the end-of-line marker. This function returns a true condition if the file pointer is at the end of a line; otherwise, a false condition is returned. The following is a loop that shows how **Eoln** is used to read a line of digits that, in turn, are stored as a character string:

```
WHILE NOT Eoln(TxtFile1) DO BEGIN
  I := I + 1;
  Read(TxtFile1, Ch);
  If Ch >= '0' AND Ch <= '9' THEN
    Str[I] := Ch;
  Write(TxtFile2, Ch);
END;
```

Handling File Processing Errors

The file processing programs presented up to this point don't perform any error-checking operations. Needless to say, the absence of error-checking routines can lead to some dangerous problems. For example, a program might try to open a file for reading that doesn't exist or might try to close a file that hasn't been opened. If you don't check for these types of errors, your program could crash unexpectedly and leave the user wondering what went wrong.

When a critical file operation is performed, such as opening a file, you'll find yourself in a much safer position if you can test the operation and check to ensure that your program can handle any errors that might occur. Fortunately, TP provides a special function called **IOResult**, which returns the status of a file operation. The format for this function is:

```
FUNCTION IOResult : Integer;
```

With TP, an internal variable is always set to an error code after each I/O operation is performed. The **IOResult** function allows your program to examine this error code. However, in using this function, you'll need to include the **$I** compiler directive to disable error-checking for a critical I/O operation. For example:

```
{$I-} Reset(TxtFile1); {$I+}
```

This directive tells the compiler to leave out the error-checking code for the procedure. If the error-checking code is not disabled, TP will generate a run-time error and automatically terminate the program. (The **$I–** turns off the error-checking function, while **$I+** turns error-checking back on.) After the procedure executes, you can then call **IOResult** to see if an error has occurred. If the function returns a value other than 0, you'll know that something went wrong.

To show how **IOResult** works, let's rewrite the file copying program presented in the previous section.

```
PROGRAM CopyFile2;
{ Sample program to copy a file with error checking }
VAR
  TxtFile1, TxtFile2 : Text;
  FName              : String;
  Ch                 : Char;

BEGIN
  Writeln('Enter the filename of the file to copy');
  Readln(FName);
  Assign(TxtFile1, FName); { Initializes the file variable }
  {$I-} Reset(TxtFile1); {$I+} { Opens the text file to be copied }
  IF IOResult <> 0 THEN BEGIN
    Writeln('The file ', FName, ' cannot be opened');
    Exit;
  END;
  Writeln('Enter the filename of the file to create');
  Readln(FName);
  Assign(TxtFile2, FName);
  Rewrite(TxtFile2); { Opens the new text file }
  WHILE NOT Eof(TxtFile1) DO BEGIN
    Read(TxtFile1, Ch);
    Write(TxtFile2, Ch);
  END;
  Close(TxtFile1); { Closes the text file }
  Close(TxtFile2); { Closes the text file }
END.
```

Notice that the following **IF** statement is used to catch an error:

```
IF IOResult <> 0 THEN BEGIN
  Writeln('The file ', FName, ' cannot be opened');
  Exit;
END;
```

If the input file cannot be opened, **IOResult** returns a value other than 0 and our message will be printed to warn the user.

1. True or False: The **Eof** function returns the status of the end-of-line file marker.
2. What is the difference between the **Eof** and **Eoln** functions?
3. What run-time error code does TP display if you attempt to use the **Reset** procedure to access a file that doesn't exist?
4. What do the **$I–** and **$I+** directives do?

1. True
2. The **Eof** function returns the end-of-file status, while **Eoln** returns the end-of-line status.
3. Run-time error (2)
4. The **$I–** directive disables code generation for run-time file I/O errors, while **$I+** enables the error-checking.

Searching Text Files

Using the procedures and functions introduced thus far, we've written a program that searches a text file for a specified string. To implement the searching feature, we've used the **Pos** string function. Recall that this function takes two arguments:

```
FUNCTION Pos(SearchStr, SourceStr : String) : Integer;
```

The first argument is matched with the source string, and the function returns the index position of the search string in the source string. To search a file, we'll read one line at a time and compare the line read with a search string. If a match is found, the program displays the line from the file and the index position of the match. The complete program is:

```
PROGRAM SearchFile;
{ Searches lines in a file for a text phrase }
VAR
  TxtFile : Text;
  FName, SearchStr, CurrentLine : String;
  MatchPos, LCount              : Integer;

BEGIN
  Writeln('Enter the filename of the file to search');
  Readln(FName);
  Assign(TxtFile,FName); { Initializes the file variable }
  {$I-} Reset(TxtFile); {$I+} { Opens the text file to search }
  IF IOResult <> 0 THEN BEGIN
    Writeln('The file ', FName, ' cannot be opened');
    Exit;
  END;
```

```
Writeln('Enter the search text');
Readln(SearchStr);
LCount := 0;
Writeln;
WHILE NOT Eof(TxtFile) DO BEGIN
  Readln(TxtFile, CurrentLine);
  LCount := LCount + 1;
  MatchPos := Pos(SearchStr, CurrentLine);
  IF MatchPos <> 0 THEN BEGIN
    Writeln(CurrentLine);
    Writeln('Match found in line ', LCount, ' at position ', MatchPos);
  END;
END;
Close(TxtFile); { Closes the text file }
END.
```

Figure 10.2 shows the matching lines that will be displayed if we search the file that contains the SEARCHFILE program for the string *BEGIN*.

Using Binary Files

As discussed in the introduction, binary files are typically used to store data that is represented as a standard Pascal data type. This means that you can process files of integers, reals, booleans, enumerated types, and records. Let's start with a simple example. The following program creates a file of integers:

Figure 10.2   This is the output of SEARCHFILE after searching for the string *BEGIN*.

```
Enter the filename of the file to search
file4.pas
Enter the search text
BEGIN

BEGIN
Match found in line 9 at position 1
  IF IOResult <> 0 THEN BEGIN
Match found in line 14 at position 25
  WHILE NOT EOF(TxtFile) DO BEGIN
Match found in line 22 at position 29
    IF MatchPos <> 0 THEN BEGIN
Match found in line 26 at position 27

Elapsed time = 00:00:07.91 Program returned(0). Press any key
```

```
PROGRAM WriteNums;
{ Writes integers to a binary file }
TYPE
  NumList = ARRAY[1..15] OF Integer;
CONST
  Numbers : NumList = (1,2,3,4,5,6,7,8,9,10,11,12,13,14,15);
VAR
  IntFile : FILE OF Integer;
  FName   : String;
  I,N     : Integer;

BEGIN
  Writeln('Enter a filename');
  Readln(FName);
  Assign(IntFile,FName); { Initializes the file variable }
  Rewrite(IntFile);      { Opens a new binary file }
  FOR I := 1 TO 15 DO
    Write(IntFile, Numbers[I]);
  Writeln('Numbers written to the file');
  Close(IntFile);
  Reset(IntFile);
  Writeln('The data stored in the file is:');
  FOR I := 1 TO 15 DO BEGIN
    Read(IntFile, N); { Reads number from file }
    Write(N);         { Writes number to screen }
  END;
  Close(IntFile);
END.
```

This program opens a new binary file, writes a set of numbers to the file, closes the file, opens the file for reading, and reads the numbers that were written. For the most part, the file is accessed as though it were a text file; that is, **Assign** is used to initialize the file variable, **Rewrite** is used to create the file, the **Write** and **Read** procedures are called to write and read data, and **Close** is used to close and save the file. Thus, how are binary files processed differently from text files?

The difference lies in the way the file variable is declared. In the WRITENUMS program, note that the variable, **IntFile**, is declared as:

```
VAR
  IntFile : FILE OF Integer;
```

Here, the keywords **FILE OF** indicate that the variable will be used to access a file. The **Integer** keyword indicates that the data stored in the file is of type **Integer**. The following statements illustrate how other types of binary file variables can be declared:

```
BolFile  : FILE OF Boolean;
SIntFile : FILE OF ShortInt;
RlFile   : FILE OF Real;
```

A binary file can also be created with a user-defined type, such as:

```
TYPE
   Computers = (ibm_pc, apple_mac, sun_386, micro_express, tandy, ast);
VAR
   CompFile : FILE OF Computers;
```

In this case, the file variable **CompFile** allows us to create and use a file that contains data from the enumerated type **Computers**.

Note A typed file can store only data components that have the same type as the file variable. For example, you can't write a real value to a file of integers. To mix data types in a binary file, you must create a file of records, which we'll go over in the next section.

1. Write a variable declaration statement to access a file of an array of integers. The array should hold 100 elements.
2. True or False: The format of a typed binary file is determined by the type of data that the file stores.
3. True or False: The **Assign** procedure is used to initialize a binary file variable.

1. The following statement accesses a file of an array of 100 integers:

```
TYPE
   Nums = ARRAY[1..100] OF Integer;
VAR
   NumFile : Nums;
```

2. True
3. True

Working with Record-Oriented Files

You can observe the real power of typed binary files when you use files of records. Recall that records allow us to combine different data elements in one package. For example, in Chapter 7 we created this record to hold the information for an electronic index card system:

```
TYPE
  Card = RECORD
    Title : STRING[20];
    Entry : ARRAY [1..5] OF STRING[Max_row];
  END;
```

We can now use this record to declare a file variable, for example:

```
VAR
  FILE OF Card;
```

Data can then be read or written from and to the file by using a record variable. The advantage of this method is that the data read and write operations are greatly simplified. Rather than reading or writing each component, only one file access is required to read a record.

To show how record-oriented files are processed, let's modify the card index program presented in Chapter 7 so that records can be saved and retrieved from files. We'll add a number of procedures, including **ViewRecords**, **AddRecords**, **SaveRecords**, and **SelectOpt**, to incorporate the file processing capabilities. Here's the complete program. Test it on your computer:

```
PROGRAM CardFile;
USES
  Crt;
CONST
  Num_of_cards = 100; { Maximum number of cards }
  Max_row = 70;
TYPE
  Card = RECORD
    Title : STRING[20];
    Entry : ARRAY [1..5] OF STRING[Max_row];
  END;
  FileStat = (reading, writing, closed);
VAR
  Deck : ARRAY [1..Num_of_cards] OF Card;
  Crd_num, I : Integer;
  CrdFile    : FILE OF Card;
  FName      : String;
  FStat      : FileStat;

PROCEDURE ViewRecords;
BEGIN
  Writeln('Enter the name of the card file to view');
  Readln(FName);
  IF FStat <> closed THEN Close(CrdFile);
  Assign(CrdFile, FName);
  Reset(CrdFile);
```

```
      Writeln('The file ', FName, ' has been opened for viewing');
      FStat := reading;
      Crd_num := 0;
      REPEAT
        Crd_num := Crd_num + 1;
        IF Crd_num <= Num_of_cards THEN BEGIN
          Read(CrdFile, Deck[Crd_num]); { Reads record from file }
          ClrScr;
          GotoXY(35, 2);
          Write('Card Number ', Crd_num : 2);
          GotoXY(21, 5);
          Write('TITLE: ');
          WITH Deck[Crd_num] DO BEGIN
            Writeln(Title);
            GotoXY(1, 8);
            Write('Line 1: ');
            Writeln(Entry[1]);
            GotoXY(1, 9);
            Write('Line 2: ');
            Writeln(Entry[2]);
            GotoXY(1, 10);
            Write('Line 3: ');
            Writeln(Entry[3]);
            GotoXY(1, 11);
            Write('Line 4: ');
            Writeln(Entry[4]);
            GotoXY(1, 12);
            Write('Line 5: ');
            Writeln(Entry[5]);
          END;
          GotoXY(20, 20);
          Writeln('Press the Enter key to continue');
          Readln;
        END;
      UNTIL Eof(CrdFile);
    END;

PROCEDURE AddRecords;
Var
  Cd : Integer;

BEGIN
  REPEAT
    Writeln('Enter the number of cards to add');
    Readln(Crd_num);
  UNTIL (Crd_num > 0) AND (Crd_num < 100);
  FOR Cd := 1 TO Crd_num DO BEGIN
    ClrScr;
    GotoXY(35, 2);
```

```pascal
      Write('Card Number ', Cd : 2 );
      GotoXY(21, 5);
      Write('TITLE: ');
      Readln(Deck[Cd].Title );
      GotoXY(1, 8);
      Write('Line 1: ');
      Readln(Deck[Cd].Entry[1]);
      GotoXY(1, 9);
      Write('Line 2: ');
      Readln(Deck[Cd].Entry[2]);
      GotoXY(1, 10);
      Write('Line 3: ');
      Readln(Deck[Cd].Entry[3]);
      GotoXY(1, 11);
      Write('Line 4: ');
      Readln(Deck[Cd].Entry[4]);
      GotoXY(1, 12);
      Write('Line 5: ');
      Readln(Deck[Cd].Entry[5]);
   END;
END;

PROCEDURE  SaveRecords;
VAR
  Cd : Integer;

BEGIN
  IF FStat = writing THEN BEGIN
    FOR Cd := 1 TO Crd_num DO
      Write(CrdFile, Deck[Cd]);
      Writeln(Crd_num, ' records written to the file');
      Close(CrdFile);
      FStat := closed;
    END
  ELSE
    Writeln('You must first open a new card record file');
END;

FUNCTION SelectOpt : Integer;
VAR
  Opt : Integer;

BEGIN
  REPEAT
    ClrScr;
    Writeln('The card file program');
    Writeln;
    Writeln('Enter an option');
    Writeln;
    Writeln('1. Open a new card file');
```

```
      Writeln('2. View records in a card file');
      Writeln('3. Add records');
      Writeln('4. Save records to a card file');
      Writeln('5. Quit the program');
      Readln(Opt);
    UNTIL (Opt >= 1) AND (Opt <=5); { Ensures response is ok }
    SelectOpt := Opt;
  END;


BEGIN
   TextBackground(Blue);
   TextColor(LightGray);
   Crd_num := 0;      { No cards have been added }
   FStat := closed;   { A file has not been opened }
   REPEAT
     I := SelectOpt; { Gets a menu option }
     CASE I OF
       1: BEGIN
         IF FStat <> closed THEN
         Close(CrdFile); { Closes any open card file }
         Writeln('Enter the name of a new card file');
          Readln(FName);
         Assign(CrdFile, FName);
         Rewrite(CrdFile);
         Writeln('The file ', FName, ' has been opened');
          FStat := writing;
       END;
       2: ViewRecords;
       3: AddRecords;
       4: SaveRecords;
     END;
   UNTIL I = 5;
END.
```

When the program starts, the **SelectOpt** procedure is called to display the menu shown in Figure 10.3 and to ask the user to select an option. The first option allows a new file to be created to store the card data that is entered. The second option allows the user to view the records. The third option is provided so that card data can be added. Each time data is added, it is stored in memory as a record assigned to the **Deck** array. To write the array of records to a disk file, the user simply selects the fourth option.

Working with Random Access Files

In our record-oriented card file program, we always read the records by starting at the beginning of the file and working our way to the end of the file. This task was accomplished by using the following loop in the **ViewRecords** procedure:

Figure 10.3   The SelectOpt procedure displays this menu.

```
The card file program

Enter an option

1. Open a new card file
2. View records in a card file
3. Add records
4. Save records to a card file
5. Quit the program
```

```
REPEAT
  Crd_num := Crd_num + 1;
  IF Crd_num <= Num_of_cards THEN BEGIN
    Read(CrdFile, Deck[Crd_num]); { Reads record from file }
  ...
UNTIL Eof(CrdFile);
```

As shown, the loop continues to execute until the end of the file is encountered. This approach, however, has one major drawback: The program must read the entire file even if we only want to view a single record. Fortunately, TP provides a way to get around this problem. We can use the **Seek** procedure to move the position of the file pointer so that a selected record can be read. The format for this procedure is:

```
PROCEDURE Seek(FileVar : <filetype>; Position : LongInt);
```

By moving the file pointer, we can take control of the starting location where data is read and written from the file. For this reason, files processed in this manner are called *random access* files. The **Position** argument in **Seek** operates like an array index. For example, the statement

```
Seek(CrdFile, 6);
Read(CrdFile, Deck[Crd_num]);
```

will take us to the seventh record in the file. (The first record in a file is accessed as record 0.)

Let's modify our **ViewRecords** procedure to support random access of records. The new version is:

```
PROCEDURE ViewRecords;
VAR
  Rec_no : LongInt;
```

```
BEGIN
  Writeln('Enter the name of the card file to view');
  Readln(FName);
  Writeln('Enter the record number to view (0 to view all)');
  Readln(Rec_no);
  IF FStat <> closed THEN Close(CrdFile);
  Assign(CrdFile, FName);
  Reset(CrdFile);
  Writeln('The file ', FName, ' has been opened for viewing');
  FStat := reading;
  Crd_num := 0;
  IF Rec_no <> 0 THEN Seek(CrdFile, Rec_no-1);
    { Moves file pointer }
  REPEAT
    IF Rec_no = 0 THEN
      Crd_num := Crd_num + 1
    ELSE Crd_num := Rec_no;
    IF Crd_num <= Num_of_cards THEN BEGIN
      Read(CrdFile, Deck[Crd_num]); { Reads record from file }
      ClrScr;
      GotoXY(35, 2);
      Write('Card Number ', Crd_num : 2);
      GotoXY(21, 5);
      Write('TITLE: ');
      WITH Deck[Crd_num] DO BEGIN
        Writeln(Title);
        GotoXY(1, 8);
        Write('Line 1: ');
        Writeln(Entry[1]);
        GotoXY(1, 9);
        Write('Line 2: ');
        Writeln(Entry[2]);
        GotoXY(1, 10);
        Write('Line 3: ');
        Writeln(Entry[3]);
        GotoXY(1, 11);
        Write('Line 4: ');
        Writeln(Entry[4]);
        GotoXY(1, 12);
        Write('Line 5: ');
        Writeln(Entry[5]);
      END;
      GotoXY(20, 20);
      Writeln('Press the Enter key to continue');
      Readln;
    END;
  UNTIL (Eof(CrdFile)) OR (Rec_no <> 0);
END;
```

When the procedure executes, the following message is displayed:

```
Enter the record number to view (0 to view all)
```

If you enter a value other than 0, **Seek** is called to move the file pointer. Notice that we decrement the **Rec_no** variable by one to account for the fact that the first component of a random access file is referenced as element 0:

```
Seek(CrdFile, Rec_no-1);
```

When a **Read** statement is later issued, the record stored at the new file position is read, not the record at the beginning of the file.

Keep in mind that data can also be written to random access files. For example, the following statements write a new record at the fourth record position in the file:

```
Seek(CrdFile, 3);
Write(CrdFile, Deck[Crd_num]);
```

What happens to the record already stored at this location? It would be overwritten. Unfortunately, no direct method is available for inserting a record in a file without overwriting other records—unless the new record is added to the end of the file. If you then want to change the order of the file, you have to read the data into an array, reorder the records, and write the data back to the file.

To help you read and write random access files, TP provides the **FilePos** function. This routine returns the offset position of the current file pointer. For example,

```
Seek(CrdFile, 2);
P := FilePos(CrdFile);
```

assigns the value 2 to the variable **P**. In this case, **P** must be declared as a **LongInt**.

Note

In the example of random access file handling, we used a file of type records. However, TP allows you to use random access procedures, such as **Seek** and **FilePos,** with any typed binary file. For example, if you are using a file of integers and you issue the statements

```
Seek(IntFile, 4);
Read(Number);
```

you'll be able to read the fifth number in the file.

Working with Untyped Files

Earlier in this chapter, you learned that binary files can be typed and untyped. You have now seen how typed files are created and used. Thus, we should briefly explore untyped files at this point. An untyped file is treated as an unformatted sequence of bytes. TP doesn't care about the type of data stored in a file that is opened as an untyped file. In fact, you can even open a text file as an untyped file. But keep in mind that once a file has been opened as an untyped file, you can access only the data as unformatted bytes.

How is an untyped file opened? You must declare a variable using the following format

```
VAR
  BnFile1 : FILE;
```

and then use **Assign** and **Reset**, as shown:

```
Assign(BnFile1, 'New.dat');
Reset(BnFile1, 1);
```

Notice that **Reset** uses an additional argument, which specifies the number of bytes that will be accessed when a read or write operation is performed. By default, TP will access a file in 128 byte increments, which are called *file blocks*. By including the second argument with the **Reset** statement, you can override the default file-block size. Each time a file is read or written, a file block of data is moved to or from the file by using an internal file buffer, as Figure 10.4 illustrates.

Note

The file block size used to process an untyped binary file should be chosen so that the file size is an exact multiple of the file-block size. For example, if you have a file size of 2,560 bytes, a block size of 128 would be appropriate because 2,560 is a multiple of 128.

Figure 10.4 TP accesses a untyped binary file using the process shown here.

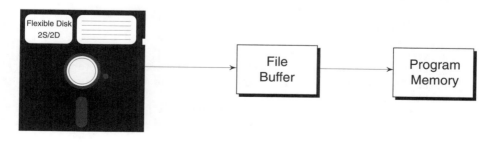

Because untyped files are processed as chunks of unformatted data, the standard **Read** and **Write** procedures can't be used for reading and writing data. However, two of TP's file block processing routines work with untyped files:

```
PROCEDURE BlockRead(FileVar : FILE; VAR Buffer; Count : Word;
                    [BytesIn : Word;]);
PROCEDURE BlockWrite(FileVar : FILE; VAR Buffer; Count : Word;
                     [BytesOut : Word;]);
```

The first procedure, **BlockRead**, is used to read or write a number of bytes from or to a file. The argument **Count** specifies the number of file blocks to read or write; then the data is stored or written to the argument **Buffer**. The fourth argument, which is optional, returns the actual number of blocks read or written. Keep in mind that the actual number of bytes read or written is calculated using the following formula:

```
File block size * Number of blocks
```

A simple program that shows how two untyped binary files can be merged is:

```
PROGRAM MergeFiles;
{ Merges two untyped binary files }
VAR
  BnFile1, BnFile2 : File;
  FName            : String;
  Ch               : Char;
  IOBuf            : ARRAY[0..127] OF Byte;
  FSize            : LongInt;
  ByteCnt          : Word;

BEGIN
  Writeln('Enter the filename of the first file');
  Readln(FName);
  Assign(BnFile1, FName); { Initializes file variable }
  Reset(BnFile1, 1);      { Opens source file }
  Writeln('Enter the filename of the second file');
  Readln(FName);
  Assign(BnFile2, FName);
  Reset(BnFile2, 1); { Opens target file }
  Seek(BnFile2, FileSize(BnFile2)); { Moves to end of the target file }
  FSize := FileSize(BnFile1); { Gets size of the source file }
  REPEAT
    BlockRead(BnFile1, IOBuf, 128, ByteCnt);
    BlockWrite(BnFile2, IOBUF, ByteCnt);
  UNTIL ByteCnt = 0;
```

```
    Writeln('The number of bytes added to the target file is ', FSize);
    FSize := FileSize(BnFile2);
    Writeln('The size of the target file is now ', FSize);
    Close(BnFile1); { Closes the source file }
    Close(BnFile2); { Closes the target file }
END.
```

First, notice that the block size supplied with the **Reset** procedures is 1. Each time the **BlockRead** procedure is executed, as shown

```
BlockRead(BnFile1, IOBuf, 128, ByteCnt);
```

the procedure will read 128 bytes or less. (Remember that the actual number of bytes read is returned in the fourth argument, **ByteCnt**.) This same argument is used with **BlockWrite** to add data to the end of the text file:

```
BlockWrite(BnFile2, IOBUF, ByteCnt);
```

The **REPEAT** loop keeps reading 128 bytes or less of data until the **ByteCnt** argument contains the value 0, which indicates that the program has reached the end of the file.

The file merging program also uses the **FileSize** function to calculate the number of bytes stored in the target file after the two files have been merged. This function returns a LongInt value that represents the file size in bytes.

Note

> The **FileSize** function can be used with both typed and untyped binary files. **FileSize** returns the number of records in a typed file or the number of blocks in an untyped file.

Summary

In this chapter you learned how to work with text and binary files. The chapter started with basic procedures for processing text files, including **Assign**, **Reset**, and **Rewrite**. Then, you saw how to use **Read** and **Write** to read and write file data. The second part of the chapter covered both typed and untyped binary files. As explained, typed files are used to store data elements represented as simple and user-defined Pascal data types, while untyped files are used to process data as unformatted bytes.

Exercises

1. Write a program to read a text file that contains a whole number on each line in the file. The program should read each line as a string and convert the string to an integer.

2. Write a program that appends one text file to another.

3. Use the **FindFirst** procedure to write a routine called CreateFile that checks to see whether a file already exists before it is opened.

Answers

1. The following program, READNUMS, reads a text file that contains a whole number on each line in the file. This program reads each line as a string and converts the string to an integer:

```
PROGRAM ReadNums;
{ Reads a text file of numbers }
CONST
   Digits : SET OF Char = ['0'..'9'];
VAR
   TxFile               : Text;
   FName, Line          : String;
   Ch                   : Char;
   LineNum, Code, I     : Integer;
   NumArray             : ARRAY[1..100] OF Integer;

BEGIN
   Writeln('Enter the filename');
   Readln(FName);
   Assign(TxFile,FName); { Initializes the file variable }
   Reset(TxFile);        { Opens the source file }
   LineNum := 0;
   WHILE NOT Eof(TxFile) DO BEGIN
     I := 0;
     WHILE NOT Eoln(TxFile) DO BEGIN
       Read(TxFile,Ch);
       IF Ch IN Digits THEN BEGIN
         I := I + 1;
         Line[I] := Ch;
       END;
     END;
     Line[0] := Chr(I);
     Read(TxFile,Ch);
     LineNum := LineNum + 1;
     VAL(Line, I,Code);
     NumArray[LineNum] := I;
   END;
   Writeln('The numbers read are:');
   FOR I := 1 TO LineNum - 1 DO
     Writeln(NumArray[I]);
   Close(TxFile); { Closes the source file }
END.
```

2. The following program, APPENDTFILES, appends one text file to another:

```
PROGRAM AppendTFiles;
{ Appends two text files }
VAR
  TxFile1, TxFile2 : Text;
  FName            : String;
  Ch               : Char;

BEGIN
  Writeln('Enter the filename of the first file');
  Readln(FName);
  Assign(TxFile1, FName); { Initializes file variable }
  Reset(TxFile1);          { Opens the source file }
  Writeln('Enter the filename of the second file');
  Readln(FName);
  Assign(TxFile2, FName);
  Append(TxFile2); { Opens the target file }
  While NOT Eof(TxFile1) DO BEGIN { Moves to end of target file }
    Read(TxFile1, Ch);
    Write(TxFile2, Ch);
  END;
  Close(TxFile1); { Closes the source file }
  Close(TxFile2); { Closes the target file }
END.
```

3. The following routine, CreateFile, uses the **FindFirst** procedure that checks to see whether a file already exists before it is opened.

```
FUNCTION CreateFile : Boolean;
VAR
  FName : String;
  FRec  : SearchRec;

BEGIN
  Writeln('Enter a filename');
  Readln(FName);
  FindFirst(FName, $3F, FRec);
  IF DosError <> 0 THEN
    CreateFile := True
  ELSE
    CreateFile := FALSE
END;
```

Dynamic Data Structures

I n previous chapters, you've learned how to define simple variables, arrays, and records. These variables are always defined at the beginning of the functions or procedures that use them. But there's a disadvantage to this approach. Sometimes you don't know how big the job is going to be. For this reason, you'll find that you have to guess high in specifying the size of data structures to ensure that you've got the "worst case" covered. If you happen to have a very large program and/or limited amounts of memory, static data structures may actually prohibit you from solving certain problems on a computer. Another source of waste can be large data structures required for intermediate processing of data. After this intermediate processing has been completed, the data structures are no longer needed. Unfortunately, they remain in memory, creating excess baggage.

To eliminate these storage-related problems, you need a way to create data structures using the free memory in your computer. Such a scheme would also allow variables to disappear back into free memory when they are no longer needed. In this way, the space can be recycled for later use. Perhaps, at this point, you're hanging on the edge of your seat, wondering whether this approach to memory use is available with TP. Relax, TP provides a concept known as *dynamic memory allocation*, one of the advanced features of the TP language. However, before we explore the details of this approach, such as where dynamic memory comes from and how to request it, you'll learn how to let TP know that your program is going to use these variables.

In this chapter, you'll learn how to use memory allocation techniques to create dynamic data structures. The chapter starts by showing you how to work with pointer variables. Then, we'll explore the **New**, **Dispose**, **GetMem**, and **FreeMem** procedures. In the second part of the chapter, you'll see how memory allocation techniques are applied to create dynamic arrays and records.

After completing this chapter, you'll know how to:

• Work with pointer variables

• Allocate and deallocate memory

• Use data structures including dynamic arrays, records, and linked lists

Introducing Pointers

In Chapter 8, we explored two methods for passing arguments to functions and procedures: pass by value and pass by reference. Remember that, when an argument is passed by reference, the *address* of the argument (variable) is passed to the lower-level routine so that the argument can be modified. You can use another technique for referencing a variable's address: *pointers*. To understand what pointers do, take a look at Figure 11.1, which shows the relationship between a variable's contents and its address. When you execute statements such as

```
I := 10;
```

or

```
J := I;
```

you are accessing the contents of a variable. The compiler automatically looks up the variable's address and accesses its contents. A pointer, however, allows you to determine the variable's address yourself. Later, you'll see why this can be useful for creating and processing dynamic data structures.

A pointer variable must be associated with a specific type of variable or record. To create a pointer, place the ∧ symbol in front of the variable's data type. Some examples of pointer declarations are:

```
TYPE
  WeeklyData = ARRAY[1..52] OF Real;
VAR
  IntgrPtr : ^Integer; { Declares pointer for an integer }
  RealPtr : ^Real;     { Declares pointer for a real }
  CharPtr : ^Char;     { Declares pointer for a character }
  StrngPtr : ^String;  { Declares pointer for a string }
  WklyDataPtr : ^WeeklyData; { Pointer to a real array }
```

As you can see, it's easy to declare pointer variables. In fact, they are declared using the same naming conventions as those for standard variables. It is a good idea to include a label in the name to identify the variable as a pointer rather than a standard variable. In previous examples, we appended *Ptr* to the end of the variables to provide a label.

Figure 11.1   You can use a pointer to access a variable.

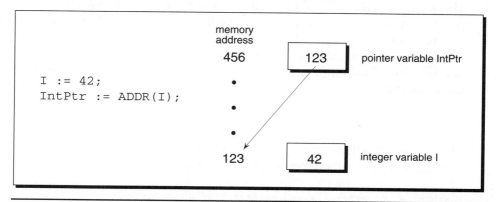

Although we've now defined a group of pointer variables, they don't point to anything in particular. An error would occur if we were to try to use one of them right now. For our definitions to be useful, we must first initialize each pointer so that it actually points to something.

Initializing Pointers

After a pointer has been created, you must set it to point to a particular variable. Pointer variables must be initialized before they are used. If you attempt to use an uninitialized pointer, you'll encounter unpredictable results, including corrupted data or a program crash. These two basic approaches are available to you for assigning an address to a pointer:

```
IntgrPtr := Addr(DaysInYear);
```

or

```
IntgrPtr := @DaysInYear;
```

In this case, we're assuming that **DaysInYear** is declared as an integer. Both statements perform the same operation—they assign the address of the integer variable **DaysInYear** to the pointer variable **IntgrPtr**. You can use whichever form you like; however, it is a good idea to be consistent. TP allows you to mix assignment styles, but the person who has to debug your program might wish you hadn't!

Imagine that you're ready to initialize a pointer, but you don't want to assign the pointer to any specific variable. Test the following statement:

```
IntgrPtr := NIL;
```

The keyword **NIL** is a value TP uses to represent an unassigned state for a pointer. Later in this chapter, you'll learn how to use this state to mark the end of a linked list.

Another way to initialize a pointer is to copy the value of one pointer into another. For example, the following statement assigns the value of **IntgrPtr** to **OtherIntPtr**:

```
OtherIntPtr := IntgrPtr;
```

This statement will compile properly only if both variables have been defined as pointers to the same type of variable. For example,

```
RealPtr := IntgrPtr; { Wrong pointer type }
NormalVar := IntgrPtr; { Not a pointer variable }
```

are both examples of illegal statements. The first statement attempts to assign the address of an integer to a real pointer. The second statement attempts to assign the address of an integer to some nonpointer variable.

In reality, your computer can't tell the difference between the address stored in an integer pointer variable and the address stored in a string pointer. Languages such as C allow you to mix pointers if you wish. Pascal, however, enforces strong data typing. For this reason, TP is more restrictive than other languages in the way it handles pointer variables. In particular, TP doesn't allow you to increment, decrement, or otherwise manipulate the contents of pointer variables. You can assign values to pointers, set pointers to **NIL**, or compare pointer values—but these are your only options. Here are some examples of valid and invalid pointer assignments:

```
VAR
  IntPtr, IntPtr2 : ^Integer;
  I : Integer;

BEGIN
  I := 10; { Okay }
  IntPtr := @I; { Okay }
  IntPtr := IntPtr + 10; { You can't do this }
  IntPtr := I;    { You can't do this }
  I := IntPtr;    { You can't do this }
  IntPtr2 := NIL { Okay }
  IF IntPtr = IntPtr2 THEN { Okay }
    Writeln('Pointers reference the same memory location');
```

1. True or False: Pointers can be used to reference only variables of built-in data types, such as **Integer**, **Real**, **Char**, and so on.
2. Given the following declarations

```
VAR
  StrPtr1, StrPtr2 : ^String;
  R1Ptr : ^Real;
  IntPtr, I : Integer;
  Num : Real;
```

which of the following assignments are valid?

   a. `IntPtr := @I;`
   b. `StrPtr1 := StrPtr2;`
   c. `R1Ptr := @Num;`
   d. `R1Ptr := Addr(Num);`

3. True or False: Pointers can be incremented.
4. Explain the function of the ^ in variable declarations.

1. False; pointers can also reference user-defined data types, such as records and arrays.
2. Only the assignment **IntPtr := @I;** is invalid.
3. False
4. The **^** tells TP that a variable will be used as a pointer.

Using Pointers

You've seen how to define pointers and how to assign valid values to them. Now let's examine how pointers are actually used. Consider the following statement:

```
RealPtr^ := 3.1415;
```

Here, the constant is assigned to the *location* whose address is held by **RealPtr**. You can also retrieve the contents of a location referenced by a pointer. To do so, you use a statement such as:

```
ColorSetting := GreenLuminosityPtr^;
```

The contents of the location pointed to by **GreenLuminosityPtr** will be transferred to a variable named **ColorSetting**, as shown in Figure 11.2. If you feel ambitious, you can transfer the contents of one pointer-referenced location to another pointer-referenced location by using such statements as:

```
DestinationPtr^ := SourcePtr^;
ModifiedDataPtr^ := InputDataPtr^ + 6.25;
FractPart := Frac(RealNumberPtr^);
```

Figure 11.2 TP allows you to retrieve the contents of a location referenced by a pointer.

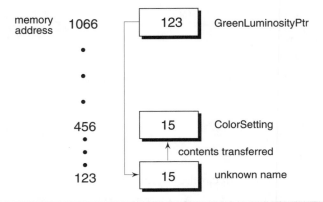

In the first statement, the contents of the location pointed to by **SourcePtr** will be assigned to the location pointed to by **DestinationPtr**. In the second example, the contents of the location pointed at by **InputDataPtr** will be retrieved and the constant 6.25 will be added to that value. The result of this computation will then be stored at the location pointed to by **ModifiedDataPtr**. The third statement calls the built-in function **Frac** to obtain the fractional part (the numbers to the right of the decimal point) of a real number pointed to by **RealNumberPtr**.

Note

> If you're using a pointer variable to reference another variable, such as
>
> ```
> IntPtr := @I;
> ```
>
> the notation **IntPtr^** simply accesses the value of **I**. As an example, these statements produce the same results:
>
> ```
> J := I;
> J := IntPtr^;
> ```

Pointers can be used wherever standard variables are allowed. One other variation for pointer use is available to you. Examine the following code:

```
TYPE
   MonthlyActivity = ARRAY[1..12] OF Integer;VAR  MonthPtr : ^MonthlyActivity;
   I : Integer;
BEGIN
   NEW(MonthPtr);
   FOR I := 1 TO 12 DO
   BEGIN
     Writeln('Please enter the value for month ', I:2);
     Read(MonthPtr^[I]);
   END;
```

Here, we have defined an integer array and a pointer that can be used to reference the array. Because TP knows **MonthPtr** can refer only to an integer array of 12 elements, it can figure out how to access individual elements within the array. It therefore allows us to follow references to that pointer with square brackets and index variables so we can retrieve or initialize individual elements of the array. That's flexibility.

At this point, you might be wondering why you would want to use pointers rather than the actual variable names. Pointers are most powerful when used with a concept known as *dynamic memory allocation*, which creates temporary variables. But before we get into the details involved in allocating memory, we'll take a quick look inside the memory of a typical computer.

1. True or False: The ^ symbol allows you to access the contents of the memory location that the pointer variable references.

2. What value is displayed by the following code segment? Assume that **IntPtr** and **IntPtr2** are declared as integer pointers.

```
I := 100;
IntPtr := @I;
IntPtr2 := IntPtr;
Write(IntPtr2^);
```

1. True
2. 100

A Look Inside Personal Computer Memory

We can make some useful and reliable generalizations about any personal computer that runs a Microsoft Disk Operating System or compatible operating system. For instance, DOS expects certain things to be at specific locations in memory.

Figure 11.3 illustrates the general way in which memory is allocated in a personal computer. As shown, the memory at the bottom is reserved to hold addresses for the various *interrupt handlers*. An interrupt handler is used to respond to unexpected events that occur within your computer.

The next area shown in Figure 11.3 includes the portions of DOS that always remain in memory: the resident DOS utilities. These DOS programs, for example, allow you to perform operations such as a directory listing of a floppy disk. Another area is also available for terminate and stay resident (TSR) programs. If you have a Microsoft mouse installed in your system, you probably have a TSR called MOUSE that you invoke either manually or in a batch file when you boot your system.

The next area in memory contains the TP program. If you run your own program within the TP environment, the machine instructions for that program will use the next available memory locations.

Above this, you should still have free memory. This area of read/write memory is available for use by your program.

The areas near the top of the memory space in Figure 11.3 (Free Memory) provide access to I/O devices, such as the CRT controller card and serial/parallel ports.

Past the top of the illustration is an area where read only memory is reserved for access by your computer whenever it starts up.

For our discussion in this chapter, we're chiefly interested in the area marked free memory because TP uses this space for dynamic variables. Fortunately, DOS is a good bookkeeper; it knows or can easily determine where the beginning and end of the various slices of memory are located. Because this information is available, TP can figure out where free memory starts and how much is available.

Figure 11.3 This illustration shows the general memory organization for the personal computer.

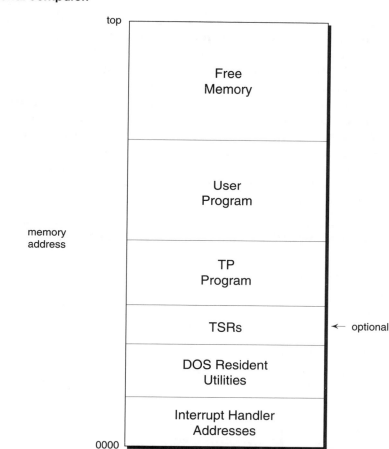

Microsoft Windows handles memory differently than DOS, but the basic idea is the same. TP keeps track of the free memory available in the system.

Dynamic Memory Allocation Techniques

Now you know, at least conceptually, where free memory is located. But what good is this knowledge without an ability to access the memory? Fortunately, TP provides four statements—**New**, **Dispose**, **GetMem**, and **FreeMem**—that allow us to allocate, manage, and deallocate dynamic memory:

```
PROCEDURE New(VAR PointerVar : <Any_pointer>);
PROCEDURE Dispose(VAR PointerVar : <Any_pointer>);
```

```
PROCEDURE GetMem(VAR PointerVar : <Any_pointer>; ByteCnt : Word);
PROCEDURE FreeMem(VAR PointerVar : <Any_pointer>; ByteCnt : Word);
```

Notice that the procedures have been paired to show their relationship to one another. You use the **New** and **Dispose** procedures to allocate and deallocate memory for a single variable or a specific component, such as an array or a record. The **GetMem** and **FreeMem** procedures allocate and eliminate a sequential block of memory so it can be accessed as if it were a fixed-length array. Now, let's look at the steps performed by TP whenever memory is requested.

When **New** or **GetMem** is invoked, TP looks for sufficient memory to satisfy the request. If memory can't be allocated, a run-time error will be generated. If it succeeds in finding available memory, a pointer is adjusted to point to the new bottom of free memory after the request has been satisfied. A pointer is then returned that points to the beginning of the allocated area, as shown in Figure 11.4. This pointer can now be used as shown earlier in this chapter. Unfortu-

Figure 11.4 Use New or GetMem to create a dynamic pointer.

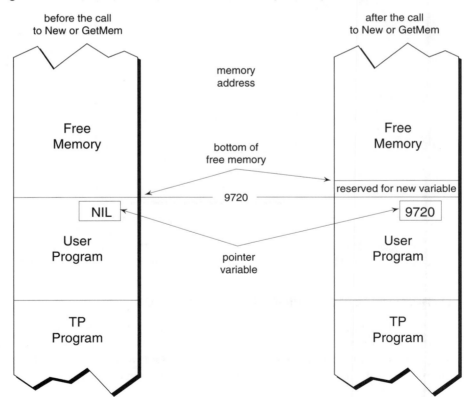

nately, TP does not save this pointer value anywhere. Thus, you have to ensure that you don't reassign the pointer. Otherwise, you won't be able to access the memory location again. If you lose access to the location, you might also lose valuable data. See if you can find the flaw in the following example:

```
IntPtr : ^Integer;

BEGIN
  New(IntPtr);
  IntPtr^ := 42;
  { Continues using the pointer variable }
  New(IntPtr);
  IntPtr^ := 6;
```

The location containing 42 becomes an orphan when the second **New** call is made. Figure 11.5 illustrates the steps that occur in this simple example. First, a memory location is allocated for an integer pointer by the first call to **New**. Next, the value of 42 is placed in the allocated memory location. If we later call **New** and provide **IntPtr** as the argument, TP will assign a *different* address to the pointer variable. Unfortunately, there is no way to return to the previous location, which still contains the 42. If this program fragment is executed repeatedly, free memory might eventually be exhausted. To avoid this situation, you can use one of three possible solutions:

- If the variable will no longer be needed by the program, deallocate it by using the **Dispose** procedure.

- If only a few pointer variables are used, assign them separate and unique names.

Figure 11.5   Repeated calls to New assigns different addresses to the pointer variable.

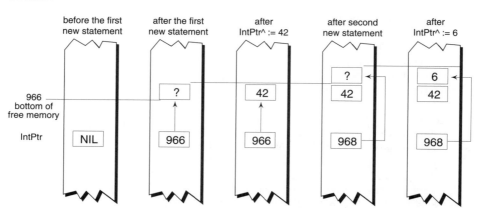

- If you are planning on collecting many dynamic variables, consider defining them as elements in a dynamic memory array rather than as individual variables. If this is impractical, consider defining an array of pointers where you can at least store the pointers for later use.

1. What is the difference between **New** and **Dispose**?
2. What's wrong with the following code section?

```
GetMem(BufPtr, 256);
FOR I := 1 TO 256 DO
   BufPtr^[I] := ' ';  { Uses the allocated memory }
FreeMem(BufPtr, 250);
```

3. What procedure should be used to allocate memory for a variable whose size is not known at compile-time?

1. **New** allocates memory for a variable, while **Dispose** deallocates the memory.
2. The memory allocated for the **BufPtr** variable is not the same size as the memory area that is deallocated by **FreeMem**.
3. **GetMem**

Allocation of Dynamic Arrays

The previous section showed how to allocate a simple variable. But how can you allocate larger structures, such as an array? It turns out that you have two options. If the array is of a specific size, you can use the same techniques explained in the previous section (using **New**). If the array is of indefinite size, you allocate a "worst case" number of elements and use the **GetMem** and **FreeMem** procedures. For example:

```
TYPE
   DailyTemp : ARRAY[1..365] OF Real;
VAR
   I : Integer;
   DailyAvgTempPtr : ^DailyTemp;
   DailyLowTempPtr : ^DailyTemp;
   DailyHiTempPtr : ^DailyTemp;

BEGIN
   GetMem(DailyAvgTempPtr, 365 * SizeOf(Real));
   GetMem(DailyLowTempPtr, 365 * SizeOf(Real));
   GetMem(DailyHiTempPtr, 365 * SizeOf(Real));
   Writeln('Please enter the high, low and average');
   Writeln('temperatures for each day...');
   FOR I := 1 TO 365 DO BEGIN
```

```
      Writeln('Day number ', I:3);
      Read(DailyHiTempPtr^[I]);
      Read(DailyLowTempPtr^[I]);
      Read(DailyAvgTempPtr^[I]);
   END;
```

This program fragment tells TP to allocate sufficient memory for three arrays of reals, where each array contains 365 elements. These elements will then be read one at a time. If we define the average daily temperature as half of the sum of the daily high and daily low, then we can calculate the average temperature by replacing

```
Read(DailyAvgTempPtr^[I]);
```

with

```
DailyAvgTempPtr^[I] := (DailyHiTempPtr^[I] + DailyLowTempPtr^[I]) / 2.0;
```

Once we are done with these data arrays, we can get rid of them by invoking:

```
FreeMem(DailyAvgTempPtr, 365 * SizeOf(Real);
FreeMem(DailyLowTempPtr, 365 * SizeOf(Real);
FreeMem(DailyHiTempPtr, 365 * SizeOf(Real);
```

It is important that the parameters passed to **FreeMem** match those of **GetMem** in order to avoid problems. If you pass a size parameter to **FreeMem** that is smaller than what was originally allocated, you will end up with unreachable locations similar to those described in the previous section. If you pass **FreeMem** a size that is larger than what was originally requested, the results will be unpredictable and could result in a real mess if two pointers end up pointing to the same memory location! The secret to using dynamic memory allocation is consistency. If you organize your program well, it will perform well.

Dynamic Records

It is also possible to allocate records dynamically. The following program defines a small record. It then assigns specific values to the elements within the record and prints the contents of the locations:

```
PROGRAM DynRecord;
TYPE
  TemplateRcrdPtr = ^MyRecord;
  MyRecord = RECORD
    WidgetCount : Integer;
    UnitCost : Real;
```

```
    END;
VAR
   MyRcrdPtr : TemplateRcrdPtr;

BEGIN
   New(MyRcrdPtr);
   MyRcrdPtr^.WidgetCount := 14;
   MyRcrdPtr^.UnitCost := 27.50;
    Writeln(MyRcrdPtr^.WidgetCount:5,  MyRcrdPtr^.UnitCost:10:4);
END.
```

The first line defines a pointer type called **TemplateRcrdPtr** and identifies it as pointing to a record called **MyRecord**. The following four lines then define the contents of the record as the integer **WidgetCount** and the real **UnitCost**. The statement after the **VAR** defines a pointer variable of the same type as **TemplateRcrdPtr**. The first line of the main program invokes **New** to allocate storage for the record. The subsequent lines then assign constant values to the two elements in the record and print the contents of the record. If you run this small program, you'll actually see 14 and 27.5000 printed on the screen.

Unfortunately, single records are not very useful. The following program is very similar to DYNRECORD, but defines an array of ten records. Each record consists of an integer, which is set to the index value for that array element, and a real, which is assigned the square of the index value:

```
PROGRAM SquaresRecord;
TYPE
   TemplateRcrdPtr = ^MyRecord;
   MyRecord = ARRAY[1..10] OF RECORD
     Number : Integer;
     SqrOfNum : Real;
   END;
VAR
   MyRcrdPtr : TemplateRcrdPtr;
   I : Integer;

BEGIN
   New(MyRcrdPtr);
   FOR I := 1 TO 10 DO BEGIN
     MyRcrdPtr^[I].Number := I;
     MyRcrdPtr^[I].SqrOfNum := I * I;
     Write(MyRcrdPtr^[I].Number:5);
      Writeln(MyRcrdPtr^[I].SqrOfNum:15:4);
   END;
END.
```

With the exception of the **ARRAY** information in the record definition and the change of a few variables, the statements in the DYNRECORD and

SQUARESRECORD programs are very similar. Even the call to **New** is the same as in the previous program. The significant difference occurs when we begin to manipulate the elements of the records; now we must also contend with an array index. The elements are accessed by first using the pointer variable name, then the ∧ symbol, then the array index information within square brackets, then a period to denote an element of a record, and finally the element name within the record.

If you run this program, you will see two columns on the screen. The first column consists of the numbers 1 through 10, while the second consists of the squares of these numbers.

Problems with Pointers and Dynamic Allocation

We would now like to summarize the limitations and problems that can occur when you use pointers. First, if a pointer to a location is lost, it may be impossible to release that location to free memory for the remainder of the program. (The exception to this is the **MARK** statement, which will be covered later in the chapter.)

Another potential problem involves the consistency of arguments passed to **Dispose** and **FreeMem** calls. If the parameters to these procedures don't match those of the **New** and **GetMem** statements that created them, serious problems can result.

Note

> One limitation must be kept in mind. The memory allocated by a given **New** or **GetMem** command cannot exceed 65,520 bytes of memory.

Another limitation stems from TP's strong data typing. Pascal is very stubborn about refusing to allow you to manipulate pointers. Some languages, such as C, allow you to overlay various types of records or arrays in order to perform unusual operations. If you are contemplating using these techniques, you'll discover that TP doesn't provide any direct way to perform such overlays. For those sufficiently skilled and ambitious, there is a relatively simple solution: assembler language routines. One procedure is required to assign the contents of one type of pointer (say, for an integer array) to that of a different type (real). Another procedure might accept a pointer and a signed integer offset; this routine would then modify the pointer by adding the integer to it.

Linked Lists

One of the most powerful applications of pointers lies in the construction of linked lists. Imagine that you have created a group of records on index cards that could be sorted in some manner. For example, you may want to organize the records beginning with the one with the earliest date to the most recent date (chronological order). Or you may wish to sort from largest transaction to smallest transaction (if you are ranking customers based on annual purchases from your company).

The point is that you have some methodical criteria for wanting to place a certain index card in front of another in your file box. If a new card is created, you can use the previously established sorting algorithm to decide where in your box the particular card should be placed.

Now imagine that you want a flexible system to perform the same operation with electronic records in your computer; linked lists solve this problem easily.

Singly Linked Lists

Figure 11.6 illustrates the concept of a singly linked list. The basic idea is that each record holds one pointer that leads to the next record. In order to travel through the list, you must be able to find the first record, which will then contain a pointer to the second record. This "chaining" or linking process is

Figure 11.6 When you want to continually point to the next record in a chain of records, you can singly list the records.

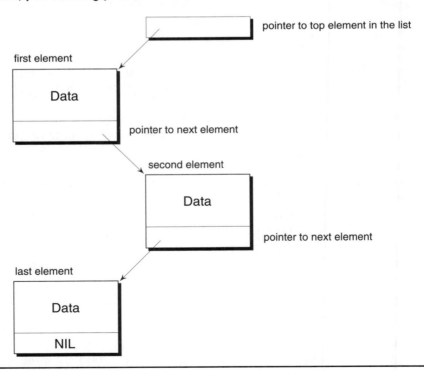

then repeated for all remaining records. Notice that the pointer in the last record should be set to some default value (such as **NIL**) since it really doesn't point to anything.

When you use singly linked lists, it is very easy to insert an additional record in the middle of a list. Figure 11.7 illustrates how a new record can be inserted in the list by changing the pointers of the affected records. Notice that, because of the independence provided by pointers, it doesn't matter where the records physically reside in memory or in what order they were created.

The following program creates a simple six-record singly linked list:

```
PROGRAM SnglLnkdLst;
  { Illustrates the operation of a singly linked list }
TYPE
  RcrdPtr = ^SnglRecord;
  SnglRecord = RECORD
    Identifier : Integer;
    DownRecPtr : RcrdPtr;
  END;
VAR
  FirstPtr, SecondPtr, ThirdPtr : RcrdPtr;
  I : Integer;

BEGIN
  { Begins by creating the first record and setting
    the Identifier field to a unique value }
  New(FirstPtr);
  FirstPtr^.Identifier := 1;
  SecondPtr := FirstPtr;
  FOR I := 2 TO 6 DO BEGIN
    {Creates five more records }
    New(ThirdPtr);
    SecondPtr^.DownRecPtr := ThirdPtr;
    ThirdPtr^.Identifier := I * 2;
    ThirdPtr^.DownRecPtr := NIL;
    SecondPtr := ThirdPtr;
  END;
  SecondPtr := FirstPtr;
  FOR I := 1 TO 6 DO BEGIN
    Writeln('Record number ',I:2,' Identifier ',
            SecondPtr^.Identifier:2);
    ThirdPtr := SecondPtr^.DownRecPtr;
    SecondPtr := ThirdPtr;
  END;
END.
```

At the outset, the program seems to have an illegal statement since the second element in the record definition is a pointer of the same type as the

Figure 11.7   You can insert a new record anywhere in a singly linked list of records.

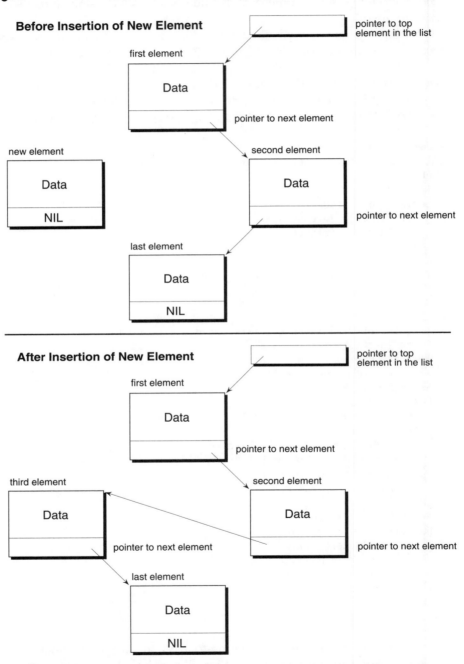

record. However, this is legal because we are simply telling TP that the pointer at that spot in the record will point to another record identical to this one. Because definitions within a **TYPE** statement do not allocate memory storage, there is nothing vague or unresolvable about this.

We also define several pointers to be of the same type as the record since we will be using them to keep track of the various records. The **FirstPtr** variable will always point to the top record. This is the only way we can trace our way through the list. The other two pointers will be used to point to the current record and the record to be created next.

In the first **FOR** loop, we create the five lower records and initialize the **DownRecPtr** element in the previous record to point to the new record. We also initialize the **Identifier** field to a unique value that we can retrieve later. The second **FOR** loop walks us through from the first record to the sixth, and prints out the value of the **Identifier** field to prove that the program successfully created these records and that it found them all in the correct order.

1. How would you modify the singly linked example program to stop the second loop when it reaches the last element? (Hint: Look at the value of the last pointer in our program.)

1. You can change the loop that processes list notes from

```
FOR I:=1 TO 6 DO BEGIN
...
END;
```

to

```
WHILE DownRecPtr <> NIL DO BEGIN
...
END;
```

Notice that we use the **NIL** pointer constant to test for the end of the list.

Doubly Linked Lists

Figure 11.8 illustrates the operation of a doubly linked list, which operates identically to a singly linked list when moving from the top record down. The twist is that each record now holds a second pointer that points up to the record above it. With doubly linked lists, you no longer have to keep track of the top of the list; if you have a pointer to any record in the list, you can find your way to all other elements in the list by using either the up pointer or down pointer, as desired.

Figure 11.8 A doubly linked list allows you to find your way to elements above and below the current location.

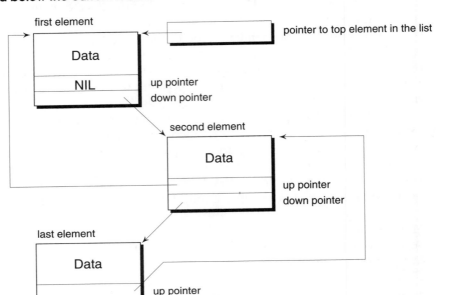

The following program, DBLLNKDLST, is similar to, SNGLLNKDLST, shown previously. DBLLNKDLST first creates and initializes the six records, then traverses the list from the first record to the last one. However, when it reaches the bottom of the list, the program begins to backtrack up the list by using the up pointer. If you run this program, you will observe that the identifier's numerical order for the second set is the reverse of the order created in the forward direction.

```
PROGRAM DblLnkdLst;
{ Illustrates the operation of a doubly linked list }
TYPE
   RcrdPtr = ^DblRecord;
   DblRecord = RECORD
     Identifier : Integer;
     DownRecPtr : RcrdPtr;
     UpRecPtr : RcrdPtr;
   END;
VAR
   FirstPtr, SecondPtr, ThirdPtr : RcrdPtr;
   I : Integer;

BEGIN
   { Begins by creating the first record and setting
```

```
      the Identifier field to a unique value }
   New(FirstPtr);
   FirstPtr^.Identifier := 1;
   FirstPtr^.DownRecPtr := NIL;
   FirstPtr^.UpRecPtr := NIL;
   SecondPtr := FirstPtr;
   FOR I := 2 TO 6 DO BEGIN
     { Creates five more records }
     New(ThirdPtr);
     SecondPtr^.DownRecPtr := ThirdPtr;
     ThirdPtr^.Identifier := I * 2;
     ThirdPtr^.UpRecPtr := SecondPtr;
     ThirdPtr^.DownRecPtr := NIL;
     SecondPtr := ThirdPtr;
   END;
   Writeln('First we will travel down the tree');
   SecondPtr := FirstPtr;
   FOR I := 1 TO 6 DO BEGIN
     Writeln('Record number ', I:2, ' Identifier ',
             SecondPtr^.Identifier:2);
     ThirdPtr := SecondPtr^.DownRecPtr;
     FirstPtr := SecondPtr;
     SecondPtr := ThirdPtr;
   END;
   SecondPtr := FirstPtr; { Points to bottom record }
   Writeln('Now we will travel up the tree');
   FOR I := 1 TO 6 DO BEGIN
     Writeln('Identifier ', SecondPtr^.Identifier:2);
     ThirdPtr := SecondPtr^.UpRecPtr;
     SecondPtr := ThirdPtr;
   END;
END.
```

Binary Trees

The last type of linked list that we'll discuss is called the *binary tree*. Figure 11.9 illustrates the general construction of such a list. It is called a binary tree because each node can have, at most, two lower-level nodes directly connected to it. You can think of a binary tree as a doubly linked list that has two down pointers: one for the left branch and one for the right branch. Binary trees become extremely important when you wish to sort large numbers of records in either ascending or descending order. In order to insert a new record into the sorted binary tree, it may be necessary to reassign many connections between records; this can get complicated and is beyond the scope of this book. We mention it here to give you an idea of the power of linked lists and TP. If you are interested in this topic, we suggest that you first read introductory sorting theory material before attempting to build and maintain binary trees.

Figure 11.9 Binary trees allow you to sort large numbers of records in either ascending or descending order.

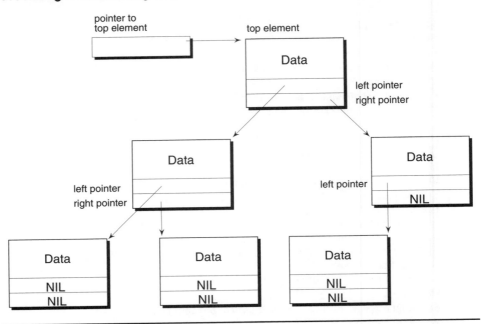

The MARK and RELEASE Statements

The **MARK** and **RELEASE** statements are used to group certain dynamically allocated variables together so they can all be eliminated at the same time. Take a look at Figure 11.10, which shows what happens when variables are allocated and subsequently freed. As you can see, when variables are released they create "holes" in memory where information is no longer stored. To put these areas to use, TP keeps a structure called a *freelist* in high memory. As each variable, array, or record is released, the address and length of the released area is placed in the freelist. Now if the program requests additional variables, TP will first search for a suitable area in the "holes" pointed to by the freelist before allocating new memory. If a suitable space is not found in the freelist, TP will then attempt to allocate space starting at the bottom of free memory.

When you invoke **MARK** with a pointer, the value returned in the pointer is the current bottom of free memory. If you now begin to allocate new dynamic variables, they will most likely be created above this location. When you invoke the **RELEASE** statement with the pointer from the **MARK** call, the bottom of free memory is set to the location passed in the pointer. This means that all variables allocated above the **MARK** address are implicitly released to the

Figure 11.10 Using MARK and RELEASE creates holes in memory.

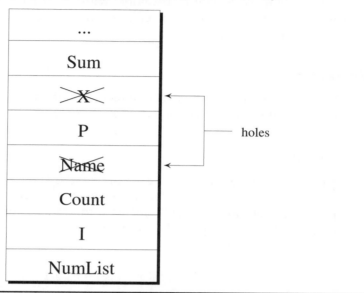

system. The pointers to those locations might still be valid, but shouldn't be reused since there may be collisions with variables defined after the release. The **RELEASE** statement also clears the freelist. Thus, if you have "holes" in the memory area below the bottom of free memory, these locations will be lost for the remainder of the program.

It should be clear from the preceding discussion that **MARK** and **RELEASE** operations should be applied with care. They are most useful when you have a function or procedure that needs to allocate a large amount of storage temporarily, but repeatedly. In these situations, you can call **MARK** before the call to the routine that will request the memory, and then call **RELEASE** on return. Please note that **RELEASE** is much faster than issuing several **FreeMem** and **Dispose** commands. The type of pointer used in the **MARK** and **RELEASE** commands is unimportant because it isn't used in either memory-access or computation operations (which are the categories of operations in which TP performs most type checking).

Summary

In this chapter, you learned how to use memory allocation techniques to create and process dynamic data structures. We started with a discussion of the pointer variable, which allows us to access a variable by referencing the variable's memory location. Next, you learned how to use pointer variables with the **New** and **GetMem** procedures to allocate memory and with **Dispose** and **FreeMem** to deallocate memory. With these basic tools—pointers and memory allocation routines—you can construct dynamic data structures such as arrays, records, and linked lists.

Exercises

1. How can you modify the dynamic record program DYNRECORD to insert a new record between the third and fourth records?

Answers

1. First, let the program create the set of records. Then, create a new record of the same type and use the Identifier element to tell you where to perform the pointer modifications. Finally, increase the loop count of the second **FOR** loop to allow you to print the extra element.

Object-Oriented Programming

he programs that have been presented up until this point are based on simple structured programming techniques. As you've seen, structured components, such as records, procedures, and functions, are useful tools for constructing reliable and easy-to-follow programs. There is, however, another programming method supported by TP that we haven't explored yet—object-oriented programming (OOP).

Although OOP has been around for many years, it is rapidly becoming the style of choice for many programmers. Why? Because it offers powerful, high-level features that allow you to better manage how your code interacts with your data. The net result is that OOP makes it easier to write and maintain programs.

In this chapter, you'll be introduced to the basic concepts of OOP and you'll learn how to use the OOP features provided with TP. This chapter starts by presenting the building blocks of OOP—object types, objects, instance variables, methods, messages, and inheritance. Next, you'll learn how to create and use a simple object to draw boxes. After you've mastered the basics, you'll see how to use OOP techniques to create a set of useful window tools that, in turn, can be used to support simple scrollable windows.

After you complete this chapter, you'll know how to:

- Use OOP techniques to write useful programs
- Define and use object types and objects
- Create methods for objects
- Use inheritance to derive new object types
- Create a set of window tools using objects
- Add extensions to object-oriented tools by deriving new object types

What Is OOP?

OOP is a programming style that uses objects for building blocks, much like the way structured programming relies on functions and procedures. Essentially, OOP is an evolutionary step up from traditional methods of programming in which data and the procedures that process the data are treated as separate components.

The best feature about this higher-level programming approach is that it provides a more natural method for representing and solving real-world problems. Rather than writing your code as a set of procedures and functions that can be called from a main program, you can combine your data and the routines that process the data into separate packages called *objects*.

For example, assume that you need to write a program to display user-interface components, such as menus and selection buttons. Using the traditional structured approach, you would need to determine your data requirements and organize the data into data structures. As an example, the following record might be used to represent a menu:

```
TYPE
  MenuRec = RECORD
   X, Y      : Integer; { Menu location }
   NumItems : Integer; { Number of menu items }
   Items     : Array[1..10] OF String;
END;
```

In this case, the record stores the menu coordinates, the number of menu items, and the actual list of menu items.

Now that the data is organized, you need to define the procedures and functions to process the menus. An example of a procedure to display a menu is:

```
PROCEDURE DisplayMenu(Menu1 : MenuRec);
VAR
  I : Integer;

BEGIN
  GotoXY(Menu1.X, Menu1.Y);
  FOR I := 1 TO Menu1.NumItems DO
    DisplayItem(Menu1.Items[I]);
END;
```

Notice that the procedure is designed around the **MenuRec** record. Can you see the limitation of this approach? A wide gap still exists between the data structure and the procedure. It would be more efficient to combine the two components into one neat package. That's where objects come in handy. The objects provided by the OOP approach allow us to remove this gap. The following program shows how our menu procedure and record can be combined in an object type.

```
TYPE
  MenuObj = Object
    X, Y      : Integer; { Menu location }
    NumItems : Integer; { Number of menu items }
    Items     : Array [1..10] OF String;
    PROCEDURE Init(X, Y   : Integer; NumI : Integer;
                            List : MenuItems);
    PROCEDURE DisplayMenu;
  END;
```

As Figure 12.1 shows, the object type contains the data components, such as **X**, **Y**, **NumItems** and the procedure **DisplayMenu**, as well as a new procedure called **Init**, which is used to initialize menu objects. However, you might now be wondering why this is so important. Are objects really all that useful? Absolutely. Since objects are very modular and function like indepen-

Figure 12.1 **The menu object contains these components.**

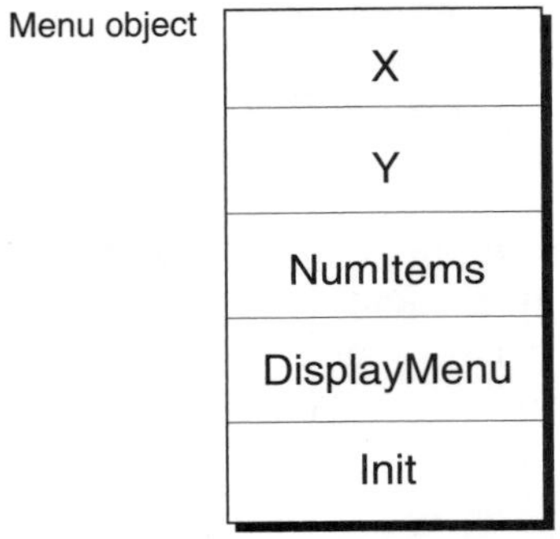

Menu object

X
Y
NumItems
DisplayMenu
Init

dent programs, they can easily be modified, extended, and used to create other types of objects. For example, you could use the simple menu object type to create more complex menu objects, such as scrollable menus.

The more you work with objects, the more you'll realize how well they can help you write code that is more structured, yet also flexible.

The Ingredients of OOP

These seven important components comprise the core of OOP:

- Object types
- Objects
- Instance variables
- Methods
- Messages
- Inheritance
- Constructors and destructors

As you learn how to use these OOP ingredients, you'll be introduced to such concepts and techniques as encapsulation, data hiding, message passing, and deriving objects.

Object Types and Objects

When you first start to learn about OOP, it's easy to get confused by all the new terminology. One question that you might already have is: "What is the difference between an object type and an object?"

In TP, an *object type* serves as a template for creating objects, which are simply the combination of data and the code that operates on the data. Actually, an object type is a user-defined data type that is defined in the **TYPE** section of a program. After an object type has been defined, its name can then be used to declare variables that serve as the objects. A variable that is declared from an object data type is considered to be an *instance of the object type*. You'll see how this is done after I present the other OOP ingredients.

Note

TP allows you to create two types of objects: *static* and *dynamic*. By default, all objects are allocated statically and they are stored in the data section of a program. Dynamic objects, however, are allocated on the heap while a program is running. Later in this chapter, you'll learn how to use the **New** and **Dispose** procedures to create, use, and deallocate dynamic objects.

Instance Variables, Methods, and Messages

Each object type that you create may contain two components: data elements, which are called *instance variables*, and procedures and functions, which are called *methods*. The instance variables in the **MenuObj** definition are:

```
X, Y     : Integer; { Menu location }
NumItems : Integer; { Number of menu items }
Items    : Array[1..10] OF String;
```

The two methods are:

```
PROCEDURE Init(X, Y : Integer; NumI : Integer; List : MenuItems);
PROCEDURE DisplayMenu;
```

This technique of packaging instance variables and methods in a object type is called *data hiding* or *encapsulation*. The methods are used to access the instance variables so that the details involved in implementing an object are hidden from the user. For example, you don't need to know how the menu object type is implemented in order to use it. You can create an object by defining a variable of the menu object type, initialize the object by assigning it values, and then use the object to display menus.

The term *message passing* is used to refer to the process of calling a method. When a method is called, we say that a specific *message* is passed to an object. The object receives a message and then determines which method to call.

Inheritance

Inheritance is a property that allows new objects to be created from existing objects. Let's return to our menu example to see how this technique works. Assume that you want to add some new features to the simple menu, such as color and the ability to display menu items in multiple columns. Rather than starting from scratch, you can use the original menu object type to derive a new menu object type that contains the new features. As Figure 12.2 shows, the new object type would inherit all of the instance variables and methods from the original object type.

Inheritance is one of the more important features of OOP. As you gain more experience working with OOP, you'll discover that it is possible to create code that can be easily adapted to work with different applications.

Note

When inheritance is used to create new object types, the term *base object type* will be used to refer to the original object type and the term *derived object type* or *subobject type* to refer to the object type that inherits the data and methods from the base object type.

Constructors and Destructors

TP provides two useful keywords, **CONSTRUCTOR** and **DESTRUCTOR**, that allow you to create special types of methods. These methods are especially useful for initializing and deallocating dynamic objects. A constructor is a special procedure that initializes an object before it is used. A destructor, on the other hand, is the constructor's counterpart; it cleans up after an object is no longer needed.

The initialization procedure, **Init**, used in the **MenuObj** example could be written as a constructor:

```
CONSTRUCTOR Init(X, Y : Integer; NumI : Integer; List : MenuItems);
```

Notice that the keyword **CONSTRUCTOR** replaces the keyword **PROCEDURE**.

Figure 12.2 Inheritance is the process of securing all of the instance variables and methods from the original object type.

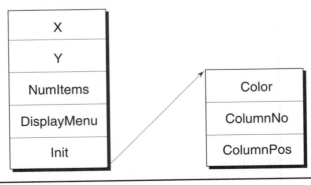

1. What is the difference between an object type and an object?
2. What are the two components that can be included in an object type definition?
3. List the instance variables and methods in the following object type definition:

```
TYPE
  Button = OBJECT
    Color     : Integer;
    Name      : String;
    LocX, LocY : Integer;
    PROCEDURE Init;
    FUNCTION GetSize : Integer;
  END;
```

4. True or False: Inheritance allows you to derive base object types from subobject types.
5. True or False: An object allows you to combine data and operations.

1. An object type is a template defined in the **TYPE** section of a program. An object, however, is an instance of an object type (a variable defined from an object data type).
2. Instance variables and methods
3. The instance variables are **Color**, **Name**, **LocX**, and **LocY**. The methods are **Init** and **GetSize**.
4. False
5. True

Creating Your First Object Type

You've now been introduced to the technical terms of OOP and you're probably ready to put OOP to work. Let's now examine how these OOP components are combined and create a simple program that draws different types of boxes on the screen. We'll define a general box object type, then we'll use it to create box objects. As you work with the box objects, you'll start to see some of the important benefits of OOP.

If you intend to write a program using structured techniques to display boxes, you would probably start by coding the data structures needed as records. You would do this because records provide a useful structure for grouping related data elements. However, since we're using OOP techniques, we'll need to combine both the data and the operations that will be required to process the data. We'll package these components as an object type. Here is a list of the components needed to create a box object type:

- The coordinates of a box
- The box color
- The style of the box's border
- Routines to initialize, draw, and erase a box

Fortunately, an object type definition in TP is very similar to a record declaration. Therefore, you won't have to learn a new syntax. The object type declaration is always placed in the **TYPE** section of a program. Here is the complete object type definition needed to create objects for drawing boxes on the screen:

```
Box    = Object
  X1, Y1, X2, Y2 : Integer;          { Box coordinates }
  Color          : Byte;             { Box color }
  Style          : BStyle;           { Box border style }
  PROCEDURE Init(PX1, PY1, PX2, PY2 : Integer; PColor : Byte;
                  PStyle : BStyle);  { Initializes the box }
  PROCEDURE Draw;                    { Draws the box }
  PROCEDURE Erase;                   { Erases the box }
END;                                 { Box }
```

As Figure 12.3 indicates, the **Box** object type contains data and procedures. The keyword **OBJECT** tells the compiler that this structure will be used to declare variables called *objects*. Notice that the format of this declaration looks like a record. In fact, the following program shows how we could represent this object type as a record:

```
TYPE
  Box = RECORD
    PX1, PY1, PX2, PY2 : Integer; { Box coordinates }
    PColor          : Byte;       { Box color }
    PStyle          : BStyle;     { Box border style }
  END;
```

Notice, however, two key differences between the object type and the record definition. The **RECORD** keyword replaces **OBJECT**, and the procedure declarations are missing from the record version. Recall that a record can contain only data components. The object type, however, is much more flexible because it can contain both data and the operations to process the data. In this sense, you can think of an object type as a superset of a record. In our **Box** object type declaration, the operations are declared as simple procedures. But keep in mind that TP also allows you to include function declarations in a object definition.

To summarize how object types are structured, the general syntax required for defining one is:

```
TYPE
  <Object type name> = OBJECT
```

Figure 12.3 This illustration shows how you would use TP to represent the Box object type.

```
          TYPE
object name ──► Box = OBJECT ◄─── OBJECT keyword
        ▲   X1, Y1, X2, Y2 : Integer;
data ──┤   Color           : Byte;
        ▼   Style           : BStyle;
           PROCEDURE Init(...);        ▲
           PROCEDURE Draw;             ├── procedures (methods)
           PROCEDURE Erase;            ▼
          END;
```

```
    <Instance variables>
    <Procedure and function declarations>
END;
```

For the *Object type name*, you can use any valid Pascal identifier, but remember that the name you use cannot be the same as a Pascal keyword. The data members and procedure and function declarations are listed after the **OBJECT** definition statement. If you look closely at our **Box** object definition, you'll see that the instance variables are listed before the procedure declarations, as the general object definition indicates. This order must be followed for each object type you define.

Note   An object type may contain either instance variables only or procedure and function declarations only.

1. What new keyword is needed to declare an object type in the **TYPE** section?
2. Explain some of the similarities and differences between object types and records.
3. What names are valid object type names?

   a. Unit

   b. _Box

   c. Menu1

1. **OBJECT**
2. Object types are similar to records because they are both defined in the **TYPE** section and both are used to declare variables. The main difference between object types and records is that an object type may contain methods (procedures and functions).
3. **Menu1** is the only valid object type name.

Figure 12.4 Use this format when implementing a method.

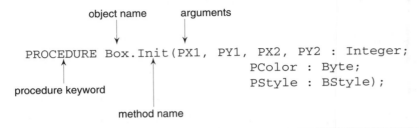

Creating Methods

In our **Box** object type declaration, each procedure was listed after the instance variables. These procedures are called *methods* because they are declared inside the body of an object type. The method declarations tell the compiler which procedures and functions are part of an object type. In this respect, they serve as placeholders. You might now be wondering where the code for a method is defined. The actual code is placed in a corresponding procedure or function definition that follows the object type definition.

Figure 12.4 shows the required components for a method implementation (definition). Notice that the object type name and method name are separated by a period. Each method definition must also list the parameters used with the method.

Recall that our **Box** object type contained three methods: **Init**, **Draw**, and **Erase**. What we need to do now is code these methods as procedures. The following method illustrates how **Init** is written:

```
PROCEDURE Box.Init(PX1, PY1, PX2, PY2 : Integer; PColor : Byte;
                   PStyle : BStyle);
{ Initializes the box }
BEGIN
   X1    := PX1;
   Y1    := PY1;
   X2    := PX2;
   Y2    := PY2;
   Color := PColor;
   Style := PStyle;
END;
```

The important thing to keep in mind is that the procedure definition must be placed after the declaration of **Box**. The method begins with the standard **PROCEDURE** keyword, which precedes the name of the object type and the method name (**Box.Init**). If this procedure is defined without the object type name, as shown here

```
PROCEDURE Init(PX1, PY1, PX2, PY2 : Integer; PColor : Byte;
              PStyle : BStyle);
```

the compiler won't know that the procedure is part of the **Box** object type.

Within the body of this method, all of the instance variables in the object such as **X1**, **Y2**, and so on can be freely accessed.

Note

A method can be called from inside the body of another method. For example, with this statement:

```
Draw;
```

the **Init** method could call the **Draw** method.

Working with Objects

Now that you know how to use the **TYPE** and **OBJECT** keywords to create an object type, you should be ready to take the next step and use the object type to create an object. Actually, objects are declared like other Pascal variables. That is, the object type name defined in the **TYPE** section is used to specify the type of the variable. For example, the following declaration section shows how an object named **ScBox1** is created using the **Box** object type presented earlier:

```
VAR
  ScBox1 : Box;
```

The object **ScBox1** is now ready to access the components defined by the **Box** object type. For this task, all you need is the period selector. For example:

```
ScBox1.Color := Blue;
```

This statement assigns the color **Blue** to the component **Color** in the object **ScBox1**. As you gain more experience working with the OOP style, you'll discover that methods are normally used to store and retrieve values to and from object components. The advantage of this approach is that it allows us to "hide" the details involved in storing data in an object.

For example, recall the definition of the **Init** method, which was designed to perform one important task: initialize an object. When **Init** is called with a statement like

```
ScBox1.Init(5, 5, 40, 20, Red, Single);
```

it performs the equivalent of the following statements:

```
ScBox1.X1     := 5;
ScBox1.Y1     := 5;
ScBox1.X2     := 40;
...
ScBox1.Style := Single;
```

As you can see, the initialization method hides the details of each assignment statement for us. To store data in the object, all we need do is access a single method. When you define new object types, it is always a good idea to include a method for initializing objects.

Passing Messages

In the previous section, you saw that an object's method could be called by using this format:

```
ScBox1.Init(5, 5, 40, 20, Red, Single);
```

In this case, the procedure **Init** is called, which is assigned to the object type **Box**. In OOP terminology, we say that the message **Init** is sent to the object **ScBox1**. What does this message do? It causes the method **Init** to execute so that the object's instance variables can be initialized.

Box Drawing, Object Style

Now that you've learned how to define and use object types, objects, and methods, let's put these components together to create our box-drawing program. This program uses the object type **Box** to create two objects named **ScBox1** and **ScBox2** to draw two boxes in different styles, sizes, and colors. Here is the complete program:

```
PROGRAM ObjExample;
USES
  Crt,Graph;
CONST
  BoxChar : ARRAY[1..2, 1..6] OF Char = { Codes for box border }
    ((#218, #196, #191, #179, #192, #217),
     (#201, #205, #187, #186, #200, #188));
TYPE
  BStyle = (Single, Double, Hide);
  Box    = Object
    X1, Y1, X2, Y2 : Integer;          { Box coordinates }
    Color          : Byte;             { Box color }
    Style          : BStyle;           { Box border style }
    PROCEDURE Init(PX1, PY1, PX2, PY2 : Integer; PColor : Byte;
              PStyle : BStyle);        { Initializes the box }
```

```
  PROCEDURE Draw;                   { Draws the box }
  PROCEDURE Erase;                  { Erases the box }
END;                                { Box }

(********       Methods for Box object       ********)
PROCEDURE Box.Init(PX1, PY1, PX2, PY2 : Integer; PColor : Byte;
               PStyle : BStyle); { Initializes the box }
BEGIN
  X1    := PX1;
  Y1    := PY1;
  X2    := PX2;
  Y2    := PY2;
  Color := PColor;
  Style := PStyle;
END;

PROCEDURE Box.Draw;
{ Draws a border for the box }
VAR
  B, I  : Integer;
  BColor : Byte;

BEGIN
  TextColor(Color);
  IF Style = Single THEN B := 1 { Sets border index }
  ELSE IF Style = Double THEN B := 2
  ELSE IF Style = Hide THEN BEGIN
    B := 1;
    BColor := GetBkColor;
    TextColor(BColor);
  END;
  GotoXY(X1, Y1);
  Write(BoxChar[B, 1]);          { Draws UL corner }
  FOR I := 1 TO  (X2 - X1) - 1 DO BEGIN
    GotoXY(X1 + I, Y1);
    Write(BoxChar[B, 2]);        { Draws top }
  END;
  GotoXY(X2, Y1);
  Write(BoxChar[B, 3]);          { Draws UR corner }
  FOR I := Y1 + 1 TO Y2 - 1 DO BEGIN
    { Draws sides }
    GotoXY(X1, I);
    Write(BoxChar[B, 4]);
    GotoXY(X2, I);
    Write(BoxChar[B, 4]);
  END;
  GotoXY(X1, Y2);
  Write(BoxChar[B, 5]);          { Draws LL corner }
  FOR I := 1 TO (X2 - X1) - 1 DO BEGIN
```

```
      GotoXY(X1 + I, Y2);
      Write(BoxChar[B, 2]);        { Draws Bottom }
    END;
    GotoXY(X2, Y2);
    Write(BoxChar[B, 6]);          { Draws LR corner }
  END;

PROCEDURE Box.Erase;
{ Erases the box }
VAR
  SaveStyle : BStyle;

BEGIN
  SaveStyle  := Style;
  Style := Hide;
  Draw;
  Style := SaveStyle;
END;

{ Main program section }
VAR
  ScBox1 : Box;
  ScBox2 : Box;

BEGIN
  ClrScr;
  ScBox1.Init(5, 5, 40, 20, Red, Single);
  ScBox2.Init(20, 21, 60, 24, Blue, Double);
  ScBox1.Draw;
  ScBox2.Draw;
  Readln;
  ScBox1.Erase; { Erases the first box }
  Readln;
END.
```

Figure 12.5 shows the boxes that are drawn by the program. The larger box is generated by the object **ScBox1**. Because this program introduces many new features, I will take the time to describe it in a little more detail than previous programs that we've written.

The main program body follows the steps outlined in Figure 12.6. Once the two objects are initialized, all of the actions are set in motion by passing messages to the objects. (Remember that we use the phrase "passing a message to an object" to indicate that a method is called.)

The real workhorse of the program is the method **Draw**, which draws a box by using extended ASCII codes. Notice that we don't have to pass parameters to this method because the data we need, such as the coordinates of the box or the border style, is already stored in the object. (The **Init** method, which is called before **Draw**, initializes the object.)

Figure 12.5 The program OBJEXAMPLE draws these boxes on the screen.

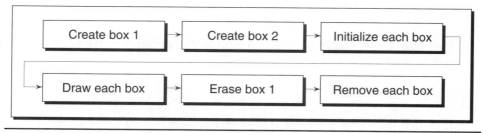

Figure 12.6 These are the tasks performed by the main program.

The first major task that **Draw** performs is to determine which border style should be used to draw the box. As the following code shows, the variable **B** is set to 1 or 2, depending on the setting of the **Style** instance variable:

```
IF Style = Single THEN B := 1
ELSE IF Style = Double THEN B := 2
ELSE IF Style = Hide THEN BEGIN
  B := 1;
  BColor := GetBkColor;
  TextColor(BColor);
END;
```

If **Style** is set to **Hide**, which indicates that a box should be erased, the **GetBkColor** function is called to determine the background color. This is done to set the standard text color to the background color. Because this function is provided with the **Graph** unit, the following statement must be included at the beginning of the program to access this unit, as well as the **Crt** unit:

```
USES Crt, Graph;
```

The remainder of the code in **Draw** is responsible for drawing the box. Each component of the box is displayed by calling a **Write** procedure:

```
Write(BoxChar[B, 1]);
```

Here, the variable **B** references half of the **BoxChar** array. (The particular half referenced depends on which border style is used. The first half of the array contains the codes for a single-line border, while the second half contains the codes for a double-line border.)

The remaining method, **Erase**, is used to remove a box that has previously been drawn. To eliminate the need to duplicate code, a little trick is used here. First, the current border style of the box object is saved:

```
SaveStyle := Style;
```

Then, the style is set to **Hide** to indicate that the box should be erased:

```
Style := Hide;
```

After the **Draw** method is called, the **Style** instance variable is reset to its previous setting:

```
Style := SaveStyle;
```

1. Which messages are passed to objects in the box-drawing program?
2. Change the box-drawing program so that it can draw a border in both a background and foreground color.

1. The messages **Init**, **Draw**, and **Erase** were passed to the object **ScBox1**, while the messages **Init** and **Draw** were passed to **ScBox2**.
2. To support drawing boxes in a background color, you must add a new instance variable to the **Box** object type, as shown in the following program:

```
Box = Object
  X1, Y1, X2, Y2 : Integer; { Box coordinates }
  Color          : Byte;    { Box color }
```

```
        BkColor        : Byte;     { Background color }
        Style          : BStyle;   { Box border style }
    ...
```

In addition, the following procedure must be added to the **Draw** method:

```
TextBackground(BkColor);
```

Using Dynamic Objects

In our first real OOP program, all of the objects used were static. That is, they were created by declaring a variable from an object type. Objects, like records, however, have another dimension to them—they can be allocated dynamically. The storage space for a dynamic object is created on the heap during program execution.

To declare a dynamic object you must use a pointer. For example:

```
VAR
  ScBox1 : ^Box;  { Declaring an object pointer }
```

Notice that the pointer symbol, (^), is placed before the name of the object type.

Before a dynamic object (pointer) can be used, you must allocate memory for it by using the **New** procedure:

```
New(ScBox1);   { Allocate memory for the object }
```

As Figure 12.7 shows, this statement creates a copy of the components from the **Box** object type. Each of the components, such as **X1**, **Y1**, **Color**, **Style**, or the method **Init**, can now be accessed by using the pointer variable **ScBox1** as the reference. If we create another object with the statement

```
New(ScBox2);
```

a second memory area will be set aside to hold the components for this object.

Once memory has been allocated for the object, you can access it by using the standard pointer notation:

```
ScBox1^.Draw;
```

In this case **ScBox1** serves as a pointer to access the **Draw** method associated with this object.

When you are finished using a dynamic object in a program, you should always deallocate the storage space created for the object. This task is easily accomplished with the **Dispose** procedure:

Figure 12.7   You must allocate memory for a dynamic object before you can use it.

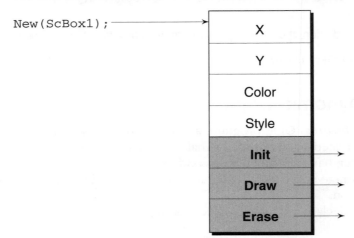

```
Dispose(ScBox1);
```

To show you the actual steps involved in using dynamic objects, I have designed a new version of the main body of the box drawing program for dynamic objects:

```
{ Main program section }
VAR
  ScBox1 : ^Box;
  ScBox2 : ^Box;

BEGIN
  ClrScr;
  New(ScBox1);     { Allocate memory for the objects}
  New(ScBox2);
  ScBox1^.Init(5, 5, 40, 20, Red, Single);
  ScBox2^.Init(20, 21, 60, 24, Blue, Double);
  ScBox1^.Draw;
  ScBox2^.Draw;
  Readln;
  ScBox1^.Erase; { Erases the first box }
  Readln;
  Dispose(ScBox1); { Deallocate memory for the objects }
  Dispose(ScBox2);
END.
```

To create a dynamic object you must use the **New** function to allocate memory for an object before you attempt to use the object. When you have finished using an object in a program, you should use the **Dispose** procedure to free the memory allocated for the object.

Note

You should include the compiler directive **{M+}** in all programs that use the TP object-oriented extensions. This directive tells the compiler to check an object when one of its methods is executed to ensure that memory has been allocated for the object.

Working with Inheritance

Thus far, all of the objects used in our programs have also been created from simple object types. However, we can also use another technique to create objects: inheritance. Recall that, earlier in this chapter, you learned that inheritance is the property that allows you to use existing object types to define new object types. In this section, we'll explore the basics of inheritance so that you can see how to use this powerful technique to create useful object types.

Creating Subobject Types

An object type that has been derived from another object type is called a *subobject type*. A subobject type is defined using the basic syntax for specifying a standard object type. The only difference is that the main object type name is included in the definition. The appropriate format is:

```
TYPE
  <Object type name> = OBJECT(<Base object type>)
    <Data members>
    <Procedure and function declarations>
  END;
```

As I mentioned earlier, the original object type is called the *base object type*, while the new object type is called a *derived object type* or *subobject type*. The following program defines a base object type called **AddMachine**. This object type, which contains methods for adding and subtracting numbers, is then used to derive a new object type called **Calculator**.

```
PROGRAM ObjFamily;
TYPE
  AddMachine = OBJECT
    Total   : Real;    { Stores the running total }
    OpCount : Integer; { Counts the number of operations }
    PROCEDURE Init(X : Real; Op : Integer);
    PROCEDURE Add(Y : Real);
    PROCEDURE Sub(Y : Real);
```

```
    PROCEDURE Print;
  END;

  Calculator = OBJECT(AddMachine)
    Previous : Real;
    PROCEDURE Mult(Y : Real);
    PROCEDURE Divide(Y : Real);
  END;

(********        Methods for AddMachine        ********)
PROCEDURE AddMachine.Init(X : Real; Op : Integer);
BEGIN
  Total := X;
  OpCount := Op;
END;

PROCEDURE AddMachine.Add(Y : Real);
BEGIN
  Total := Y + Total;
  Inc(OpCount);
END;

PROCEDURE AddMachine.Sub(Y : Real);
BEGIN
  Total := Total - Y;
  Inc(OpCount);
END;

PROCEDURE  AddMachine.Print;
BEGIN
  Writeln('The running total is ', Total);
  Writeln('The number of operations performed are ', OpCount);
END;

(********        Methods for Calculator        ********)
PROCEDURE Calculator.Mult(Y : Real);
BEGIN
  Previous := Total;
  Total := Total * Y;
  Inc(OpCount);
END;

PROCEDURE Calculator.Divide(Y : Real);
BEGIN
  Previous := Total;
  Total := Total / Y;
  Inc(OpCount);
END;
```

```
VAR
  Machine1 : AddMachine;
  Machine2 : Calculator;

BEGIN
  Machine1.Init(200.0, 0); { Initializes adding machine object }
  Machine2.Init(500.0, 0); { Initializes calculator object }
  Machine1.Print;
  Machine2.Print;
  Machine1.Add(42.27);
  Machine1.Print;
  Machine2.Mult(22.0);
  Machine2.Print;
END.
```

As Figure 12.8 shows, the derived object type **Calculator** inherits all of the instance variables and methods from the base object type **AddMachine**. Because of the inheritance, an object created from the **Calculator** object type can call any of the methods in **AddMachine** or use any of its instance variables. Objects created from the base object type, however, cannot use the instance variables or methods defined in the derived object type. For example, the statement

```
Machine1.Mult(20, 2);
```

Figure 12.8 The Calculator object type inherits all instance variables and methods from the the AddMachine base object type.

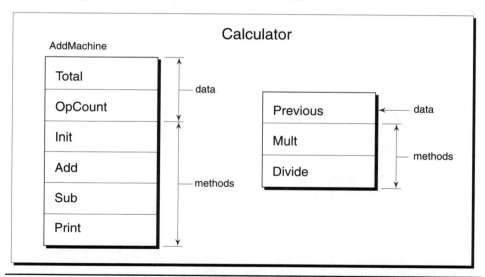

would generate a compiler error because **Machine1** is an object derived from the **AddMachine** object type, and the **Mult** method is not supported by this object type.

Overriding Methods

One interesting problem can occur when you use inheritance to derive new object types—the inherited object types must use the methods defined in the base object type. For example, in our previous program the objects derived from the **Calculator** object type will always call the **Init**, **Add**, **Sub**, and **Print** methods by default because these methods are inherited.

Now assume that we want to use a different **Print** method with the **Calculator** object type. To do this, you can simply provide a new version of the method that you want to override. Applying this technique, our **Calculator** object type would be changed to:

```
Calculator = OBJECT(AddMachine)
    Previous : Real;
    PROCEDURE Mult(Y : Real);
    PROCEDURE Divide(Y : Real);
    PROCEDURE Print;
  END;
```

The derived object would now use the version of the **Print** method defined in this object type. A new version of the calculator program that shows how the overridden method is used is:

```
PROGRAM ObjFamily;
TYPE
  AddMachine = OBJECT
    Total    : Real;    { Stores the running total }
    OpCount  : Integer; { Counts the number of operations }
    PROCEDURE Init(X : Real; Op : Integer);
    PROCEDURE Add(Y : Real);
    PROCEDURE Sub(Y : Real);
    PROCEDURE Print;
  END;
  Calculator = OBJECT(AddMachine)
    Previous : Real;
    PROCEDURE Mult(Y : Real);
    PROCEDURE Divide(Y : Real);
    PROCEDURE Print;
  END;

(********        Methods for AddMachine        ********)
PROCEDURE AddMachine.Init(X : Real; Op : Integer);
```

```
  BEGIN
    Total := X;
    OpCount := Op;
  END;

  PROCEDURE AddMachine.Add(Y : Real);
  BEGIN
    Total := Y + Total;
    Inc(OpCount);
  END;

  PROCEDURE AddMachine.Sub(Y : Real);
  BEGIN
    Total := Total - Y;
    Inc(OpCount);
  END;

  PROCEDURE AddMachine.Print;
  BEGIN
    Writeln('The running total is ', Total);
    Writeln('The number of operations performed are ', OpCount);
  END;

  (********          Methods for calculator          ********)
  PROCEDURE Calculator.Mult(Y : Real);
  BEGIN
    Previous := Total;
    Total := Total * Y;
    Inc(OpCount);
  END;

  PROCEDURE Calculator.Divide(Y : Real);
  BEGIN
    Previous := Total;
    Total := Total / Y;
    Inc(OpCount);
  END;

  PROCEDURE Calculator.Print;
  BEGIN
    Writeln('The previous total is ', Previous);
    Writeln('The running total is ', Total);
    Writeln('The number of operations performed are ', OpCount);
  END;

VAR
  Machine1 : AddMachine;
  Machine2 : Calculator;
```

```
BEGIN
  Machine1.Init(200.0, 0);  { Initializes adding machine object }
  Machine2.Init(500.0, 0);  { Initializes calculator object }
  Machine1.Print;
  Machine2.Print;
  Machine1.Add(42.27);
  Machine1.Print;
  Machine2.Mult(22.0);
  Machine2.Print;
END.
```

Because the **Print** method has been overridden, the program can now display the previous total computed by the calculator, which is stored in the instance variable **Previous**.

The only problem now lies in determining how the **Calculator** object can access the **Print** method defined in the base object type **AddMachine**. To solve this problem, we want to be able to have access to the method that has been overridden. To support such a feature, TP allows you to include the name of the object type in the method call. An example of how it can be used is:

```
PROCEDURE  Calculator.Print;
BEGIN
  Writeln('The previous total is ', Previous);
  AddMachine.Print;
END;
```

In this case, the **Print** method assigned to the **Calculator** object type is called. This method executes a **Writeln** statement and then calls the **Print** method in the **AddMachine** object type. This technique used to access methods is illustrated in Figure 12.9.

Figure 12.9 Accessing methods

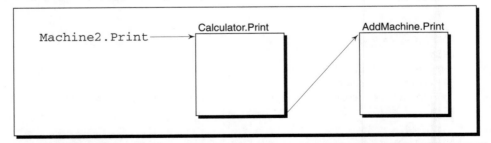

1. What is the difference between a base object type and a subobject type?
2. How are subobject types created?
3. Is the definition of the following subobject type, which is derived from the **AddMachine** object type presented earlier, valid?

```
TYPE
  NewMachine = OBJECT(AddMachine)
    Memory : Real;
     PROCEDURE NewMachine.Init(X : Real; Op : Integer; Memory : Real);
  END;
```

1. A base call is used to derive a subobject type. The subobject type inherits all of the instance variables and methods from a base object type.
2. A subobject type is created by defining an object type in the **TYPE** section of a program and by including the name of the base object type from which the subobject type is derived in the object type definition.
3. Yes, even though the method **NewMachine.Init** is different because it contains a different number of parameters than the **Init** method in the **AddMachine** object type.

Building Tools with Objects

One of the benefits of objects is that you can use them to create programming tools that are very flexible. In this section, you'll learn how to use OOP techniques to create a set of general-purpose tools for displaying windows and for reading and writing strings. To develop these tools, we'll create a general window object that contains methods for drawing a window border, checking window coordinates, and reading and writing strings. We'll also need a set of low-level screen routines for accessing the display. Figure 12.10 shows the components that we'll include in the window tools.

Figure 12.10 These are the components of the window tools we'll be using in this section.

Low-Level Screen Routines	Object Methods
WritechAttr	Init
ReadchAttr	MkBrdr
ScrollAbs	CoordChk
	GetCurPos
	DisplayStr
	ReadStr

To create the toolset, we'll first need to write the low-level screen routines. Next, we'll define a general window object type and write the methods needed to support the object type. After the tools are finished, you'll see how to use them with some sample programs.

Creating Low-Level Screen Routines

Our first task is to write the screen routines needed to support the window object tools. Rather than using the standard **Read** and **Write** procedures, let's create a few low-level procedures so that we can access the screen using the functions stored in the ROM BIOS. TP provides access to these powerful video functions via the **Intr** procedure. These functions perform a number of tasks, including moving and reading the cursor, writing and reading characters and strings with different attributes, and scrolling the screen. To access ROM BIOS functions, the **Intr** procedure is called with the following two arguments:

```
Intr($10, Regs);
```

Here, **$10** indicates that the interrupt called is 10h—the service routines for controlling the personal computer's video. The argument **Regs** contains the values for the registers. Each video function requires different register settings; however, the **AH** register always contains the function code for the video routine you wish to access.

Table 12.1 lists the procedures that we'll create to access some of the ROM BIOS video functions. Notice that procedures are included for reading and writing characters and for scrolling the screen.

Let's start with the **WriteChAttr**. To code this procedure, two of the ROM BIOS functions must be called:

```
Interrupt: 10h
Function Code: AH = 15
Description: Determines the current video state, including video mode and
             active video page
Register Inputs :  None required
Register Outputs:  BH = Video page number
                   AL = Video mode
                   AH = Number of columns on screen
```

Table 12.1   Low-Level Screen Routines

Procedure	Description
WriteChAttr	Writes one or more characters and attributes, starting at a specified screen location
ReadChAttr	Reads a character and attribute from a specified screen location
ScrollAbs	Scrolls a specified region up one line

```
Interrupt: 10h
Function Code: AH = 9
Description: Writes a specified number of characters, with attributes, at
             the current cursor position
Register Inputs:  BH = Video page number
                  BL = Attribute
                  AL = Character code
                  CX = Number of characters to display
Register Outputs: None
```

The first interrupt tells us the video mode and page settings for our monitor. We'll need this information to call the second function, **AH=9**, to display characters. The complete procedure is:

```
PROCEDURE WriteChAttr(Ch,Atr : Byte; NChar : Integer);
{ Writes one or more characters starting at current screen location }
VAR
  Regs : Registers;

BEGIN
  Regs.AH := 15;     { Determines video page }
  Intr($10, Regs);   { Calls the video interrupt }
  Regs.BL := Atr;    { Stores attribute }
  Regs.AL := Ch;     { Character to display }
  Regs.CX := NChar;  { Number of characters to display }
  Regs.AH := 9;      { Displays character with attribute }
  Intr($10, Regs);   { Calls the video interrupt }
END;
```

Notice that the **Intr** procedure is called twice. The first call returns with the video page stored in the **BH** register. Then, the registers are assigned the values stored in the parameters **Ch**, **Atr**, and **NChar**. Here is a sample call that illustrates how a series of five + characters is displayed in black, starting at the current cursor position:

```
WriteChAttr(#43, 7, 5);
```

The companion procedure with **WriteChAttr** is **ReadChAttr**. To use this procedure, which reads only a single character and its attribute, we'll need to make a call to the following ROM BIOS interrupt:

```
Interrupt: 10h
Function Code: AH = 8
Description: Reads a character and its attribute at the current cursor
             position
Register Inputs:  BH = Video page number
Register Outputs: AH = Attribute
                  AL = Character code
```

Using this interrupt, the version of **ReadChAttr** is:

```
PROCEDURE ReadChAttr(VAR Ch, Atr : Byte);
{ Determines the character and its attribute at current screen location }
VAR
  Regs : Registers;

BEGIN
  Regs.AH := 15;    { Determines video page }
  Intr($10, Regs); { Calls the video interrupt }
  Regs.AH := 8;     { Reads character and attribute }
  Intr($10, Regs); { Calls the video interrupt }
  Ch := Regs.AL;    { Gets the character }
  Atr := Regs.AH;   { Gets the attribute }
END;
```

This time, notice that the parameters **Ch** and **Atr** are **VAR** parameters.

The final screen procedure is **ScrollAbs**, which scrolls a specified screen region up one line. For scrolling the screen, the ROM BIOS actually provides a general-purpose scrolling function that can be called to scroll the screen up a specified number of lines. The description of the interrupt function is:

```
Interrupt: 10h
Function Code: AH = 6
Description: Scrolls the screen up a specified number of lines.
Register Inputs: AL  = Number of lines to scroll
                 BH  = Attribute for blank line
                 CL  = Column position of upper-left corner
                 CH  = Row position of upper-left corner
                 DL  = Column position of lower-right corner
                 DH  = Row position of lower-right corner
Register Outputs: None
```

Because we only need a procedure to scroll a screen region up one line, we'll set the register **AL** to 1. The other registers are assigned values by using parameters, as shown in the following format:

```
PROCEDURE ScrollAbs(X1, Y1, X2, Y2, Atr : Byte);
{ Scrolls the specified screen region up one line }
VAR
  Regs : Registers;

BEGIN
  Regs.AH := 6;     { Function code to scroll screen }
  Regs.BH := Atr;   { Stores attribute for blank line}
  Regs.AL := 1;     { Scrolls one line }
  Regs.CL := X1;    { Upper-left corner to scroll }
  Regs.CH := Y1;
```

```
   Regs.DL := X2;    { Lower-right corner to scroll }
   Regs.DH := Y2;
   Intr($10, Regs); { Calls the video interrupt }
END;
```

Now that you've seen the low-level screen tools, you might be wondering how they will be used to support text windows. Because each window displayed will have a border, **WriteChAttr** is needed to display the extended ASCII line characters in creating a border. This procedure is also used by the window object type method, **DisplayStr**, which is presented in the next section. The **ReadChAttr** procedure is used by the method **ReadStr** for reading strings at a specified window location. Finally, **ScrollAbs** is used in the **DisplayStr** method so that text in a window can be scrolled as it is displayed.

Building Window Objects

You are now ready to see the window object type, **ScWindow**, and its methods. For our general toolset, only one window object type is required:

```
ScWindow = Object
   X1, Y1, X2, Y2    : Byte; { Window coordinates }
   BrdAttr, BrdStyl  : Byte; { Window attributes }
   Color             : Byte; { Text color }
   { Window object methods }
   PROCEDURE Init(WX1, WY1, WX2, WY2, WBrdAttr, WBrdStyl, WColor : Byte);
   PROCEDURE MkBrdr;
   PROCEDURE CoordChk(WX1, WY1, WX2, WY2 : Byte);
   PROCEDURE GetCurPos(VAR X, Y : Byte);
   PROCEDURE DisplayStr(X, Y : Byte; DspStr : String);
   PROCEDURE ReadStr(X, Y : Byte; VAR InStr : String; VAR Atr : Byte);
END;
```

As shown, this object type is not much different from other object types that have been introduced. The first three lines contain the declarations for the instance variables, while the remainder of the object type consists of the method declarations. Table 12.2 lists each method, along with a brief description.

Table 12.2 Window Methods

Method	Procedure
Init	Initializes a window object
MkBrdr	Draws a window border
CoorChk	Tests the coordinates of a window
Get CursPos	Returns the cursor position relative to a window object
DisplayStr	Displays a string in the window object at a specified location
ReadStr	Reads a string in a window object at a specified location

---

As with all other objects created in this chapter, the **Init** procedure is needed to initialize the object. For our window objects, **Init** also makes calls to **CoordChk** and **MkBrdr** to check the coordinates of the window and to draw a box. Take a look at an example. First, you'll need to start with a declaration:

```
VAR
  Win1 : ScWindow;
```

Then, you can create a window object and display the window:

```
New(Win1);
Win1.Init(5, 5, 40, 10, 80, 1, Blue);
```

In this case, notice that the window is drawn with a single-line border. If you changed the **Init** call to

```
Win1.Init(5, 5, 40, 10, 80, 2, Blue);
```

the window would be drawn with a double-line border.

After a window object has been created, you can read and write strings from and to the window by using the **ReadStr** and **DisplayStr** methods. For example, the following statement displays a string starting at the fifth column and second row of the window object:

```
Win1.DisplayStr(5, 2, 'Message displayed at Column 5 Row 2');
```

As you work with window objects, keep in mind that the row and column coordinates are addressed using relative coordinates. This coordinate system is illustrated in Figure 12.11. Here, the upper-left corner of the window is (5, 5,) and therefore the window coordinate (5, 2) actually references screen location (10, 7). Because the window coordinates are stored in each window object, it's easy to read and write text from and to a window.

To understand better how the coordinate addressing system works, take a close look at the **GetCurPos** method, which is used to determine the current position of the cursor in relation to a window object:

```
PROCEDURE ScWindow.GetCurPos(VAR X, Y : Byte);
{ Determines the position of the cursor inside the window }
BEGIN
  X := WhereX - X1; { Adjusts for window coordinates }
  Y := WhereY - Y1;
END;
```

Here the TP functions **WhereX** and **WhereY** are used to determine the absolute screen coordinates of the cursor. To calculate the cursor position

Figure 12.11 A window's coordinates are relative to the upper-left corner of the window, not the screen.

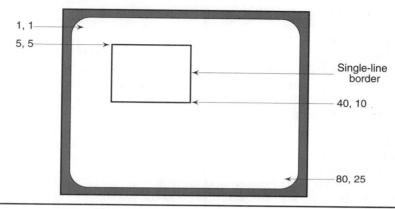

relative to the window, we simply subtract the window object's upper-left corner from the absolute screen location. That's all there is to it.

The Window Tools

The following is the complete set of window tools. You should type in this unit, save it in the file WINTOOLS.PAS, and compile the file.

```
UNIT WinTools;

INTERFACE
USES Crt, Dos;
CONST
  BoxChar : ARRAY[1..2, 1..6] OF Byte =
    { Codes for window border }
    ((218, 196, 191, 179, 192, 217),
     (201, 205, 187, 186, 200, 188));
TYPE
  ScWindow = Object
    X1, Y1, X2, Y2    : Byte; { Window coordinates }
    BrdAttr, BrdStyl : Byte; { Window attributes }
    Color            : Byte; { Text color }
    { Window object methods }
    PROCEDURE Init(WX1, WY1, WX2, WY2, WBrdAttr, WBrdStyl,
                   WColor : Byte);
    PROCEDURE MkBrdr;
    PROCEDURE CoordChk(WX1, WY1, WX2, WY2 : Byte);
    PROCEDURE GetCurPos(VAR X, Y : Byte);
    PROCEDURE DisplayStr(X, Y : Byte; DspStr : String);
```

```
      PROCEDURE ReadStr(X, Y : Byte; VAR InStr : String; VAR Atr : Byte);
END;

PROCEDURE WriteChAttr(Ch, Atr : Byte; NChar : Integer);

IMPLEMENTATION
(*******          Screen tools          *********)
PROCEDURE WriteChAttr(Ch, Atr : Byte; NChar : Integer);
{ Writes one or more characters starting at current screen location }
VAR
  Regs : Registers;

BEGIN
  Regs.AH := 15;     { Determines video page }
  Intr($10, Regs);   { Calls the video interrupt }
  Regs.BL := Atr;    { Stores attribute }
  Regs.AL := Ch;     { Character to display }
  Regs.CX := NChar;  { Number of characters to display }
  Regs.AH := 9;      { Displays character with attribute }
  Intr($10, Regs);   { Calls the video interrupt }
END;

PROCEDURE ReadChAttr(VAR Ch, Atr : Byte);
{ Determines the character and its attribute at current screen location }
VAR
  Regs : Registers;

BEGIN
  Regs.AH := 15;     { Determines video page }
  Intr($10, Regs);   { Calls the video interrupt }
  Regs.AH := 8;      { Reads character and attribute }
  Intr($10, Regs);   { Calls the video interrupt }
  Ch := Regs.AL;     { Gets the character }
  Atr := Regs.AH;    { Gets the attribute }
END;

PROCEDURE ScrollAbs(X1, Y1, X2, Y2, Atr : Byte);
{ Scrolls the specified screen region up one line }
VAR
  Regs : Registers;

BEGIN
  Regs.AH := 6;      { Function code to scroll screen }
  Regs.BH := Atr;    { Stores attribute for blank line}
  Regs.AL := 1;      { Scrolls one line }
  Regs.CL := X1;     { Upper-left corner to scroll }
  Regs.CH := Y1;
  Regs.DL := X2;     {Lower-right corner to scroll }
  Regs.DH := Y2;
```

```
    Intr($10, Regs);   { Calls the video interrupt }
END;


(*********          Window object methods          **********)
PROCEDURE ScWindow.Init(WX1, WY1, WX2, WY2, WBrdAttr, WBrdStyl,
                        WColor : Byte);
{ Initializes a window object and draws its border }
BEGIN
  CoordChk(WX1, WY1, WX2, WY2);
  TextColor(WColor); { Sets the text color }
  X1 := WX1;     { Saves the window attributes }
  Y1 := WY1;
  X2 := WX2;
  Y2 := WY2;
  Color := WColor;
  BrdStyl := WBrdStyl;
  BrdAttr := WBrdAttr;
  MkBrdr;         { Draws window border }
END; { ScWindow.Init }


PROCEDURE  ScWindow.MkBrdr;
{ Draws a border for the window }
VAR
  I : Integer;


BEGIN
  IF BrdStyl < 1 THEN BrdStyl := 1 { Uses default border }
  ELSE IF BrdStyl > 2 THEN BrdStyl := 2;
  GotoXY(X1, Y1);
  WriteChAttr(BoxChar[BrdStyl, 1],BrdAttr, 1);
  { Draws UL corner }
  GotoXY(X1 + 1, Y1);
  WriteChAttr(BoxChar[BrdStyl, 2], BrdAttr, (X2-X1)-1);
  { Draws top }
  GotoXY(X2, Y1);
  WriteChAttr(BoxChar[BrdStyl, 3], BrdAttr, 1);
  { Draws UR corner }
  FOR I := Y1 + 1 TO Y2 - 1 DO BEGIN { Draws sides }
    GotoXY(X1, I);
    WriteChAttr(BoxChar[BrdStyl, 4], BrdAttr, 1);
    GotoXY(X2, I);
    WriteChAttr(BoxChar[BrdStyl, 4], BrdAttr, 1);
  END;
  GotoXY(X1, Y2);
  WriteChAttr(BoxChar[BrdStyl, 5], BrdAttr, 1);
  { Draws LL corner }
  GotoXY(X1 + 1, Y2);
  WriteChAttr(BoxChar[BrdStyl, 2], BrdAttr, (X2 - X1) - 1);
  { Draws bottom }
```

```
    GotoXY(X2, Y2);
    WriteChAttr(BoxChar[BrdStyl, 6], BrdAttr, 1);
    { Draws LR corner }
END;

PROCEDURE ScWindow.CoordChk(WX1, WY1, WX2, WY2 : Byte);
{ Tests the window coordinates to assure they are in range }
BEGIN
  IF (WX1 < 1) OR (WX2 > 80) THEN
  BEGIN
    Writeln('Row coordinate is out of range');
    Exit;
  END
  ELSE IF (WY1 < 1) OR (WY2 > 25) THEN
  BEGIN
    Writeln('Column coordinate is out of range');
    Exit;
  END
END;

PROCEDURE ScWindow.GetCurPos(VAR X, Y : Byte);
{ Determines the position of the cursor inside the window }
BEGIN
  X := WhereX - X1; { Adjusts for window coordinates }
  Y := WhereY - Y1;
END;

PROCEDURE ScWindow.DisplayStr(X, Y : Byte; DspStr : String);
{ Displays a string using a specified attribute }
VAR
  I : Integer;

BEGIN
  X := X + (X1); { Adjusts for window coordinates }
  Y := Y + (Y1);
  GotoXY(X, Y);
  FOR I := 1 TO Length(DspStr) DO BEGIN
    IF X = X2 THEN BEGIN { Advances to the next line }
      Y := Y + 1;
      X := X1 + 1;
      GotoXY(X, Y);
    END;
    IF Y = Y2 THEN BEGIN
      { Scrolls the screen up one line }
      Y := Y2 - 1;
      ScrollAbs(X1, Y1, X2 - 2,
                Y2 - 2, 0);
      GotoXY(X, Y);
    END;
```

```
      WriteChAttr(Ord(DspStr[I]), Color, 1);
      { Displays character }
      X := X  +  1; { Advances cursor }
      GotoXY(X, Y);
    END;
  END;


  PROCEDURE ScWindow.ReadStr(X, Y : Byte; VAR InStr : String;
                              VAR Atr : Byte);
  VAR
    Ch : Byte;
    I  : Integer;

  BEGIN
    X := X1 + X; { Adjusts for window coordinates }
    Y := Y1 + Y;
    I := 1;
    GotoXY(X, Y);
    ReadChAttr(Ch, Atr);          { Reads the first character}
    WHILE Ch <> 32 DO BEGIN
      InStr[I] := Chr(Ch);        { Stores the character read}
      I := I + 1;                 { Advances the string index }
      X := X + 1;
      IF X = X2 THEN BEGIN { Checks for text wrap }
        Y := Y + 1;
        X := X1 + 1;
      END;
      GotoXY(X, Y);
      ReadChAttr(Ch, Atr);
    END;
    InStr[0] := Chr(I - 1); { Stores length of string }
  END;

END.
```

Using the Window Tools

Our first program illustrates how two different windows can be displayed by creating two window objects:

```
PROGRAM Windows1;
USES WinTools, Crt;
VAR
  TestWin1 : ScWindow;
  TestWin2 : ScWindow;
  WinStr   : String;
  StrAtr   : Byte;
```

```
BEGIN
  ClrScr;
  TestWin1.Init(10, 2, 40, 20, 80, 2, Blue);
  TestWin1.DisplayStr(1, 2, 'This text is displayed in window 1');
  Readln;
  TestWin1.DisplayStr(1, 17, 'This long line is going to be scrolled');
  Readln;
  TestWin2.Init(42, 5, 80, 10, 60, 1, Red);
  TestWin2.DisplayStr(1, 1, 'This text is displayed in window 2');
  Readln;
  TestWin1.ReadStr(1, 1, WinStr, StrAtr);
  TestWin2.DisplayStr(1, 2, 'The word read in window 1 is:');
  TestWin2.DisplayStr(1, 3, WinStr);
  Readln;
END.
```

When you run the program, you'll see that each window is displayed separately. The **Init** method is used to initialize the two window objects **TestWin1** and **TestWin2**. Then, the **Display** method is used to write a string in each window. Notice that when the second string is displayed in **TestWin1**, the window region is scrolled to make room for the long string. Finally, the **ReadStr** method is called to read the first word in **TestWin1,** which is then displayed in **TestWin2**.

Deriving Window Methods

The window tools included in **WinTools** were easy to write because only one window object type was required, **ScWindow**. But assume that we want to create a different style of window—one that contains a title. At first, you might think the best way to handle this situation is to return to the original window object type and modify it to support titles. Is there a better approach? Yes; we can use the window object type to derive a new window type. The following program shows how this is accomplished:

```
TYPE
  TitleWin = OBJECT(ScWindow)
    Title : String;
    PROCEDURE Setup(WX1, WY1, WX2, WY2, WBrdAttr, WBrdStyl,
                    WColor : Byte; WTitle : String);
    PROCEDURE MkBrdr;
  END;
```

Can you tell what's been done here? Inheritance is used to create a new window object type named **TitleWin**. As Figure 12.12 shows, this new object type inherits all of the instance variables and methods from the base object type

Figure 12.12 The derived object type TitleWin inherits all of the instance variable and methods from the base object type ScWindow.

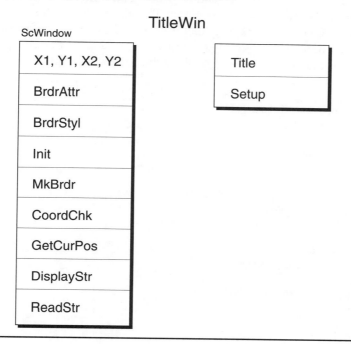

ScWindow. Of course, a new variable, **Title**, has been added to store the window's title and a method, **Setup**, has been added to initialize objects created from the **TitleWin** object type.

By deriving this new window, we've also introduced one slight problem. How do we draw the window's border and include the title? After all, we can't use the **MkBrdr** method from the **ScWindow** object type. To solve this dilemma, we'll override the **MkBrdr** method like we did with the **Calculator** object type in the previous section. The new method will draw the border and add the title, but with one slight twist. There's a hidden problem here. In order to reuse code, we will want our **TitleWin Setup** method to call the **ScWindow Init** method and this routine in turn makes a call to **MkBrdr**. But which **MkBrdr**? The way the program is written now, any call to **ScWindow.Init** will result in a call to **ScWindow.MkBrdr**. Of course, we can always manually call the **TitleWin.MkBrdr** method when we are using **TitleWin** objects and **ScWindow.MkBrdr** when we are using **ScWindow** objects, but that seems a little awkward. Fortunately, there's another solution—we can make **MkBrdr** a *virtual* method.

Virtual Methods and Constructors

Up until now, we've been making use of *static* methods in our programs and examples. A static method is one that TP can resolve at the time the program is compiled. When using objects that inherit and override methods, TP sometimes must wait until the program is running to be able to determine exactly which version of a method to use. Consider the following example:

```
TYPE
{define object classes}
  BaseObj = Object
  PROCEDURE Method1;
  PROCEDURE Method2;
  END;

  DerivedObj = Object(BaseObj)
  PROCEDURE Method2;
  END;

{Implement Objects}
PROCEDURE BaseObj.Method1;
BEGIN
  WriteLn('Inside BaseObj.Method1');
  Method2;
END;

PROCEDURE BaseObj.Method2;
BEGIN
  WriteLn('Inside BaseObj.Method2);
END;

PROCEDURE DerivedObj.Method2
BEGIN
  WriteLn('Inside DerivedObj.Method2);
END;
```

In this example, **Method1** will always call **BaseObj.Method2**, even if it's called from a **DerivedObj** object. This because **Method2** is *statically bound* to the **BaseObj** class. To solve this problem, we want **Method2** to be *dynamically bound*. We do this by using the **Virtual** keyword when declaring **Method2**:

```
TYPE
  BaseObj = Object
  PROCEDURE Method1;
  PROCEDURE Method2; virtual;
  END;
```

```
DerivedObj = Object(BaseObj)
PROCEDURE Method2; virtual;
END;
```

When TP encounters the **virtual** keyword, it automatically knows to use something called a *Virtual Method Table* (VMT) to resolve method calls for objects of that particular class. Objects that do not use or inherit virtual methods do not need a VMT. But how does TP know when to create a VMT for an object class? Whenever you define an object that uses virtual methods, you must include a constructor method for that object. You might remember from earlier in this chapter that a consuctor method is like any other method, but uses the **CONSTRUCTOR** keyword. Applying this concept to our box drawing objects means making a couple of changes to our **WinTools** unit:

```
TYPE
   ScWindow = Object
      X1, Y1, X2, Y2    : Byte; { Window coordinates }
      BrdAttr, BrdStyl : Byte; { Window attributes }
      Color             : Byte; { Text color }
      { Window object methods }

      {Make Init a CONSTRUCTOR method}
      CONSTRUCTOR Init(WX1, WY1, WX2, WY2, WBrdAttr, WBrdStyl, WColor : Byte);

      {Make MkBrdr a virtual method}
      PROCEDURE MkBrdr; virtual;

      {No other changes are necessary}
      PROCEDURE CoordChk(WX1, WY1, WX2, WY2 : Byte);
      PROCEDURE GetCurPos(VAR X, Y : Byte);
      PROCEDURE DisplayStr(X, Y : Byte; DspStr : String);
      PROCEDURE ReadStr(X, Y : Byte; VAR InStr : String; VAR Atr : Byte);
END;
```

The first change shown here involves changing the **Init** method from a **PROCEDURE** to a **CONSTRUCTOR**. We would call this method as we would any other. A note of warning: You should call an object's constructor before using any of its other methods or data. This makes constructors ideal for initializing an object's data. The second change we made was making **MkBrdr** virtual. Notice that the **virtual** keyword appears after the semi-colon in the procedure definition and is followed by another semi-colon.

Using our knowledge of virtual methods and constructors, we can now implement our new **TitleWin** class:

```
PROGRAM Windows2;
USES WinTools, Crt;
TYPE
  TitleWin = OBJECT(ScWindow)
    Title : String;
    PROCEDURE Setup(WX1, WY1, WX2, WY2, WBrdAttr, WBrdStyl,
                    WColor : Byte; WTitle : String);
    PROCEDURE MkBrdr; virtual;
  END;

PROCEDURE TitleWin.Setup(WX1, WY1, WX2, WY2, WBrdAttr, WBrdStyl,
                         WColor : Byte; WTitle : String);
{ Initializes a window object, draws border, adds title }
BEGIN
  Title := WTitle; { Stores window title }
  Init(WX1, WY1, WX2, WY2, WBrdAttr, WBrdStyl, WColor);
END; { TitleWin.Set }

PROCEDURE TitleWin.MkBrdr;
{ Draws a border for the window }
VAR
  I,SLen,LenRem : Integer;

BEGIN
  IF BrdStyl < 1 THEN BrdStyl := 1 { Uses default border }
  ELSE IF BrdStyl > 2 THEN BrdStyl := 2;
  GotoXY(X1, Y1);
  WriteChAttr(BoxChar[BrdStyl, 1],BrdAttr, 1);
  { Draws UL corner }
  GotoXY(X1 + 1, Y1);
  SLen := (((X2 - X1) - 1) - Length(Title)) DIV 2;
  LenRem := (((X2 - X1) - 1) - Length(Title)) MOD 2;
  WriteChAttr(BoxChar[BrdStyl, 2], BrdAttr, SLen+1);
  { Draws top }
  DisplayStr(SLen + 1, 0, Title);
  GotoXY(X1 + SLen + Length(Title) + 1, Y1);
  IF LenRem = 0 THEN
    WriteChAttr(BoxChar[BrdStyl, 2], BrdAttr, SLen)
    { Draws top }
  ELSE
    WriteChAttr(BoxChar[BrdStyl, 2], BrdAttr, SLen + 1);
    { Draws top }
  GotoXY(X2, Y1);
  WriteChAttr(BoxChar[BrdStyl, 3], BrdAttr, 1);
  { Draws UR corner }
  FOR I := Y1 + 1 TO Y2 - 1 DO BEGIN
  { Draws sides }
    GotoXY(X1, I);
```

```
      WriteChAttr(BoxChar[BrdStyl, 4], BrdAttr, 1);
      GotoXY(X2, I);
      WriteChAttr(BoxChar[BrdStyl, 4], BrdAttr, 1);
    END;
    GotoXY(X1, Y2);
    WriteChAttr(BoxChar[BrdStyl, 5], BrdAttr, 1);
    { Draws LL corner }
    GotoXY(X1 + 1, Y2);
    WriteChAttr(BoxChar[BrdStyl, 2], BrdAttr, (X2 - X1) - 1);
    { Draws bottom }
    GotoXY(X2, Y2);
    WriteChAttr(BoxChar[BrdStyl,  6], BrdAttr, 1);
    { Draws LR corner }
  END;

VAR
  TestWin1 : ScWindow;
  TestWin2 : TitleWin;

BEGIN
  ClrScr;
  TestWin1.Init(10, 2, 40, 20, 80, 2, Blue);
  TestWin1.DisplayStr(1, 2, 'This text is displayed in window 1');
  Readln;
  TestWin2.Setup(42, 5, 80, 10, 60, 1, Red, 'Window2');
  TestWin2.DisplayStr(1, 1, 'This text is displayed in window 2');
  Readln;
END.
```

Notice that the two objects are initialized differently. The **Init** method is called for **TestWin1**, while **Setup** is called for **TestWin2**. Instead of duplicating code we have already written, **Setup** calls **Init** to initialize the window's position and the color of the border. This re-use of code by descendent objects is one of the very powerful features of object-oriented programming. By using a virtual method, we enabled the **ScWindow** class to call the correct version of **MkBrdr**.

Summary

In this chapter, you learned how to use the OOP features that TP provides. We started by discussing the building blocks of OOP, including object types, objects, methods, instance variables, and inheritance. You then learned how to define an object type by using the **OBJECT** keyword. As presented, object types are defined by using a format similar to that of records. The main difference between an object type and a record is that a object type can contain procedures and functions, which are called methods. We also explored the powerful inheritance feature that OOP provides. You saw that the main advantage in using inheritance is its ability to derive new object types so that you can build on existing objects, rather than creating new ones from scratch.

In the last part of this chapter, we constructed a set of window tools using the OOP techniques explained earlier. We also learned about constructors and virtual methods, two very powerful object-oriented features provided in TP.

Exercises

1. List the methods and instance variables used in the following object type:

```
TYPE
  Buffer = Object
    Data   : String;
    Size   : Integer;
    Status : Boolean;
    PROCEDURE Init(Data : String; Size : Integer);
    PROCEDURE GetData;
    PROCEDURE DisplayData;
END;
```

2. What is wrong with the following object type definition?

```
TYPE
  Shape = Object
    X1, Y1, X2, Y2 : Integer;
    Color          : Integer;
    Scale          : Real := 20.1;
    PROCEDURE Shape.Init(X1, Y1, X2, Y2 : Integer);
  END;

PROCEDURE Init(X1, Y1, X2, Y2 : Integer);
BEGIN
    X1 := X1; Y1 :=Y1;
    X2 := X2; Y2 := Y2;
END;
```

3. Rewrite the **Shape** object type in step 2 so that it is correct.

4. Write a short program that will set up an object type to store current data. The object type will consist of three instance variables—Month, Day, and Year—and methods for initializing an object, setting the data, and displaying the data. Allocate the object dynamically and when the object is initialized, it should be set to the current data. (Hint: the **Dos** unit provides a routine that returns the system date.)

5. Using inheritance and the following object type definition as the base object type, derive a new object type for representing employees in a company. To do this, you'll need instance variables to store yearly salary, number of hours

worked for the current week, and a job description. Include a method to compute an employee's weekly salary.

```
TYPE
  Person = OBJECT
    FName, LName : String;
    Address      : String;
    Age          : Integer;
    PROCEDURE Init(FN, LN, Addr : String; A : Integer);
    PROCEDURE ShowData;
END;

PROCEDURE Person.Init(FN, LN, Addr : String; A : Integer);
BEGIN
    FName := FN; LNAME := LN;
    Address := Addr;
    Age := A;
END;

PROCEDURE  Person.ShowData;
BEGIN
    Writeln('Name: ', FName, ' ', LName);
    Writeln('Address: ', Address);
    Writeln('Age: ', Age);
END;
```

6. True or False: Objects with virtual methods must define or inherit a constructor method.

Answers

1. The instance variables are **Data**, **Size**, and **Status**. The methods are **Init**, **GetData**, and **DisplayData**.

2. The instance variable **Scale** cannot be initialized in the object type definition. Also, the **Init** method declared in the object type is written incorrectly. It should be:

```
PROCEDURE Init(X1, Y1, X2, Y2 : Integer);
```

The parameters passed to **Init** are also incorrect because they have the same name as the instance variables of the object type. Because of this, the compiler can't determine which variable is being accessed: the parameter or the instance variable.

3. Here is the new version of the **Shape** object type:

```
TYPE
  Shape = Object
```

```
     X1, Y1, X2, Y2    : Integer;
     Color             : Integer;
     Scale             : Real;
      PROCEDURE Shape.Init(SX1, SY1, SX2, SY2 : Integer);
   END;

PROCEDURE Shape.Init(SX1, SY1, SX2, SY2 : Integer);
BEGIN
   X1 := SX1; Y1 := SY1;
   X2 := SX2; Y2 := SY2;
   Scale := 20.1;
   END;
END;
```

4. The following program, OBJDATE, sets up an object type to store current data. The object is allocated dynamically:

```
 PROGRAM ObjDate;
USES Dos;
TYPE
  Date = Object
     Year  : Word;
     Month : Word;
     Day   : Word;
      PROCEDURE Init;
      PROCEDURE Setup(Y, M, D : Word);
      PROCEDURE Display;
    END;

PROCEDURE Date.Init;
VAR
   Dummy : Word;

BEGIN
   GetDate(Year, Month, Day, Dummy); { Initializes to current date }
END;

PROCEDURE Date.Setup(Y, M, D : Word);
BEGIN
    Year  := Y;
    Month := M;
    Day   := D;
END;

PROCEDURE Date.Display;
BEGIN
    Writeln('The date is: ', Month,'/', Day,'/', Year);
END;
```

```
VAR
  DateObj : ^Date;

BEGIN
  New(DateObj);
  DateObj^.Init;
  DateObj^.Display;
  DateObj^.Setup(1962,11,23);
  DateObj^.Display;
  Dispose(DateObj);
END.
```

5. Here is the newly derived object type:

```
TYPE
  Employee = OBJECT(Person)
    Salary        : Real;
    Hours_Per_Week : Integer;
    Job_Descrip   : String;
    PROCEDURE Setup(FN, LN, Addr : String; A : Integer;
                    Sal : Real; Hours : Integer; Job : String);
    PROCEDURE ShowPay;
  END;


PROCEDURE Employee.Setup(FN, LN, Addr : String; A : Integer; Sal :
                         Real; Hours : Integer; Job : String);
BEGIN
    Init(FN, LN, Addr, A); { Calls base object type initializer }
    Salary        := Sal;
    Hours_Per_Week := Hours;
    Job_Descrip   := Job;
  END;


PROCEDURE  Employee.ShowPay;
VAR
  Rate_Per_Hour : Real;

BEGIN
    ShowData; { Calls method in base object type }
    Writeln('The employee''s job is: ', Job_Descrip);
    Rate_Per_Hour := (Salary / 52) / 40;
    Writeln('The weekly pay is ', Rate_Per_Hour * Hours_Per_Week);
END;
```

6. True

13

Explorations with Graphics

If you've never written a graphics program, you might be surprised to learn how easy graphics are to create. TP provides a set of flexible and easy-to-use graphics procedures and functions with the **Graph** unit. This library is called the Borland Graphics Interface (BGI). Using the BGI routines, you can draw lines and other basic geometric shapes, set screen colors, configure your graphics hardware, and perform many other graphics-related tasks.

In this chapter, you'll learn how to use basic TP graphics features to write graphics programs. Because the number of available BGI routines is so large, they can't all be covered. However, this chapter will help you get started by demonstrating the basics of graphics programming. The first topic involves techniques for initializing graphics hardware. You'll learn how to use commands such as **InitGraph** to initialize your graphics programs. You'll also be provided with a quick tour of the BGI functions, procedures, and internal data. After covering the basic hardware-related topics, we'll explore other graphics programming topics, including coordinate systems, color palettes, clipping, and drawing routines.

After you complete this chapter, you'll know how to:

- Write a graphics program
- Use the basic procedures and functions in the BGI
- Use graphics hardware and video modes
- Work with graphics coordinates
- Display text in graphics mode

Writing Basic Graphics Programs

This chapter could begin by presenting the theory of graphics programming. However, the old saying "learn by doing" might provide a more interesting approach. So, let's jump right in by writing a graphics program at the outset. After looking at a simple graphics program, we'll step back and explore the basic components required in a graphics program.

Before you attempt to write and run graphics programs, you need to make sure your computer is equipped with a graphics display and adapter card. Needless to say, if you don't have the proper hardware, you won't be able to take advantage of TP's graphics features. To run a graphics program your computer must have a standard graphics card, such as CGA, VGA, EGA, MCGA, or Hercules hardware.

Figure 13.1 shows the basic steps used to write our first graphics program. We'll put these steps to work by writing a simple program that draws two basic shapes: a rectangle and a circle.

Figure 13.1 Follow these basic steps when you write a graphics program.

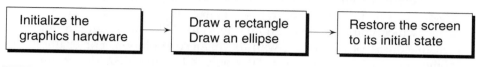

```
Program Graphics1;
USES
  Graph;
CONST
  GDriver : Integer = Detect; { Use autodetect feature }
VAR
  GMode : Integer;

BEGIN
  InitGraph(GDriver, GMode, ''); { Sets to default mode }
  Rectangle(0, 0, 399, 199); { Draws a rectangle }
  Circle(100, 100, 50); { Draws a circle inside the rectangle }
  Readln;
  CloseGraph; { Returns to original mode }
END.
```

Notice that the code begins with the **USES** section, which includes the **Graph** unit. Every graphics program must include this unit; otherwise, the compiler will not recognize the graphics routines and predefined constants that are used.

The basic command to initialize the TP graphics system is:

```
InitGraph(GDriver, GMode, '');
```

The first two parameters, **GDriver** and **GMode**, are used to select the graphics driver and the graphics mode. The last parameter specifies the path name that TP should search to locate the graphics driver files that it needs. These files come with your TP distribution disk and have the extension .BGI. If TP cannot locate these files, your program will not be able to initialize the BGI system. Because the call to **InitGraph** doesn't provide a search path, the sample program will run only if you have the graphics driver files in the same directory from which you are executing the program.

Note

To run graphics programs from directories other than the one where the driver files are stored, make sure you include the full path name for the directory where the drivers are stored. For example, this path would instruct TP that the .BGI drivers are in the directory \TP\GRAPHICS\DRIVERS:

```
'\TP\GRAPHICS\DRIVERS'
```

Before the call is made to **InitGraph**, notice that the first parameter, **GDriver**, is assigned the constant **Detect**. Why is this done? This technique allows you to initialize the graphics system in such a way that TP will itself select which graphics driver and mode to use. The driver and the mode that it selects consist of the setting with the highest resolution. For example, if your computer has VGA hardware, TP would select the VGA driver and initialize your hardware in the 640x480 mode. (Later, when we explore graphics modes, I'll provide other constants that can be used with **InitGraph**.)

After initializing the graphics system, our program draws two shapes by calling the procedures **Rectangle** and **Circle**. The first two parameters in both procedures define the upper-left corner of the rectangle and the last two parameters define the lower-right corner. You may want to experiment with these coordinates to draw different sized shapes.

Our program's final task is to switch from a graphics mode back into the video mode your computer was in before the program started. This is done by calling the **CloseGraph** procedure. **CloseGraph** is also responsible for shutting down the BGI and deallocating the memory set aside for graphics drivers, fonts, and buffers. Don't forget to include this statement in your graphics programs. Otherwise, your computer will be set to the wrong display mode after your program terminates.

Checking for Errors

To keep our graphics program simple, error-checking code was not included. If you plan to write programs that will run on different computers, you should take every precaution possible to ensure that your program will run without errors. Graphics programs require special hardware to run. For this reason alone, they are especially susceptible to initialization errors. Fortunately, there is any easy method for detecting initialization errors. To do this, you can call a special function named **GraphResult**. This function should be called immediately after **InitGraph** is called. The **GraphResult** function returns a value to indicate the status of the initialization operation.

Let's modify our first program to check for potential graphics initialization errors.

```
Program Graphics2;
{ Shows how you should check for graphics initialization errors }
USES
  Graph;
CONST
  GDriver : Integer = Detect; { Use autodetect feature }
VAR
  GMode  : Integer;
  GError : Integer;
```

```
BEGIN
  InitGraph(GDriver, GMode, ''); { Sets to default mode }
  GError := GraphResult;
  IF GError < 0 THEN BEGIN
    Writeln('Graphics initialization error');
    Halt(1);
  END;
  Rectangle(0, 0, 399, 199); { Draws a rectangle }
  Circle(100, 1000, 50); { Draws a circle inside rectangle }
  Readln;
  CloseGraph; { Returns to original mode }
END.
```

A return value of less than 0 indicates that an initialization error has occurred. In this program, we test for this condition and call the **Halt** procedure to exit the program if the initialization fails.

In addition to initialization errors, you might encounter problems while you're executing one of TP's graphics routines. To check for potential errors, you can call the **GraphResult** function after each BGI graphics operation. Here is a sample code section that illustrates how this function can be used:

```
Rectangle(0, 0, 399, 199);
Status := GraphResult;
IF Status < 0 THEN ProcessError(Status);
```

The procedure **ProcessError** refers to a routine that you could write to process the error that has occurred.

 1. What is wrong with the following graphics program?

```
Program GraphicsTest;
CONST
  GDriver : Integer = Detect; { Use autodetect feature }
VAR
  GMode : Integer;

BEGIN
  InitGraph(GDriver, GMode, ''); { Sets to default mode }
  LineTo(100, 100);              { Draws a line }
  Readln;
END.
```

2. Using the TP help system, look up the error-code constants that are returned by the **GraphResult** function. What is the name of the constant that indicates that the BGI graphics is not installed properly?

1. The program is missing the **USES Graph** statement, which is necessary for graphics programs, and the **CloseGraph** procedure, which is used to restore the screen to its default mode.

2. **grNoInitGraph**

Working with the Graph Unit

As demonstrated in our sample program, the **Graph** unit must be included in your programs so that you can make calls to the BGI graphics procedures and functions. This unit contains a number of routines and predefined constants to help you take advantage of your graphics hardware. At first, you might be overwhelmed by the number of procedures and functions provided with **Graph**. To help you navigate through these routines, you might want to use the TP help system to view the **Graph** help information.

Note: To examine the definition of any of the constants, data types, procedures, or functions in the **Graph** unit, select the Contents option from the Help menu and then select the Units category. You can then select the Graph topic to access help on either the set of BGI functions and procedures or the set of internal constants and data types.

Working with Graphics Hardware

To support the set of popular graphics adapters, including CGA, EGA, VGA, MCGA, Hercules, Monochrome Display Printer Adapter (MDPA), and AT&T graphics adapters, TP includes a number of internal display drivers. Fortunately, you don't have to worry about the technical details of your display adapter's operations in order to use the graphics routines. The graphics tools that TP provides operate at a relatively high level and therefore take care of many of the low-level tasks needed to display graphics. There are, however, some basic graphics concepts that you'll need to know before you can write graphics programs.

As Figure 13.2 shows, each display is divided into a set of very small units called *pixels* (picture elements). The screen resolution is determined by the available number of pixel rows and columns. A graphics adapter, such as the CGA, provides 640 columns by 200 rows in its highest-resolution mode. The VGA, however, which provides greater resolution, supports as many as 640 columns and 480 rows. New and improved types of video cards and monitors are being introduced regularly. Now, 800 columns by 600 rows is a fairly common resolution.

Perhaps you're wondering what pixels have to do with drawing graphics images. When you execute drawing routines such as

Figure 13.2 Pixel representation of the screen.

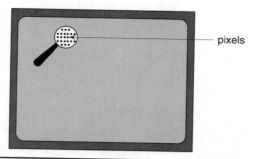

pixels

```
MoveTo(10, 10);
LineTo(100, 10);
```

the graphics system determines which pixels on the screen should be turned on. In this case, the pixels in row 10, starting with column 10 and continuing to column 100, are selected to draw the line.

Video Modes

Each graphics adapter supported by the **Graph** unit provides different, selectable modes. The resolution and number of colors available for displaying graphics are controlled by the mode you select. In our first graphics program, the highest-resolution video mode was automatically selected by calling the **InitGraph** procedure:

```
Procedure InitGraph(Var GraphDriver : Integer;
         Var GraphMode : Integer; PathToDriver : String);
```

If you want to have more control over which mode is selected for your currently installed graphics display hardware, you can specify a mode for the second parameter. To manage and simplify the large number of modes available, the **Graph** unit includes the following set of constants that provide symbolic names for the different modes:

CGAC0	EGA64Hi	MCGAC2	ATT400C3
CGAC1	EGAMonoHi	MCGAMed	ATT400Med
CGAC2	VGALo	MCGAHi	ATT400Hi
CGAHi	VGAMed	HercMonoHI	PC3270Hi
EGALo	VGAHi	ATT400C0	IBM8514Lo
EGAHi	MCGAC0	ATT400C1	IBM8514Hi
EGA64Lo	MCGAC1	ATT400C2	

This example shows how the EGA hardware can be initialized in its "low"-resolution mode.

```
InitGraph(EGA, EgaLo, '');
```

For most programs, you may want to use the autodetect setting because it ensures that the mode providing the greatest resolution for your graphics adapter will be selected.

Note

After your graphics hardware has been initialized with a call to **InitGraph**, you can later change the video mode by calling the **SetGraphMode** procedure. As an example, this call selects a mode for the CGA display hardware:

```
SetGraphMode(CGA3);
```

To determine the default graphics settings on your computer, run the following program:

```
PROGRAM Graphmode;
USES
     Graph;
VAR
   GMode, GDriver : INTEGER;
BEGIN
     GDriver := Detect; {Uses the autodetection feature}
     InitGraph(GDriver,GMode, '');
     IF GraphResult = GrOK THEN
     BEGIN
        WriteLn('Graphics Driver: ', GetDriverName);
        WriteLn('Graphics Mode: ', GetModeName(GMode));
        WriteLn('Maximum Width: ',GetMaxX);
        WriteLn('Maximum Height: ',GetMaxY);
        WriteLn('Maximum Number Of Colors: ',GetMaxColor + 1);
        ReadLn;
        CloseGraph; {Returns to original mode}
     END;
END.
```

Graphics Colors

You've now seen that graphics are drawn by selecting pixels. A natural question at this point might be: "How do I control the colors of the pixels that are turned on?" Your screen actually provides two levels of color control: foreground and background. Only one color for each of these levels can be selected at a time. When you draw a figure, such as a line or a rectangle, the pixels in the figure are set to the current foreground and background colors. How are these colors selected? We use the following two procedures:

```
PROCEDURE SetBkColor(Color : Word);
PROCEDURE SetColor(Color : Word);
```

For the **SetBkColor** routine, a color code is specified to select the background color. However, the parameter for **SetColor** is a different matter. This value is used as an index to reference a hardware color palette that contains the actual colors for your graphics adapter. For example, if we issue the statement

```
SetColor(3);
```

the third color index location in the palette is accessed to determine which color should be used to set the foreground color.

The size of the palette is determined by the graphics adapter you are using. For example, the CGA palette contains 4 entries, whereas the EGA palette contains 16. The **GetMaxColor** function used in the previous section returns the highest number value of the colors available in the current graphics mode. This range starts at 0, so on a 16 color system, and **GetMaxColor** would return 15, meaning that valid color settings would correspond to the range 0 through 15.

The CGA Mode

To access colors in the CGA mode, you can use three procedures: **SetBkColor**, **SetColor**, and **SetGraphMode**. When working in the medium-resolution CGA color mode, as many as three foreground colors and one background color can be displayed simultaneously. Table 13.1 shows the five graphics drawing modes that are supported by the CGA. You can select any of these modes by using the **SetGraphMode** procedure. For example, the statement

```
SetGraphMode(CGAC1);
```

selects the medium-resolution, four color mode.

As I mentioned earlier, the CGA provides four color entries in its color palette. You can, however, select from one of four different palettes (modes) to get different color combinations. To do this, simply call the **SetGraphMode** procedure with one of the constants listed in Table 13.1. The color sets for each of the four color modes

Table 13.1   CGA Selectable Modes

Mode Constant	Value	Resolution	Colors
CGAC0	0	320x200	4
CGAC1	1	320x200	4
CGAC2	2	320x200	4
CGAC3	3	320x200	4
CGAHi	4	640x200	2

are listed in Table 13.2. To illustrate, assume that you're operating in the medium-resolution, four color mode. If you execute the statement

```
SetGraphMode(CGAC0);
```

and then select the second palette color index

```
SetColor(2);
```

your graphics will be drawn in light red. While the palette is active, you can use either of the other two colors, light green and yellow.

As a summary, the three steps required to set a CGA mode and to select foreground and background drawing colors are:

Step 1: SetGraphMode(CGAC1); { Selects a valid CGA mode }
Step 2: SetBkColor(BackgroundColor); { Selects a background color }
Step 3: SetColor(ForeGrColor); { Chooses a palette index }

The background color can be selected from among 15 color options. To help you select background colors, the **Graph** unit provides a set of 15 constants, such as **Black**, **Blue**, **Green**, and so on, that are assigned to the special codes needed to select a background color.

The EGA and VGA Modes

The EGA and VGA graphics adapters provide more colors than the CGA. The maximum number of colors in the EGA palette is 16, while the maximum number for VGA is 256. What's unique about these palettes? They are completely definable by the user, which means you can add your own colors. Table 13.3 shows the graphics drawing modes for both the EGA and the VGA. All of these modes can be used with each adapter, except for the last three (which are provided with the VGA only).

Table 13.2 CGA Color Palettes

Palette Number	Color 1	Color 2	Color 3
0	Light Green	Light Red	Yellow
1	Light Cyan	Light Magenta	White
2	Green	Red	Brown
3	Cyan	Magenta	Light Gray

Color 0 in the color palette serves as the background color.

Table 13.3   EGA and VGA Selectable Modes

Mode	Value	Resolution	Colors
EGALo	0	640x200	16
EGAHi	1	640x350	16
EGA64Lo	0	640x200	16
EGA64Hi	1	640x350	4/16
VGALo	0	640x200	16
VGAMed	1	640x350	16
VGAHi	2	640x480	16

1. What mode is selected by the following statement?

```
SetGraphMode(EGAHI);
```

2. How many CGA graphics drawing modes are supported by TP? How many EGA modes are there?

3. What is the difference between a color palette index and a color code?

1. The high-resolution EGA mode is selected.
2. There are five CGA modes and five EGA modes.
3. A color code is the actual red-green-blue mix required to display a color. The color palette index is the palette location where the color is stored.

Using the Coordinate System

Here, we'll explore how pixels are accessed using TP's coordinate system. Actually, TP supports the simple x,y cartesian coordinate system. With this coordinate system, screen locations are addressed using rows and columns. For example, the following procedure would draw a line from the position (10,30) (row 10, column 30) to the point (100,100):

```
Line(10, 30, 100, 100);
```

The physical coordinate system uses a numbering system that is directly related to the resolution of the graphics mode in which you are working. For example, assume that you're using CGA set to the medium-resolution mode. Since the resolution of this mode is 320x200, the actual screen coordinates are represented as shown in Figure 13.3. Notice that the upper-left corner is location (0, 0) and the lower-right corner is (319, 199).

Figure 13.3 These are the screen coordinates for a system using the CGA medium-resolution graphics mode.

To access a single screen location, use **PutPixel** and **GetPixel**:

```
PROCEDURE PutPixel (X, Y : INTEGER; Pixel: WORD);
FUNCTION GetPixel(X, Y : INTEGER): WORD;
```

PutPixel turns on a pixel of the given color at the pixel row and pixel column indicated by the **X** and **Y** coordinates. **GetPixel** returns the current value of the specified screen location. **GetPixel** is useful if you wish to "twinkle" or turn a point on and off by changing a pixel's color and returning it to its original value. The following program gives a demonstration of how to use **PutPixel**:

```
Program ScreenFill;
USES
    Graph, CRT;
VAR
  GMode, GDriver : INTEGER;
  X, Y : INTEGER;
BEGIN
    GDriver := Detect; {Uses the autodetection feature}
    InitGraph(GDriver,GMode, '');
    IF GraphResult = GrOK THEN
    WHILE NOT KeyPressed DO
    BEGIN
        X := Random(GetMaxX)+1;
        Y := Random(GetMaxY)+1;
        PutPixel(X,Y,Random(GetMaxColor)+1);
    END;
END.
```

The **ScreenFill** program uses the **Random** function which returns a random integer between 0 and the parameter passed to it. These random numbers are used to calculate both the screen position and the color of a pixel element.

Drawing Lines and Basic Shapes

We'll now put the coordinate systems to work to draw some basic graphics shapes. For drawing graphics figures, TP provides three main procedures:

```
PROCEDURE Line(X1,Y1,X2,Y2 : Integer);
PROCEDURE Rectangle(X1, Y1, X2, Y2 : Integer);
PROCEDURE Ellipse(X, Y : Integer; StAngle, EndAngle : Integer;
                  XRadius, YRadius : Word);
```

From these basic shapes—lines, rectangles, and ellipses—you can create a variety of graphics figures. Each of these routines is designed to work with the current settings and drawing attributes, such as color and line style.

Lines

To draw a line in graphics mode, you could simply turn on all the pixels between two points:

```
FOR X := 100 TO 200 DO
   PutPixel(X,100,PixelColor);
```

This draws a straight horizontal line from the point (100,100) to the point (200,100). This is fine, but what if we want to draw a diagonal line? TP's graphics routines provides us with a couple of ways to draw lines:

```
PROCEDURE Line (X1, Y1, X2, Y2 : Integer);
PROCEDURE LineTo (X,Y : Integer);
```

The **Line** procedure draws a line in the current color from the point at (X1,Y1) to the point at (X2,Y2). **LineTo** draws a line from the *current point* to the point at (X,Y). But what's the current point, you might be asking. The current point (**CP**) is a value stored internally by TP and refers to the last location it wrote to. For example,

```
Line(100,100,150,150);
```

leaves the **CP** at (150,150). You can also move the **CP** by using the **MoveTo** procedure:

```
PROCEDURE MoveTo(X,Y: Integer);
```

Circles and Ellipses

TP also allows you to easily draw circles and ellipses using the **Circle** and **Ellipse** procedures:

```
PROCEDURE Ellipse (X, Y: Integer; StrtAngle, EndAngle : Word; XRadius,
                   YRadius : Word);
PROCEDURE Circle(X,Y : Integer; Radius: Word);
```

The **Circle** procedure draws a circle with a radius of **Radius** and centered at point (**X,Y**). In the **Ellipse** procedure, **X** and **Y** are also used to denote the center point of the ellipse. The **StrtAngle** and **EndAngle** parameters can be used to specify either a partial ellipse (an arc) or a complete ellipse. Use a **StrtAngle** of 0 and an **EndAngle** of 360 to create a complete ellipse. The following program shows how to use **Ellipse** to simulate a rotating circle:

```
PROGRAM RotatingCircle;

USES
    CRT, Graph;

TYPE
    WidthArray = ARRAY[0..8] OF REAL;
CONST
    XAxis : WidthArray = (1.0,0.67,0.4,0.2,0.0,0.2,0.4,0.67,1.0);
    X = 200;
    Y = 200;
    YRad = 100;
    StartA = 0;
    EndA = 360;
VAR
    I : INTEGER;
    GMode, GDriver : INTEGER;
BEGIN
    GDriver := Detect; {Uses the autodetection feature}
    InitGraph(GDriver,GMode, '');
    IF GraphResult = GrOK THEN
    BEGIN
      I := 0;
      WHILE NOT KeyPressed DO
      BEGIN
         SetColor(Black); {Erase existing ellipse}
         Ellipse(X,Y,StartA,EndA,TRUNC(YRad * Xaxis[I MOD 9]),YRad);
        INC(I);
         SetColor(Green);
         Ellipse(X,Y,StartA,EndA,TRUNC(YRad * Xaxis[I MOD 9]),YRad);
         Delay(100);
      END;
    END;
END.
```

In the **CONST** section of the program, we declare an array of reals that we use to change the width of the ellipse as a ratio of the height **YRad**. To erase the existing ellipse before drawing the new one, the program sets the current color to **Black** (the default background color) and draws a black ellipse on top of the green one. After incrementing **I** to change the width-to-height ratio, the color is again set to **Green** and the new ellipse is drawn. The **Delay** function is called to slow down the program to help smooth out the image. You may want to adjust this value or remove the call to **Delay** altogether. After all, very few graphics programs need to be slowed down!

Text in Graphics Mode

Graphics are great, but what if you need to add explanatory text? Simple, just use the **OutText** procedure provided in the **Graph** unit:

```
PROCEDURE OutText(TextString: String);
```

OutText places the text string at the location currently held by **CP**. To modify the value of **CP**, use the **MoveTo** procedure. You can use **OutText** to write out text anywhere on the graphics screen using any valid color. Our final example program shows how to write text to the screen while in graphics mode:

```
PROGRAM GraphText;

USES
    CRT, Graph;
VAR
    GraphDriver, GraphMode : INTEGER;
    ch : CHAR;

BEGIN
    GraphDriver := Detect;
    InitGraph(GraphDriver, GraphMode, '\BP\BGI');
    MoveTo(300,0);
    SetColor(White);
    OutText('Circle');
    Line(300,10,50,50);
    ch := ReadKey;
    SetColor(Green);
    Circle(50,50,40);

    SetColor(White);
    MoveTo(300,20);
    OutText('Ellipse');
    Line(300,30,175,130);
    ch := ReadKey;
    SetColor(Blue);
    Ellipse(175,130,0,360,50,25);
```

```
      SetColor(White);
      MoveTo(300,40);
      OutText('Rectangle');
      Line(300,50,200,200);

      ch := ReadKey;
      SetColor(Red);
      Rectangle(50,200,200,300);
      ch := ReadKey;
      CloseGraph;
END.
```

Summary

This chapter provided you with sufficient basic graphics programming concepts to use the **Graph** unit successfully. You now know how to use the basic procedures and functions to initialize your graphics hardware, set video modes, configure color palettes, define coordinates, draw basic figures, and write text strings in graphics mode.

Exercises

1. Write a program that uses the **GetMaxX** and **GetMaxY** functions to draw a circle which fills the screen. Depending on which key is pressed, the program should then make the circle grow larger or smaller.

2. Write a program to display all of the colors available in palette 2 of the CGA. Use the medium-resolution, four color mode (**CGAC1**).

Answers

1. The following program, CIRCLEGROW, uses the **GetMaxX** and **GetMaxY** functions to draw a circle that fills the screen, and allows for specific keypresses to make the circle grow and shrink:

```
PROGRAM CircleGrow;
USES
    CRT, Graph;
CONST
  Grow = 'g';
  Shrink = 's';
  Done = ' ';
  Change = 10;

VAR
    GraphDriver, GraphMode : INTEGER;
    ch : CHAR;
    X,Y,Rad: INTEGER;
```

```
BEGIN
     GraphDriver := Detect;
      InitGraph(GraphDriver, GraphMode, '\BP\BGI');
     X := GetMaxX DIV 2;
     Y := GetMaxY DIV 2;
     Rad := GetMaxY DIV 2;

     SetColor(Green);
     Circle (X,Y,Rad);
     ch := ReadKey;
     WHILE ch <> Done DO
     BEGIN
          SetColor(Black);
          Circle (X,Y,Rad);
          IF ch = Grow THEN
              Rad := Rad + Change
          ELSE IF ch = Shrink THEN
              Rad := Rad - Change;
          SetColor(Green);
          Circle (X,Y,Rad);
          ch := ReadKey;
     END;
END.
```

2. The following program, SHOWCOLORS, displays all of the colors available in palette 2 of the CGA:

```
Program ShowColors;
USES Graph;
CONST
   GDriver : Integer = Detect;
VAR
   GDrv, GMode, GError, I : Integer;

BEGIN
   GDrv := CGA; GMode := CGAC1;
    InitGraph(GDriver, GMode, '\TP\BGI');
   GError := GraphResult;
   IF GError < O THEN BEGIN
     Writeln('Graphics initialization error');
     Halt(1);
   END;

   FOR I := 1 TO 3 DO BEGIN
     SetColor(I);
     Rectangle(0, 0, 399, 199);
     Readln;
   END;
   CloseGraph;
END.
```

Using the Debugger

I magine that you've written a customized program that allows you to keep track of your entire CD collection. This program allows you to add, delete, modify, and search for records based on the name and type of CD. The program stores this data in a disk file so that it's always accessible. There's only one problem; any time you try to enter more than one new CD into your custom catalog, the computer seems to freeze and the keyboard beeps every time you press a key. To find out what is going on, you could print out the source code of your program and stare at each statement to see if you find a problem. Alternatively, you could put a **WriteLn** statement after each statement in your program to tell you what is going on. While either of these solutions may be of some help, there's another way that is often much easier: Use a debugger!

A *debugger* is a program that allows you to control the execution of another program. A program running another program; how is this possible? Think of it this way: The IDE is a part of a program (TP) that allows you to load and edit files. It also allows you to compile these files into executable format and then run them. What the debugger allows you to do is to see your program running one step at a time, letting you control when it executes the next statement, function, or procedure. At the same time, it enables you to look into your program's variables to examine, and even modify, the values your program is using, *while your program is still running*. If this sounds like a powerful function, it is!

This chapter explains the IDE's built-in, or *integrated*, debugger and how to use it. After you complete this chapter, you'll know:

• The three basic categories of program errors

• How to control your program's execution through breakpoints

• How to watch, examine, and modify your program variables

How the Debugger Fits in with the IDE

TP comes with a debugger built right into the IDE. That is, each time you use the IDE, the debugger is right there. You control the debugger by using the Run and Debug menus, and their shortcut keys. For the debugger to be of any use, though, you must first make sure it has certain information about your program.

Generating Debugging Output

To control execution of your program, the debugger needs the compiler to create special information about the program. You can do this in two ways. One is to display the Options menu, select Compiler, and then select Debug Information. Unless your program is very large, you will also want to make sure that the Local symbol information check box in the Debug Information dialog is checked as well. The other way to generate debug information is to use the **$D+** compiler directive inside your program code. (To turn off local symbol information, use the **$L-** compiler directive.)

If you try to debug a program in the IDE without debugging information, a warning dialog box appears. If this happens, click on No, change the compiler options, and remake the program. Debugging output is also important when using other, external debuggers such as Turbo Debugger. Turbo Debugger is a standalone program that is shipped with some versions of TP and with other Borland compiler products.

Integrated Debugger Options

To use the integrated debugger, display the Options menu and select Debugger. The Debugger dialog box shown in Figure 14.1, is displayed. Make sure the Integrated option is checked for using the debugger inside the IDE. To have TP generate debugging information for external debuggers, make sure to check the Standalone check box.

The Display swapping options control how TP displays the user screen when your program is executing. Smart swapping means that TP will switch to the user screen whenever data is sent to the output screen, or when a procedure is called. The Always option will cause the user screen to be displayed at

Figure 14.1   Use this dialog box to make your debugger selections.

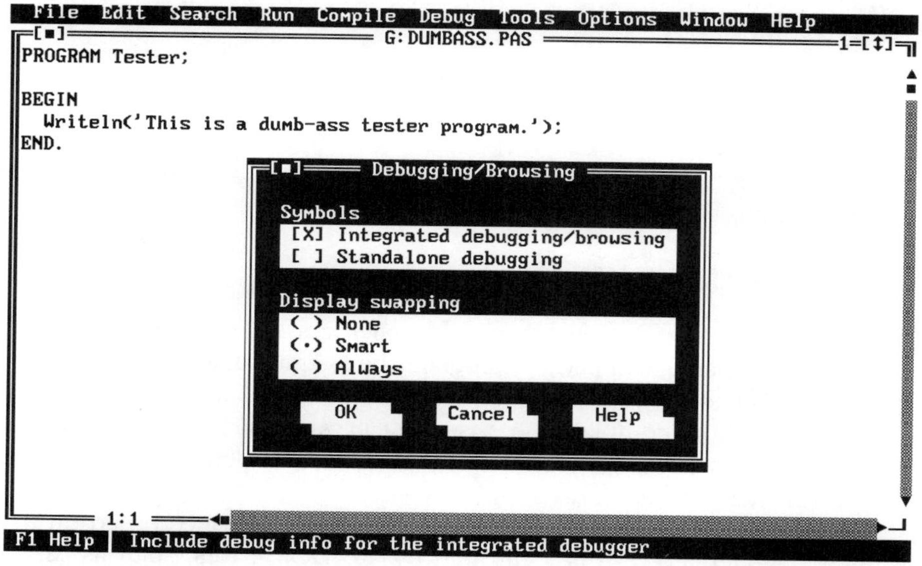

```
 File  Edit  Search  Run  Compile  Debug  Tools  Options  Window  Help
┌─[■]══════════════════ G:DUMBASS.PAS ═══════════════════1=[↕]═┑
│PROGRAM Tester;                                                    ▲
│                                                                  ■
│BEGIN                                                             ■
│  Writeln('This is a dumb-ass tester program.');
│END.
│            ┌─[■]══════ Debugging/Browsing ══════┑
│            │                                     │
│            │   Symbols                           │
│            │    [X] Integrated debugging/browsing│
│            │    [ ] Standalone debugging         │
│            │                                     │
│            │   Display swapping                  │
│            │    ( ) None                         │
│            │    (·) Smart                        │
│            │    ( ) Always                       │
│            │                                     │
│            │    ┌──────┐  ┌────────┐  ┌──────┐  │
│            │    │  OK  │  │ Cancel │  │ Help │  │
│            │    └──────┘  └────────┘  └──────┘  │
│            └─────────────────────────────────────┘
│══ 1:1 ══◄■                                              ►
 F1 Help │ Include debug info for the integrated debugger
```

each line of program execution, whether there's screen output or not. If None is checked, the debugger will never swap the screen out. You can also display the user screen at any time by selecting User screen from the Debug menu, or by pressing Alt+F5.

Overview of Bugs and Debugging

All useful programs have bugs of one type or another. It is possible for even the simplest of programs to have bugs, and still appear to operate properly. Some bugs are disastrous, causing your computer to crash or hang, resulting in lost data and aggravation. Other bugs are more subtle, resulting in minor errors in computations or unintended output. Basically, however, bugs can be classified into three major categories: compile-time errors, run-time errors, and logic errors.

Compile-time errors occur when you make a mistake entering a program. If you leave a semicolon off the end of a line in your program, the compiler will issue an message like

```
Error 85: ";" expected
```

and place the editing cursor next to the error. Other errors, such as using a **BEGIN** without a matching **END** statement or incorrect use of the language syntax, can be caught by the compiler. Because TP is a "strongly typed" language, it will complain if you try something like this:

```
VAR
    I : Integer;

BEGIN
    I := 2.01;
```

If you try to compile a program containing this assignment, the compiler will generate:

```
Error 24: Type mismatch.
```

This kind of error checking by the compiler can save you a lot of grief when working with large, complicated programs by assuring that your data types match.

Run-time errors are errors, on the other hand, which pass through the compiler without complaint because they are syntactically correct, but they are caught by TP's run-time system. This type of error is generated when you try to perform such actions as division by zero.

Run-time errors are divided into four broad categories based on the error number generated. Errors 1 through 99 are DOS errors, such as "2: File not found"; 100 through 149 are I/O errors such as "104: File not open for input"; 150 through 199 are critical errors like "150: Disk is write protected"; and 151 through 255 are fatal errors such as "200: Division by zero."

If you are running a program inside the IDE and a run-time error occurs, TP will automatically take you to the program line where the error occurred and display the error message. If a program running outside the IDE generates a run-time error, you can find the line it occurred on by starting the IDE and using the Find Error selection from the Search menu. You will need to supply the address shown in the error message (it will look something like 00A4:014B).

For an extra measure of protection when running your program, you may want to tell the compiler to generate error checking information. To create this information, simply check the appropriate boxes in the Compiler Options dialog, which is shown in Figure 14.2. Range checking will generate an error if you try to access an element of an array that doesn't exist—that is, if the index is too large or too small. Stack checking makes sure that there's enough room on the stack (an internal memory area) for each function or procedure call as it is made. I/O checking will automatically report problems with performing input or output. Overflow checking generates a fatal error when a variable's value is too large or small for its type—when a variable of type **Integer** is assigned a value greater than 32,767. When debugging a program, it's a good idea to always use these options.

Figure 14.2 Use the Compiler Option dialog to ease your debugging sessions.

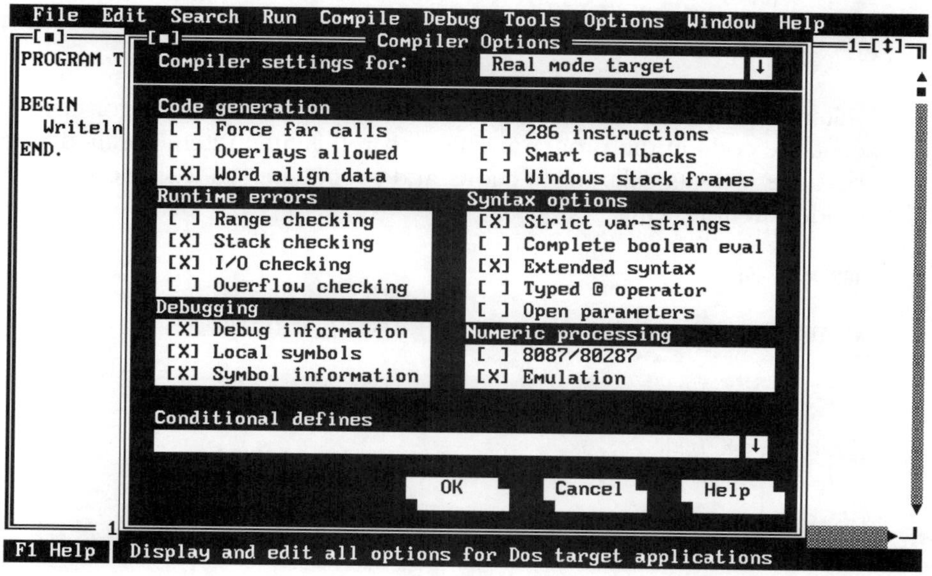

Logic errors are the third type of bug that can appear in your program, and they are the hardest to find.

This type of error is generally the most pervasive because it cannot be found automatically by the compiler or at runtime as can the other types of errors. Sometimes the results of a logic error are obvious and it is easy to find the cause. Other times, the results are more subtle and consequently more difficult to track down. The rest of this chapter demonstrates how to use TP's integrated debugger to find and correct this type of bug.

Run Menu Options

The IDE's Run menu contains six options. The first, Run, does exactly that; it runs your program to completion. Run will also check to make sure your program is up to date and will recompile it if necessary. To see any output from your program, use the Alt+F5 shortcut key.

The next item in the Run menu is Step over. *Stepping* allows you to execute a single line of TP code at a time. Take a look at this short program:

```
PROGRAM SRoot;
VAR
   X : Real;
BEGIN
   Write('Enter a value: ');
   ReadLn(X);
   X := Sqrt(X);
   WriteLn('Square root is: ', X);
END.
```

Stepping through this program would take four steps, one for each line of executable code in the program. The reason this menu item is called Step *over* is because it treats calls to functions and procedures as a single line of code. Consider the following:

```
PROGRAM Bigger;

FUNCTION BiggerOne (X : INTEGER, Y: INTEGER) : INTEGER;
BEGIN
    IF X > Y THEN
        BiggerOne := X;
    IF Y > X THEN
        BiggerOne := Y;
END;

VAR
    A, B : INTEGER;
    Result : INTEGER;
```

```
BEGIN
     Write('Enter first value: ');
     ReadLn(A);
     Write('Enter second value: ');
     ReadLn(B);
     WriteLn;
     Result := BiggerOne(A,B);
     WriteLn('The bigger one is: ',Result);
END.
```

Stepping would only show you the execution of the program lines between the **BEGIN** and the **END** in the main program body. To see what was going on inside the **BiggerOne** function, you would need to *trace* into it. The Trace into command allows you to execute a single line of TP code at a time, much like Step over. The difference here is that using Trace into will show the program executing each line of code it can find.

Note

For the debugger to be able to show the TP source of a particular part of your program, it must be compiled with debugging information turned on. If, for some reason, you want to skip a portion of your program in the debugger, you can use the **$D-** compiler directive inside the portion you want to ignore.

The Go to cursor command tells the debugger to execute the current program until it reaches the line where the editor cursor is positioned. This is handy if you already have an idea as to where to start looking in your program for the problem. To try the Go to cursor command, use the normal editing keys to position the cursor and select the command from the menu, or use the F4 shortcut key. You must position the cursor on a program line that generates executable code. If you don't, you'll see an error message like the one shown in Figure 14.3. Remember, variable and constant declarations do not generate code; neither do comments. Also, if you put the cursor on a line that is never executed, the debugger will not be able to stop execution there, and your program will continue to completion.

Suppose you used the Go to cursor command and discovered that you'd missed the place you wanted to stop by a couple of lines. If the line you wanted to examine was further along in the program, you could step over or trace into to the correct spot. But if you've gone too far, you could select another of the Run menu's commands, Program reset. Using Program reset effectively "clears the decks" so your program can start again from the beginning. This is a particularly useful feature if you want to go back and try a part of your program again with different input variables, or if you accidentally step too far and need to start again.

Figure 14.3 **An error message will be displayed if the cursor is not positioned on a program line.**

The final option on the Run menu is Parameters. These are values that are passed to your program at startup time. If you use the DOS DIR command like this:

```
DIR *.PAS
```

the *.PAS is called a *command-line parameter*. Your TP programs can also make use of command-line parameters using the **ParamCount** and **ParamStr** functions. If your program uses parameters, you can use the debugger to examine and change the values the program uses. The Program Parameters dialog has a history list so you can choose from the previous settings you've used.

What If Your Code Changes?

Sometimes in the middle of a debugging session, you may want to make a change in your program code. Running the debugger from within the IDE makes this easy. Simply make the changes, save the program file and rebuild your program. If you accidentally change the program source code, the debugger will warn you with the dialog box shown in Figure 14.4. The safest thing to do is to click on Yes to rebuild your program. If you click on No, you run the risk of confusing the debugger about what your program really looks like.

Figure 14.4 This warning dialog is displayed if you change your source code while debugging your program.

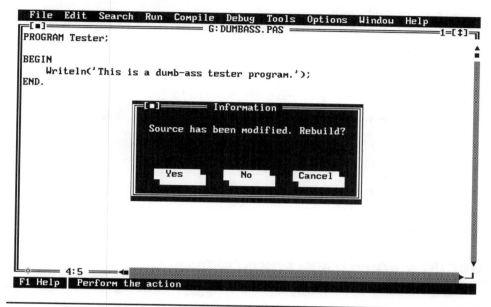

Execution Bar

The execution bar is a colored highlight that shows the current point of execution in your TP program. It first appears when you press F7 or F8 or use the Run menu to start the debugging session. You can control the color of the execution bar by using the Color dialog box in the Environment Options menu. Choose the Source position item in the Editor group and pick the new color.

1. True or False: A debugger will help you find syntax errors in your program.
2. Rearrange this program code for stepping to make it easier to determine if the second part of the statement is executed:

   ```
   IF (X > Y) THEN X := Limit;
   ```

3. Trace through the BIGGER program given earlier in this chapter to see if you can see and correct the hidden bug (Hint: see what happens if A and B are the same value).

1. False, the compiler checks for syntax errors.
2. Because the debugger treats entire lines of program code as a single statement, you must put the assignment statement on a line by itself. If X is greater than Y, the

execution bar will appear on the next line; otherwise it will skip the assignment statement:

```
IF (X > Y) THEN
   X := Limit;
```

3. If A and B are equal, no specific value is returned from the **BiggerOne** function. This is called "falling off the end of a function," and is a common source of errors. The value returned from the function is unpredictable and can cause all kinds of problems. A better way of writing the **BiggerOne** function might be:

```
FUNCTION BiggerOne (X : INTEGER, Y: INTEGER) : INTEGER;
BEGIN
    IF X > Y THEN
        BiggerOne := X
    ELSE
        BiggerOne := Y;
END;
```

This version ensures that a value is always returned from the function.

Debug Menu—Using Breakpoints

So far in this chapter you've learned enough to be able to control execution of your program by stepping and tracing. There is a third way to control execution and that's by using *breakpoints*. A breakpoint is a position in the code of a program where execution halts based on a specified condition. You already learned about one type of breakpoint when you used the Go to cursor command in the previous section. This type of breakpoint is called an *unconditional breakpoint*. Whenever your running program encounters an unconditional breakpoint, it halts execution of the program and positions the execution bar on the program line where the breakpoint is set.

As you might have guessed, in addition to unconditional breakpoints, there are also *conditional breakpoints*. The IDE suspends execution of your program at a conditional breakpoint only when the specified condition evaluates to True. This condition can be based on the value of program variables (such as "X := 0" or "Y > Z"), or it can be based on the number of times a particular line of code has been executed previously. The first type is very useful when you wish to run your program until a specific condition has been met. The second type is useful when dealing with loops or program segments that are frequently called.

You can use the Debug menu to set and modify breakpoints in your program. To set a new breakpoint, select Add breakpoint, as shown in Figure 14.5. In the Add Breakpoint dialog box, you can specify a condition that will trigger the breakpoint when it evaluates to True. This means the condition must be a boolean expression. There is a history list for conditions so that you can select a breakpoint condition you've used before.

Figure 14.5 Use the Add breakpoint command to set a conditional breakpoint in your program.

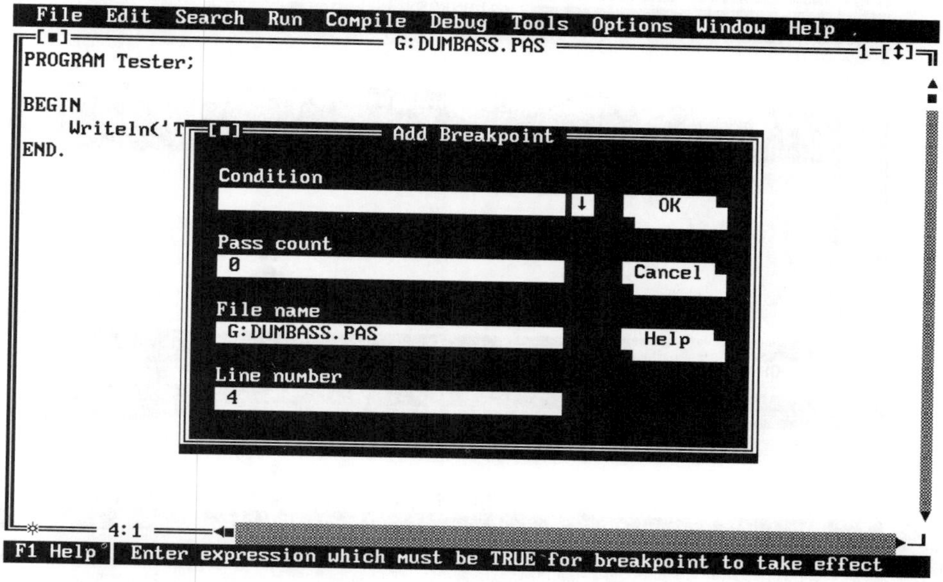

Also in the Add Breakpoint dialog box, you can specify a pass count, which indicates how many times the breakpoint should be skipped before execution is halted. The effect of using both a condition and a pass count is cumulative, meaning that the condition must evaluate to True for the number of times in the pass count before execution is halted. You can use the File name and Line number controls in the dialog box to set a breakpoint at a place other than where the cursor is currently positioned.

Note
▼

To break into a runaway program, use Ctrl+Break. This action gets the debugger's attention and enables it to stop the program at the currently executing line. You can then use the Step over and Trace into commands to continue running the program, or you can reset the program by selecting the Program reset command.

Modifying Breakpoints

Once a breakpoint is set, it remains in effect until it is *cleared* or until you close TP. Clearing a breakpoint removes it from the list of breakpoints maintained by the IDE's debugger. Clearing and modifying breakpoints is done in the Breakpoints dialog box, shown in Figure 14.6. Select Breakpoints from the

Figure 14.6   Use this dialog box to modify existing breakpoints.

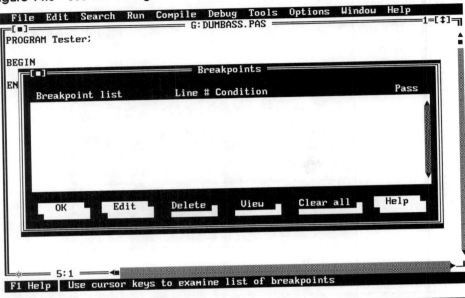

Debug menu to display this dialog box. To remove a specific breakpoint, highlight it and click on the Delete button. To remove all the breakpoints from your program, click on the Clear all button. Highlighting a breakpoint in the dialog and using the View button will take you to the line of code where the breakpoint is situated. To modify an existing breakpoint, use the Edit button.

Note

> Because breakpoints only affect the debugger, you don't need to restart your program if you want to change or add breakpoints in the middle of a debugging session.

Using the Call Stack

Another useful debugging tool is the *call stack*. You can display the Call Stack window by using the Debug menu or the Alt+F3 shortcut key. The Call Stack window shows the sequence of procedures or functions your program called to reach the currently executing line of code. The currently running procedure is at the top of the list. Your main program is at the bottom of the list. Each entry in the list displays the name of the procedure that called it and the parameters that were used to call it. To display the currently active line of any procedure, highlight the line and press Enter. The main window will then display it. The Call Stack can be especially useful when used with a breakpoint to tell you what route your program took to get to a particular piece of code.

Watching Variables

The debugger also provides a watch window, which allows you to monitor, or *watch*, program variables and expressions as your program executes. To display the watch window, select Watch from the Debug menu. The watch window behaves like any other window in the IDE; you can resize it, close it, switch to it and from it by using the Alt+*number* keys. You can also use the Debug menu to add items to the watch window.

To add a variable to the Watch window, use Add watch... from the Debug menu. Alternatively, if the watch window is currently active, pressing the Insert key will let you add a variable. Variables in the watch window will update as their values change during the course of the program. You can watch any variable, constant, or expression in this way. To remove a value from the watch window, simply highlight it and press the Delete key.

Examining and Modifying Values

Sometimes you might find it useful to be able to examine a particular variable's value, and if necessary to change it while your program is running. If you find this to be true, simply select Evaluate/Modify from the Debug menu to display the Evaluate and Modify dialog box. Entering a value in the Expression portion of the dialog will display its calculated value in the Result portion. If the expression being evaluated is a program variable, you are able to change its value by entering an expression of the same type. This means that if you are examining the value of a variable that has been declared as type **Integer**, you can change it to any integer value. This is a very powerful feature because it allows you to test specific conditions in your code while your program is running.

Note

> You can also use the Evaluate and Modify dialog box to calculate expressions, not just examine variables. If your program contained the line
>
> ```
> SomeProcedure(A * B + 15);
> ```
>
> you could find out what the value of **A * B +15** was by entering it in the Evaluate portion of the Evaluate and Modify dialog box.

Summary

In this chapter, you've learned what a debugger is and what it can do. You've also found out how to control execution of your program and restart it when necessary. We touched on examining and changing variable values when your program is running, and how to watch several variables simultaneously. As you write more and more complicated programs (which produce more and more complicated bugs), you'll develop techniques and insights into how and why your program might be behaving in that unexpected way. TP's integrated debugger is a powerful tool, certainly, but as you gain experience, you'll discover that the very best debugger available is the one right between your ears!

Exercises

1. True or False: You can set a breakpoint on any line in your program.
2. What information does the Call stack window provide?
3. If your program is in an infinite loop and you have no breakpoints set, how can you break into the program?
4. Use the Watch window to find out why this program never terminates:

```
PROGRAM Count;
CONST
      Fred = 'String';

FUNCTION ReturnOrdinalSuffix(VAR Number : INTEGER) : STRING;

BEGIN
      Number := Number MOD 100;
      IF (Number > 9) AND (Number < 20) THEN
      {Must be a 'teen'}
             ReturnOrdinalSuffix := 'th'
      ELSE
      BEGIN
            Number := Number MOD 10;
            CASE Number OF
                    1 : ReturnOrdinalSuffix := 'st';
                    2 : ReturnOrdinalSuffix := 'nd';
                    3 : ReturnOrdinalSuffix := 'rd';
            ELSE
                    ReturnOrdinalSuffix := 'th';
            END;
      END;
END;

VAR
    I,J : INTEGER;
    Str : STRING;
BEGIN
      FOR I := 1 TO 20 DO
      BEGIN
            Str := ReturnOrdinalSuffix(I);
            Write(I,Str,'      ');
      END;
END.
```

Answers

1. False; you can only set a breakpoint on a line of your program that contains executable code. You cannot set a breakpoint on blank lines, comments, or variable declarations.

2. The Call stack window shows the path of procedures and functions that your program called to reach the currently executing procedure or function. It only shows active pathways, meaning that it does not show procedures that have already returned to the calling program.

3. Use Ctrl+Break to get into the debugger when running from inside the IDE.

4. The problem with this program is that **ReturnOrdinalSuffix** modifies the value which is passed to it. This is not necessarily bad, but because we are passing it a loop index, the program will never end. Every time **ReturnOrdinalSuffix** is given the value 20, it modifies it to 0 and the loop starts all over again. You can fix this by changing the function declaration to

```
FUNCTION ReturnOrdinalSuffix(Number : INTEGER) : STRING;
```

so that it works with a copy of the variable instead.

Index